The changing spaces of television acting

The changing spaces of television acting

From studio realism to location realism in BBC television drama

Richard Hewett

MANCHESTER UNIVERSITY PRESS

Copyright © Richard Hewett 2017

The right of Richard Hewett to be identified as the author of this work has been asserted by him in accordance with the Copyright, Designs and Patents Act 1988.

Published by Manchester University Press
Altrincham Street, Manchester M1 7JA, UK
www.manchesteruniversitypress.co.uk

British Library Cataloguing-in-Publication Data is available

ISBN 978 1 7849 9298 9 hardback
ISBN 978 1 5261 4863 6 paperback

First published by Manchester University Press in hardback 2017

This edition published 2020

The publisher has no responsibility for the persistence or accuracy of URLs for any external or third-party internet websites referred to in this book, and does not guarantee that any content on such websites is, or will remain, accurate or appropriate.

Typeset by Out of House Publishing

Contents

List of figures	*page* vi
Acknowledgements	xii
Introduction	1
1 Scaling down in early studio realism	25
2 Refining studio realism	70
3 The genesis of location realism	117
4 The age of location realism	165
5 The return of studio realism?	223
Conclusion	238
References	243
Index	261

Figures

1.1	Isabel Dean in *The Quatermass Experiment*: 'Contact has been Established', tx. 18/07/1953 (BBC/BBC Worldwide DVD)	*page* 33
1.2	Isabel Dean in *The Quatermass Experiment*: 'Contact has been Established', tx. 18/07/1953 (BBC/BBC Worldwide DVD)	33
1.3	Isabel Dean in *The Quatermass Experiment*: 'Contact has been Established', tx. 18/07/1953 (BBC/BBC Worldwide DVD)	35
1.4	Isabel Dean in *The Quatermass Experiment*: 'Contact has been Established', tx. 18/07/1953 (BBC/BBC Worldwide DVD)	35
1.5	Isabel Dean and Edward Jewesbury in *I, Claudius*: 'The Queen of Heaven', tx. 25/10/1976 (BBC/BBC Worldwide DVD)	39
1.6	Isabel Dean and Edward Jewesbury in *I, Claudius*: 'The Queen of Heaven', tx. 25/10/1976 (BBC/BBC Worldwide DVD)	39
1.7	Moray Watson in *The Quatermass Experiment*: 'Contact has been Established', tx. 18/07/1953 (BBC/BBC Worldwide DVD)	41
1.8	Van Boolen and Iris Ballard in *The Quatermass Experiment*: 'Contact has been Established', tx. 18/07/1953 (BBC/BBC Worldwide DVD)	53

1.9	Iris Ballard in *The Quatermass Experiment*: 'Contact has been Established', tx. 18/07/1953 (BBC/BBC Worldwide DVD)	54
1.10	Iris Ballard in *The Quatermass Experiment*: 'Contact has been Established', tx. 18/07/1953 (BBC/BBC Worldwide DVD)	54
1.11	Van Boolen in *Quatermass and the Pit*: 'The Halfmen', tx. 22/12/1958 (BBC/BBC Worldwide DVD)	56
1.12	Reginald Tate and W. Thorp Devereux in *The Quatermass Experiment*: 'Contact has been Established', tx. 18/07/1953 (BBC/BBC Worldwide DVD)	63
1.13	Reginald Tate and W. Thorp Devereux in *The Quatermass Experiment*: 'Contact has been Established', tx. 18/07/1953 (BBC/BBC Worldwide DVD)	63
1.14	Reginald Tate and W. Thorp Devereux in *The Quatermass Experiment*: 'Contact has been Established', tx. 18/07/1953 (BBC/BBC Worldwide DVD)	64
1.15	Reginald Tate and W. Thorp Devereux in *The Quatermass Experiment*: 'Contact has been Established', tx. 18/07/1953 (BBC/BBC Worldwide DVD)	64
2.1	William Russell and William Hartnell in *Doctor Who*: 'An Unearthly Child', tx. 23/11/1963 (BBC/BBC Worldwide DVD)	78
2.2	Jacqueline Hill, William Russell and William Hartnell in *Doctor Who*: 'An Unearthly Child', tx. 23/11/1963 (BBC/BBC Worldwide DVD)	79
2.3	William Russell, Jacqueline Hill and William Hartnell in *Doctor Who*: 'An Unearthly Child', tx. 23/11/1963 (BBC/BBC Worldwide DVD)	79
2.4	William Hartnell in *Doctor Who*: 'An Unearthly Child', tx. 23/11/1963 (BBC/BBC Worldwide DVD)	81
2.5	William Hartnell in *Doctor Who*: 'An Unearthly Child', tx. 23/11/1963 (BBC/BBC Worldwide DVD)	81

2.6 Heather Lyons and Mavis Ranson in *Doctor Who*: 'An Unearthly Child', tx. 23/11/1963 (BBC/BBC Worldwide DVD) — 88

2.7 William Russell and Cyril Smith in *The Adventures of Sir Lancelot*: 'The Knight with the Red Plume', tx. 24/09/1956 (Sapphire Films for ITCP/Network DVD) — 90

2.8 Carole Ann Ford in *Doctor Who*: 'An Unearthly Child', tx. 23/11/1963 (BBC/BBC Worldwide DVD) — 93

2.9 William Russell and Jacqueline Hill in *Doctor Who*: 'An Unearthly Child', tx. 23/11/1963 (BBC/BBC Worldwide DVD) — 97

2.10 Carole Ann Ford in *Doctor Who*: 'An Unearthly Child', tx. 23/11/1963 (BBC/BBC Worldwide DVD) — 97

2.11 Carole Ann Ford in *Doctor Who*: 'An Unearthly Child', tx. 23/11/1963 (BBC/BBC Worldwide DVD) — 103

2.12 William Russell in *Doctor Who*: 'An Unearthly Child', tx. 23/11/1963 (BBC/BBC Worldwide DVD) — 105

2.13 Jacqueline Hill in *Doctor Who*: 'An Unearthly Child', tx. 23/11/1963 (BBC/BBC Worldwide DVD) — 105

2.14 William Hartnell in *Doctor Who*: 'An Unearthly Child', tx. 23/11/1963 (BBC/BBC Worldwide DVD) — 107

2.15 William Russell and William Hartnell in *Doctor Who*: 'An Unearthly Child', tx. 23/11/1963 (BBC/BBC Worldwide DVD) — 107

2.16 Carole Ann Ford and William Hartnell in *Doctor Who*: 'An Unearthly Child', tx. 23/11/1963 (BBC/BBC Worldwide DVD) — 108

2.17 Jacqueline Hill, Carole Ann Ford, William Hartnell and William Russell in *Doctor Who*: 'An Unearthly Child', tx. 23/11/1963 (BBC/BBC Worldwide DVD) — 108

3.1 Peter Bowles in *Survivors*: 'The Fourth Horseman', tx. 16/04/1975 (BBC/BBC Worldwide DVD) — 130

3.2 Chris Tranchell, Ian McCulloch and Lucy Fleming in *Survivors*: 'Law and Order', tx. 18/06/1975 (BBC/BBC Worldwide DVD) — 135

3.3 Ian McCulloch in *Survivors*: 'Law and Order', tx. 18/06/1975 (BBC/BBC Worldwide DVD) — 135

3.4   Lucy Fleming in *Survivors*: 'Law and Order',
      tx. 18/06/1975 (BBC/BBC Worldwide DVD)   136
3.5   Carolyn Seymour in *Survivors*: 'The Fourth Horseman',
      tx. 16/04/1975 (BBC/BBC Worldwide DVD)   140
3.6   Carolyn Seymour in *Survivors*: 'The Fourth Horseman',
      tx. 16/04/1975 (BBC/BBC Worldwide DVD)   140
3.7   Carolyn Seymour in *Survivors*: 'The Fourth Horseman',
      tx. 16/04/1975 (BBC/BBC Worldwide DVD)   141
3.8   Shot of the kitchen table in *Survivors*: 'The Fourth
      Horseman', tx. 16/04/1975 (BBC/BBC
      Worldwide DVD)   141
3.9   Carolyn Seymour in *Survivors*: 'The Fourth Horseman',
      tx. 16/04/1975 (BBC/BBC Worldwide DVD)   142
3.10 Carolyn Seymour in *Survivors*: 'The Fourth Horseman',
      tx. 16/04/1975 (BBC/BBC Worldwide DVD)   142
3.11 Carolyn Seymour in *Survivors*: 'The Fourth Horseman',
      tx. 16/04/1975 (BBC/BBC Worldwide DVD)   143
3.12 Carolyn Seymour in *Survivors*: 'The Fourth Horseman',
      tx. 16/04/1975 (BBC/BBC Worldwide DVD)   143
3.13 Carolyn Seymour in *Survivors*: 'Law and Order',
      tx. 18/06/1975 (BBC/BBC Worldwide DVD)   152
3.14 Talfryn Thomas in *Doctor Who*: 'The Green Death
      Episode One', tx. 19/05/1973 (BBC/BBC
      Worldwide DVD)   154
3.15 Talfryn Thomas in *Dad's Army*: 'My British Buddy',
      tx. 07/11/1973 (BBC/BBC Worldwide DVD)   154
3.16 Talfryn Thomas in *Survivors*: 'The Fourth Horseman',
      tx. 16/04/1975 (BBC/BBC Worldwide DVD)   156
3.17 Talfryn Thomas in *Survivors*: 'Law and Order',
      tx. 18/06/1975 (BBC/BBC Worldwide DVD)   157
3.18 Talfryn Thomas in *Survivors*: 'Law and Order',
      tx. 18/06/1975 (BBC/BBC Worldwide DVD)   158
3.19 Talfryn Thomas in *Survivors*: 'Law and Order',
      tx. 18/06/1975 (BBC/BBC Worldwide DVD)   159
3.20 Talfryn Thomas in *Survivors*: 'Law and Order',
      tx. 18/06/1975 (BBC/BBC Worldwide DVD)   159
4.1   Christopher Eccleston in *Doctor Who*: 'Rose',
      tx. 26/03/2005 (BBC/BBC Worldwide DVD)   176

4.2 Christopher Eccleston in *Doctor Who*: 'The Doctor Dances', tx. 28/05/2005 (BBC/BBC Worldwide DVD)   179
4.3 Julie Graham in *Survivors*: 'Episode 1', tx. 23/11/2008 (BBC/BBC Worldwide DVD)   181
4.4 Julie Graham in *Survivors*: 'Episode 1', tx. 23/11/2008 (BBC/BBC Worldwide DVD)   181
4.5 Julie Graham in *Survivors*: 'Episode 1', tx. 23/11/2008 (BBC/BBC Worldwide DVD)   181
4.6 Julie Graham in *Survivors*: 'Episode 1', tx. 23/11/2008 (BBC/BBC Worldwide DVD)   182
4.7 Julie Graham in *Survivors*: 'Episode 1', tx. 23/11/2008 (BBC/BBC Worldwide DVD)   182
4.8 Julie Graham in *Survivors*: 'Episode 1', tx. 23/11/2008 (BBC/BBC Worldwide DVD)   183
4.9 Julie Graham and Shaun Dingwall in *Survivors*: 'Episode 1', tx. 23/11/2008 (BBC/BBC Worldwide DVD)   184
4.10 Julie Graham and Shaun Dingwall in *Survivors*: 'Episode 1', tx. 23/11/2008 (BBC/BBC Worldwide DVD)   184
4.11 Julie Graham in *Survivors*: 'Episode 1', tx. 23/11/2008 (BBC/BBC Worldwide DVD)   184
4.12 Carolyn Seymour in *Survivors*: 'Gone Away', tx. 30/04/1975 (BBC/BBC Worldwide DVD)   190
4.13 Ian McCulloch, Carolyn Seymour and anonymous actor in *Survivors*: 'Gone Away', tx. 30/04/1975 (BBC/BBC Worldwide DVD)   190
4.14 Chahak Patel in *Survivors*: 'Episode 2', tx. 25/11/2008 (BBC/BBC Worldwide DVD)   191
4.15 Julie Graham, anonymous actor, Chahak Patel and Paterson Joseph in *Survivors*: 'Episode 2', tx. 25/11/2008 (BBC/BBC Worldwide DVD)   192
4.16 Barry Stanton and Brian Peck in *Survivors*: 'Gone Away', tx. 30/04/1975 (BBC/BBC Worldwide DVD)   193
4.17 Annie Lovett and Anthony Flanagan in *Survivors*: 'Episode 2', tx. 25/11/2008 (BBC/BBC Worldwide DVD)   193

4.18 Billie Piper in *Doctor Who*: 'Father's Day',
tx. 14/05/2005 (BBC/BBC Worldwide DVD) — 207

4.19 Billie Piper in *Doctor Who*: 'Father's Day',
tx. 14/05/2005 (BBC/BBC Worldwide DVD) — 207

4.20 Christopher Eccleston and Richard Wilson in
Doctor Who: 'The Doctor Dances', tx. 28/05/2005
(BBC/BBC Worldwide DVD) — 215

4.21 Christopher Eccleston in *Doctor Who*: 'The Doctor
Dances', tx. 28/05/2005 (BBC/BBC Worldwide DVD) — 216

5.1 Jason Flemyng, Adrian Dunbar and Mark Gatiss
in *The Quatermass Experiment*, tx. 02/04/2005
(BBC/Simply Home Entertainment) — 224

5.2 Jason Flemyng and Adrian Dunbar in *The Quatermass Experiment*, tx. 02/04/2005 (BBC/Simply Home Entertainment) — 227

5.3 Jason Flemyng in *The Quatermass Experiment*,
tx. 02/04/2005 (BBC/Simply Home Entertainment) — 227

5.4 Ben Hardy, Adam Woodyatt, Mimi Keene (obscured)
and Laurie Brett in *EastEnders*, tx. 20 February
2015 (BBC) — 234

Acknowledgements

In preparing this book I was greatly aided by the expertise provided by the various staffs of the British Library, the BFI Reading Room and the City of Westminster Libraries, and in particular the tireless efforts of Louise North at the BBC Written Archives Centre. Thanks are also due to James Thornton for kindly allowing me access to the RADA Library, and to Andy O'Dwyer at the BBC, Louise McMullan at Equity and Edward Hicks at RADA for their assistance and advice.

Introductions to potential interviewees were kindly provided by Professor Andrew Higson at the University of York, Dick Fiddy at the British Film Institute, Susanna Capon, formerly at Royal Holloway, and television producer Matt Bouch. Thanks also to Dr Billy Smart for supplying me with an advance copy of his PhD thesis. The material provided by my subjects – who represent the great and the good of British television drama from the 1950s to the present day – has been invaluable, and I thank them each for taking the time to speak to me, and in many cases to review transcripts of our conversations: Howard Burch, Richard Clark, Kenneth Cope, Julia Dalkin, Lucy Fleming, Jason Flemyng, Tony Garnett, Mark Gatiss, Andrew Gunn, Graeme Harper, Charlie Higson, Adrian Hodges, Waris Hussein, Peter James, Louise Jameson, Denis Lill, the late Roger Lloyd Pack, Patrick Malahide, Kevin McNally, Derek Paget, Jamie Payne, Professor Jonathan Powell, Alvin Rakoff, Trevor Rawlins, Phillip Rhys, Kemal Sylvester, Suzan Sylvester, Colin Teague, Andrew Tiernan and Moray Watson, who sadly passed away shortly before the book went to press; his patience and courtesy did much to settle my first interview nerves. I would like to extend special thanks to Christopher Morahan, who not only agreed to my use of excerpts from our interview, but took the time to read through the manuscript and provide comments.

Colleagues who provided a much-needed sounding board are too numerous to list, but special mention must go to Doctor Cathy Johnson and Professor Roberta Pearson, for their extensive advice and support, and to Professors Jonathan Bignell and Paul McDonald, who also provided excellent feedback. Many thanks also to Matthew Frost and his team at Manchester University Press for making this project possible, and for turning my primitive cover design into such a professional piece of work.

As an early version of some of the material in Chapter 3 appeared in Volume 10.2 of *The Journal of British Cinema and Television* as 'Acting in the New World: Studio and Location Realism in Survivors', thanks are also due to the editors and reviewers for their comments.

Lastly, I would like to take this opportunity to thank my family – my parents, Ann and John Hewett, and my brother Paul – and the many friends who offered much appreciated encouragement throughout the research and writing process.

Introduction

> Creative and interpretive work demands concentration ... The effort is apparent when experienced actors are watched in rehearsal. Often the labour is a contradiction of the effortlessness that is eventually shown to the audience in performance. Indeed, at times, the rehearsal process may seem to be by far the most interesting part of the work.
>
> **(Barry 1992: 42)**

> Prior to the shooting period you don't get to meet the actors to rehearse anything ... Those few minutes before a take, that's all the time we have to quickly discover the moments we want to get out of the scene, work it through and let the crew see where we're at. Then, if we're lucky ... the director and actors will get maybe ten or maybe 15 minutes to hone it down and cover any other points.
>
> **(Harper 2007: 46)**

The comments above represent extreme contrasts in approach to British television acting, from opposite ends of a fifty-year spectrum. Michael Barry, the first person to head the BBC's screen drama output,[1] describes the rigorous rehearsal process endemic to the world of live broadcasting; a template that survived, in one form or another, decades after pre-recording had become the norm. Director Graeme Harper's latter-day production diary, however, illustrates the rapidity with which television performances were evolved in the mid-2000s, by which time the rehearsal process had been condensed to little more than a brief discussion before filming commenced.

Until recently, little work had been conducted on television acting per se, let alone the various coalescing factors that underpin and help shape it. *The Changing Spaces of Television Acting* aims to address that lack, utilising a selection of science fiction case studies from the world of BBC television drama to investigate how small screen performance and its various determinants have altered since the days of live production. Television science fiction provides a particularly useful starting point, this being a genre that is almost as old as the medium itself, and – as will be demonstrated – one that is arguably less inflected by genre-specific performance tropes than other styles such as crime drama or period adaptation. While a multi-genre analysis of television acting would doubtless prove fascinating, combining this approach with a historical overview would be well beyond the scope of a work of this length. *The Changing Spaces of Television Acting* instead focuses on science fiction case studies to provide a multi-perspectival examination of the historical development of acting in UK television drama, considering not only the performances ultimately seen on television screens, but also the ever-shifting factors that combine to shape them. In addition, it outlines broader developments within British television itself, its case studies offering a valuable index to the times in which they were produced.

One of the most notable contrasts between early television drama and the modern day is the shift from multi-camera studio (initially transmitted live, and later pre-recorded on videotape) to single camera location filming. The consequences of this were felt only gradually, and due to various other contributing factors were in a constant state of flux. However, studio and location provide a useful starting point for analysing both the changing determinants of British television acting (the cause) and the resulting screen performance (the effect). To this end, the terms 'studio realism' and 'location realism' have been developed here specifically to examine this shift. While these cannot be regarded as absolutes – audience reception of what is an acceptably 'realist' television performance can also be a determining factor – they represent an important first step towards a historical engagement with television acting.

Any use of the term 'realism' is potentially perilous, understandings being informed by time, place and medium; what is accepted as 'realistic' in one arena of performance does not necessarily transfer to another. Raymond Williams describes realism in the arts as 'a set of formal representations, in a particular medium to which we have become accustomed. The object is not *really* lifelike but by convention and repetition has been made to appear so' [original emphasis] (1983: 261). Roberta Pearson highlights the fact that any such representation of reality becomes 'a cultural construct, a matter of commonly held opinion rather than that which is presumed to have some objective existence outside the text' (1992: 28), while Jonathan Bignell offers a potential interpretation of television realism as '[a] representation of recognisable and often contemporary experience, such as in the representation of characters in whom the audience can believe' (2008: 190). Realism can therefore be understood as constantly changing in line with the world it seeks to represent; the realism of the 1950s television studio might be as distinct from that of the 1970s as it is from location realism in the 2000s. Utilising the analytical terms studio and location realism does not imply that physical sites alone were responsible for performance; rather, they are convenient prisms for tracing the journey from one to the other, through which a range of contributing factors are refracted.

The chief differences between studio and location realism are outlined in the table below, though it should be stressed that these are intended as general guidelines rather than an all-encompassing formula:

Studio realism	Location realism
Actors are working primarily in a constructed space, i.e. the studio set, providing a link with the traditional practices of theatre performance.	Actors are working primarily in a 'real' location, whether exterior or interior, as opposed to a performance space created for that purpose.[a]
Performances are prepared in advance, in a separate space such as the rehearsal room, before being transferred to the live broadcast/recording site.	Performances are evolved 'on site', with little or no prior preparation, allowing actors to respond to the environment in which they are working.
Scenes are performed in their entirety, with limited opportunity for re-takes.	Master shots aside, scenes are performed repeatedly, in segments, to accommodate different shot framings.

(cont.)

Studio realism	Location realism
Representation of reality is mediated by both space (typically an artificial, three-walled set) and technology.	Representation of reality, though mediated by technology, is less shaped by the use of an artificial or constructed performance space.
Use of voice and body are 'scaled down' from the level of projection required for the stage, but still feature a greater degree of projection than would be employed in real life.	Body and voice are used on a scale similar to that which would be employed in real life.
Physical movement is often designed to provide visual interest within the set, rather than deriving from character objectives.	Physical movement derives from the situation and character objectives; visual interest is produced by framings and editing.
Gesture is employed selectively to signify meaning and intent, though on a smaller scale than that used in the theatre.	Gesture to signify meaning and intent is minimal.
Clarity of diction is paramount.	Clarity of diction is not always required.[b]

[a] Although sets are employed in modern television drama, they are more likely to be soundstages of the type used in film-making, avoiding the 'three-walled' constructions traditionally associated with television studio drama. In addition, regular sets are often free-standing and semi-permanent, arguably becoming locations in their own right as opposed to temporarily erected artifices.

[b] This element has proved a bone of contention in recent years, the BBC's 2014 adaptation of *Jamaica Inn* receiving a storm of protests over the difficulty of understanding actor dialogue.

It would be limiting to offer this formulation as a simple binary; the likelihood is that examples in their purest forms are impossible to locate. As will be seen, a variety of performance styles co-exist at various points in British television history which would be difficult to categorise within these models. In addition, the selection of science fiction case studies potentially allows for the further proliferation of acting styles, as for example when performing the role of a non-human, or interacting with CGI imagery or special effects. However, such specific cases do not provide this book's central focus, and by identifying the key elements outlined above I believe it is possible to provide a useful starting point to consider at least the significant trends of change in acting style.

Until comparatively recently, few works existed to focus specifically on small screen acting in Britain. From 2015, Gary Cassidy and Simone Knox's series of blogs for *CST online* examining 'What Actors Do' evinced a growing interest in television performance. At the time of writing, Christopher Hogg and Tom Cantrell's forthcoming book *Acting in British Television* promises a rich exploration of contemporary style in popular genres including soap, comedy and police procedural via its use of original interview material, while their edited collection, *Exploring Television Acting*, will include my own chapter on studio and location realism in relation to television adaptations of Sherlock Holmes. Along with *The Changing Spaces of Television Acting*, such works demonstrate a growing awareness of the need for in-depth studies of British television acting. Previous case studies, such as *Crossroads: The Drama of a Soap Opera* (Hobson 1982), 'Rooms within Rooms: *Upstairs Downstairs* and the Studio Costume Drama of the 1970s' (Wheatley 2005) and 'The Quality of Intimacy: Revelation and Disguise in the Dramatic Monologue' (Goode 2006), have largely neglected acting to concentrate on narrative or visual style.[2] While performance is, refreshingly, considered in Lez Cooke's *Style in British Television Drama* (2013), which like this book chronicles the shift from multi-camera to single camera production, it is just one of several factors examined as part of *mise-en-scène*.[3] Cooke's work aside, the determinants of screen acting are usually ignored in television studies performance analysis, with John Caughie's 2000 reading of *Nineteen Eighty-Four* (BBC, 1954) a typical example. For Caughie, the cast's delivery of lines is acted 'with a clarity of diction and a "scriptedness" which are usually characterized, pejoratively, as "theatrical"' (2000a: 48). Criticising what he perceives as Peter Cushing's 'emotional "signalling"' (ibid.: 49), Caughie reserves praise only for Andre Morell as O'Brien, the enigmatic party member who wins Smith's confidence before betraying and torturing him. Interestingly, Caughie sees Morell's contained performance as better adapted to the small screen than those of his colleagues, 'detailing his characterization with what actors call "business" (a little mannerism with his spectacles), but withholding expressiveness' (ibid.: 48–49). What Caughie neglects to mention is that, as Smith – the audience's primary point of identification – Cushing has few early scenes in which his character can give vent to his feelings via dialogue; a degree of 'signalling' is therefore required for the spectator to fully comprehend the narrative thrust.

As one of the earliest surviving full-length British television dramas, it is perhaps unsurprising that *Nineteen Eighty-Four* has been utilised by several television historians, including Jason Jacobs (2000) and Lez Cooke (2003, 2013). However, Jacobs' attention to performance is tantalisingly brief, and while Cooke contextualises his reading via reference to the multi-camera set-up, non-technological determinants are largely ignored. Cooke and Jacobs do, however, offer a more positive take on Cushing's performance than Caughie, Jacobs providing a detailed analysis of the canteen scene, in which a pre-recorded voiceover of Smith's thoughts is heard over a close-up of Cushing's face, every twitch and glance signifying the character's fear of betraying his hatred of the regime.[4] However, while Cooke praises Cushing's skill in 'close up' acting (2003: 26), for Jacobs 'the gestural clarity of [his] performance does seem "theatrical", in the sense that even in close-up it seems to be "projecting"' (2000: 151). Although Jacobs is not employing the problematic term 'theatrical' in the pejorative sense pointed out by Caughie,[5] it seems a singularly inappropriate word to describe a facial performance which, if given in a theatre auditorium, would be impossible to read beyond the first few rows.[6]

In their individual ways, both Jacobs and Caughie fall into the analytical trap outlined by Roberta Pearson: 'While we cannot expect the average viewer ... to respond in the same manner as the original audience, we can expect a film critic or scholar not to use the aesthetic standards of his or her own time and culture in judging an artifact from another' (1990: 2). While it could be argued that what John Ellis has summarised as the tension between immanent reading and textual historicism (2007: 15–26) offers fruitful areas for comparison, Caughie's employment of terms such as 'stagey' and 'stilted' (2000a: 49) preclude a deeper understanding of this archive performance by failing to consider the factors that helped shape it – factors which form the basis of this book's analytical approach.

To date, a far greater amount of material has been published on cinema performance than television, with classical Hollywood typically (and perhaps understandably) providing the model for analysis. This has, however, often resulted in a concentration on the concept of stardom; what actors signify, rather than what they do on the screen. Notable works include Richard Dyer's *Stars* (1979, revised 1998), Charles Affron's *Star Acting: Gish, Garbo, Davies* (1977), and Andrew Klevan's *Film Performance: From Achievement to Appreciation* (2005), while James Naremore's *Acting in the Cinema* (1988), though following the 'star' route, is also significant for its summation of various theories of acting and performance. However, many of these works are in part compromised by an absence of background contextualisation. More recently, Ken Miller's *More Than Fifteen Minutes of Fame* (2013), while avoiding the star studies perspective, focuses instead on the relationship between screen performances (including television and the internet alongside film) and audiences, largely ignoring the question of how what actors do is influenced by determining factors.

The first book to fully consider the historical, social and industrial factors that mould screen acting is Roberta Pearson's *Eloquent Gestures: The Transformation of Performance Style in the Griffith Biograph Films* (1992), which evolved the terms 'histrionic' and 'verisimilar' to describe distinct performance styles in Biograph silent films. Few have followed Pearson's lead, though Cynthia Baron and Sharon Marie Carnicke's *Reframing Screen Performance* (2008) employs some useful examples of historicisation, as when examining actor training in the Hollywood studio era (17–32), and is laudable for utilising textual analysis to illustrate various approaches to performance, rather than as a means to its own end. This approach in particular has helped inform *The Changing Spaces of Television Acting*; though textual analysis has an important part to play in evidencing the acting styles of different periods, these can only be partially comprehended if divorced from the underlying factors that combined to shape them. This book offers an unprecedented historical overview of the working conditions of the small screen, tracing the connections between actors' background environments and the resulting television performances.

Researching historical determinants is potentially problematic, however, in that they are not fixed, and fluctuate in importance over the years. Some develop at a faster rate than others, or are of greater or lesser significance than might be expected at separate points in time; others are almost impossible to quantify. A prime determinant of any performance is the nature of the role being played, but this is so great a variable that it cannot be adequately considered in a historical overview of this type. The determinants examined herein are those that can be demonstrated to have changed over the period in question, and to have had a consequent impact on performance. When examined in individual chapters they will appear in descending order of relevance, though they are listed below in no specific order.

Technology is one of the prime factors affecting television acting. The impossibility of pre-recording in the medium's earliest years presented an entirely different set of pressures from those of the later filming process, multi-camera studio requiring a prior period of rehearsal which virtually disappeared when single camera film became the norm. However, as seen in Chapter 2, significant advances in technology did not always have the immediate impact on production practice that might have been expected.

Another key factor is actor training. Although television studies work in this field has thus far been limited, cinema academics have frequently highlighted the importance of drama theoretician Constantin Stanislavski's teachings on realism in performance,[7] Vsevolod Pudovkin (1953: 115–118, 147–148), Richard A. Blum (1984) and Sharon Marie Carnicke (1999: 75–87) each having demonstrated the Russian's relevance to film acting. A consideration of how and when Stanislavski's theories began to be taught in Britain is therefore necessary to any history of television performance, yet the paucity – until comparatively recently – of comprehensive screen training in British drama academies is arguably of equal importance, and this is highlighted in each chapter.

Actor experience is also relevant to television work, and is considered here in three ways: duration, amount and type. The chief distinction between duration and amount is length of experience as compared with the size and quantity of roles played in that time; technical considerations aside, the demands on a leading actor are very different from those on supporting players in terms of maintaining continuity of characterisation and performance. Equally relevant is the type of experience gained, which is divided here between stage, cinema, radio and television. The extent to which an actor is versed in these media can greatly inform their television performance, and brief histories are therefore provided for the various actors featured.

Experience can, of course, also influence the direction that casts are given; directors' approaches will vary depending on the grounding they have received. Whether trained internally by the BBC or hired as freelancers, a director working at one point in time might well have a preference for working procedures which had fallen out of favour by another. The change in directors' working practices is another of the key determinants to feature in each chapter; however, other factors are included individually where relevant. Chapter 2, for example, examines social realism and its effects on television acting, while Chapter 4 features a section on generational differences between actors working in contemporary television drama.

Utilising the correct terminology for performance analysis is a complex issue, as highlighted by John Caughie: 'While we have a vocabulary that describes and understands the effect of a cut or a close-up, we lack a critical language to describe and understand an expression that flits across a face or a hesitation in the voice' (2000b: 163). Various authors have made attempts either to formulate their own terminology (Pearson 1992), or to appropriate and re-apply that evolved by others to provide an overall lexis (Baron and Carnicke 2008); the creation of studio and location realism for this book is an example of the former. While various terms have been adopted, adapted or created herein for the purpose of analysis, these do not include the adjectives 'naturalistic' and 'theatrical', both of which are problematic and open to misinterpretation. In his call-to-arms article 'Nats Go Home' (1964), Troy Kennedy Martin famously selected naturalism as the prime characteristic of an era which I believe would be better categorised as studio realism, while James Naremore's definition of 'theatrical' performance as involving 'a degree of ostensiveness which marks it off from quotidian behaviour' (1988: 17) ignores the fact that what can be considered 'ostensive' is dependent on both culture and chronology. The question of theatricality is a particularly complex one. Early television's live 'immediacy' has often caused it to be aligned with a stage model, Philip Auslander claiming that the linear, limited arrangement of studio cameras replicated the static theatrical front of house or 'fourth wall' (2008: 21). For Auslander, the later increased mobility of cameras resulted in a shift towards a 'cinematic' style: 'Once [they] could enter the set and shoot from reverse angles, the syntax of televisual discourse became that of cinematic discourse' (*ibid*.). It should be noted that Auslander is writing of American television, which shifted to a single camera film model much earlier than Britain, where the process of studio multi-camera recording was retained decades after live drama had ceased. Rather than maintaining the stage-bound effect described by Auslander, however, this arrangement resulted in the development of an aesthetic which I shall argue – as others have before me[8] – was distinct both from theatre and cinema.

Given the problems relating to 'theatrical' performance, the term 'stage-derived' is used here to describe any use of voice and body in a manner or on a scale similar to that which might be seen in the theatre; a term that is not intended as in any way pejorative. I have also co-opted Jason Jacobs's term 'projected' (2000: 151) to describe both scale of physical gesture, posture, gait, etc., and the volume and articulation of voice; any employment of these greater than that required in real life is, by definition, an example of 'projection'. This can, however, be applied by degrees; the projection used in studio realism of the 1970s, for example, would be less than that seen in a stage production, but would have been significantly reduced by the time of location realism in the 2000s.

Projection aside, the consideration of voice raises another question. The period covered within these pages has seen a significant shift away from what was formerly known as Standard English, and is now commonly termed Received Pronunciation, or 'RP'; there has also been a marked increase in actors employing their own, original accents. In order to delineate between these different uses of voice, a brief taxonomy of terms has been evolved. A 'real' voice is the natural product of an actor's 'home' environment or background; that which they use in everyday life.[9] An 'adopted' voice is one that has been learned until it has become second nature, with the result that the actor's original accent has been abandoned; an example of adopted voice would be a regional actor who has studied Received Pronunciation at drama school and gone on to employ it on a daily basis. A 'recovered' voice is one which, though obliterated through the learning of an adopted voice, can be recalled and employed for any role that requires it. By contrast, a 'mimicked' voice is one temporarily employed by an actor for a role that is not their real or recovered voice; such an accent can be produced 'by ear', as the result of a natural gift for imitation, or through study, for example using phonetics. The difference between the mimicked accent and the adopted is that the former is used only for a particular role, whereas the latter has replaced the real voice in daily life. Finally, the 'put on' voice is one the actor believes to be suitable for a particular role, but is produced without the depth of study or natural ability of the mimicked.

Given the extent of Constantin Stanislavski's influence, some of the Russian's original terminology, much of which has since become standard vocabulary in western drama schools, is employed here for the purpose of analysis. For example, the expression 'given circumstances' (also termed the 'magic if') describes the imaginary situation in which the actor is placed, forcing them to consider what they would do, how they would feel, etc. and thus acting as the initial stimulant to the development of any scene (1934: 46–53). 'Objective' describes the particular aim that a character wishes to achieve (*ibid.*: 111–126), while a 'unit' or 'beat' is a subdivision or section of action, perhaps signifying that an objective has been achieved or abandoned (*ibid.*).

These, then, are the terms to be employed when analysing case studies. However, the selection of texts for examination presents another potential problem. As highlighted by Jonathan Bignell, any such programme, once chosen:

> becomes an example representing a larger context and history. Yet such a programme must therefore exceed the range it represents, and be regarded as more than typical as soon as that example is cited instead of the others which could have been chosen. This duality between representativeness and exceptionalness is necessarily the case with any example, but it becomes especially problematic for teaching and writing about television because of the nature of television as a popular medium about which everyone has an opinion and a memory.
>
> **(2006: 16)**

Other complicating factors include the perceived tension between 'serious' drama (traditionally exemplified by the single play) and 'popular' series and serials, and the difficulties attendant to the absence of developed work on broadcasters' production practices (Bignell 2007b: 37) – a lack this work takes steps to rectify.

Given the aims of this book, it is desirable that the texts used derive from demonstrably distinct 'eras'. Technology provides a useful delineator here, as television drama can be seen to have fallen loosely into four sections. Live studio drama was the norm from the inception of British television in 1936 until the early 1960s; however, the initial impossibility of recording transmitted output means that few complete examples exist prior to the early 1950s. The introduction of videotape in 1958 meant that it was now possible to pre-record programmes, though both the early difficulty and cost of editing tape meant that the majority of drama was recorded 'as live': performed continuously in story order, with a minimum of breaks. This remained common practice until the 1970s, when the increased manipulability of tape[10] – combined with a new agreement with actors' union Equity (McNaughton 2014: 16–18) – meant that it was possible to 'rehearse/record'[11] productions in segments which could then be edited together. The studio, however, remained the prime site of television drama until the early 1990s, by which time all-film – and latterly HD (High Definition) video – production had become the norm, utilising locations and soundstages of the type more traditionally employed on feature films.

With this consideration in mind, the case studies utilised are: *The Quatermass Experiment* (BBC, 1953; BBC, 2005), *Doctor Who* (BBC, 1963–89;[12] BBC, 2005–); and *Survivors* (BBC, 1975–77; BBC, 2008–10). Each fits the requirement of the original having evolved in a distinct production era, with the additional advantage that it was followed by a new version in the 2000s. While *The Quatermass Experiment* was broadcast as a live, six-part serial, *Doctor Who* was initially pre-recorded 'as live'. *Survivors* began as a multi-camera studio production with location film inserts, but from its seventh episode switched to an all Outside Broadcast (OB) location video model; an early precursor of location realism. The use of modern 're-makes' for each of these productions in the 2000s offers the perfect opportunity to illustrate changes in acting style over the period in question, providing both a chronological development and a then-and-now comparison.

The focus on BBC productions, as opposed to independent television, is one of pragmatism and accessibility, the Corporation's Written Archives Centre (WAC) offering a wealth of valuable background information, including production files, shooting scripts and Viewer Research Reports. While a comparison with independent television would be of inestimable value, ITV companies' early lack of a centralised management structure and established production procedure – combined with the difficulty of locating archives for individual companies (Johnson and Turnock 2005: 5) – means that selecting representative texts for particular historical periods becomes extremely complicated.

The question of format also requires attention. The original versions of *The Quatermass Experiment* and *Doctor Who* were both technically serials,[13] yet the first had a finite run of just six weeks, while the latter continued for twenty-six years. Only the first two episodes of *The Quatermass Experiment* were preserved in the archives, meaning that a study of the entire production is not possible, while the prodigious length of *Doctor Who*'s initial run means that a comprehensive overview would require a book-length work of its own at the very least. By contrast, *Survivors* was produced as a series, though with a continuing narrative and story strands that stretched over several episodes. This potential complicating factor has been circumvented, however, by choosing to focus solely on the opening episodes of *The Quatermass Experiment* ('Contact has been Established') and *Doctor Who* ('An Unearthly Child'), while in the case of *Survivors* two episodes from the first series have been selected to represent the different production processes employed: series opener 'The Fourth Horseman' for filmed location inserts and multi-camera studio, and the later 'Law and Order' for the all-OB location model. It should be remembered here that these episodes have been selected in order to unpack the state of British television acting at the time they were made, and not necessarily as representative narrative samples of their respective productions. One of the few early episodes of *Doctor Who* to be set in contemporary London, rather than a historical time period or an alien planet, 'An Unearthly Child' is in many ways atypical of the style the series would later adopt, and the same could be said of 'The Fourth Horseman', which depicts an England that has yet to descend into the chaos that characterises subsequent episodes of *Survivors*.

Two of the modern productions are less problematic. While the 2008 version of *Survivors* is a loose re-make, *Doctor Who* is a continuation of the original series; however, the latter avoids alienating viewers unfamiliar with the programme's history by making few explicit references in early episodes to past stories. Both *Doctor Who* and *Survivors* can be categorised as continuing series dramas which utilise the single camera film model, and so are dealt with together in a single chapter. Rather than focusing on one episode for each series, scenes from multiple episodes are utilised for analysis; a decision that is partially reflective of the fragmented nature of modern television drama, in which actors could be filming segments of different episodes on the same day.[14] Produced live as a single drama, the 2005 re-mount of *The Quatermass Experiment* is unrepresentative of modern production contexts, and therefore features in a separate chapter examining the renewed interest in live television drama in the 2000s.

The extent to which these texts are technologically representative of their time is a separate issue. While both *The Quatermass Experiment* and *Doctor Who* utilised then-current production processes, neither was allocated the latest technological facilities. The Emitron cameras used at Alexandra Palace for the former dated back to 1936, while *Doctor Who*'s early home of Lime Grove Studio B was similarly outmoded at a time when the BBC's new Television Centre was already in use. Conversely, the opening episode of *Doctor Who* could be seen as exceptional in that an initially un-transmitted 'pilot' was produced, only to be rejected for broadcast, and the move by *Survivors* to all-OB production was a similarly ground-breaking one for series drama.[15] These considerations would be significant were technology the sole determinant of studio realism, but this was demonstrably not the case. *The Quatermass Experiment* and *Doctor Who* were not the only television dramas being produced at their respectively 'old-fashioned' studios, and a range of other, intersecting factors were also at work.

While none of these programmes was shown after the 9 p.m. watershed, *The Quatermass Experiment* and *Survivors* were broadcast after 8 p.m., while *Doctor Who*'s earlier timeslot of 5.15 p.m. has often seen it categorised as a children's programme. However, Jonathan Bignell has made the case that it in fact addressed 'mixed family audiences of different age groups, sexes and social classes' (2007a: 43). It was produced under the auspices of the Drama Department, and according to Bignell represented the BBC's aim 'to continue the ... ethos of "quality" writing in terms of character, dramatic logic and thematic complexity' (2005b: 82).

Lastly – and perhaps most importantly – the point must be made that these case studies have not been selected in order to examine a particular generic style of acting. In *Genre and Performance*, actress-turned-academic Christine Cornea illustrates the extent to which the genre in which an actor is working can influence their performance, for example recognising and replicating 'familiar codes and conventions' when auditioning (successfully) for a role in a supernatural horror film (2010: 6). *The Quatermass Experiment*, *Doctor Who* and *Survivors* have frequently been grouped together as science fiction or 'telefantasy' (e.g. Cornell *et al.* 1996), genres which, as highlighted by Catherine Johnson (2007: 62–63) and Jonathan Bignell (2007b: 38–39), have until comparatively recently received scant attention as serious drama. The main exception here is *Doctor Who*, which in 1983 was the subject of a detailed study by John Tulloch and Manuel Alvarado, and since its 2005 relaunch has been examined extensively in monographs by Matt Hills (2010) and James Chapman (2013), in addition to edited collections from David Butler (2007) and Matt Hills *et al.* (2013). However, these works represent a case study-based approach, as opposed to a more general repositioning of telefantasy as a 'serious' television genre. The term 'telefantasy' is indeed a problematic one, borrowed as it is from fan discourse and comprising 'a wide range of fantasy, science fiction and horror' (Johnson 2005: 2). Johnson points out that the breadth of texts to which this can be applied makes it difficult to provide 'a clearly defined generic classification' (*ibid.*), and the texts used here are cases in point. While *The Quatermass Experiment* and *Doctor Who* both feature space travel and extra-terrestrial life, there is little obvious connection between either's narrative and that of *Survivors*, in which a virus wipes out 95 per cent of the Earth's population. Science fiction alone can clearly encompass any number of scenarios, with varying levels of realism and fantasy. However, what the episodes examined herein *do* have in common is the intrusion of the fantastic – the unknown or 'other' – into an environment which is presented at the outset as recognisably 'normal' and present day. This element, rather than resulting in 'fantastic' (i.e. unreal) performances – which might be the case for telefantasy series set in the future, or on alien worlds (as is the case in other episodes of *Doctor Who*) – requires a grounding in realism as strong as that found in any other television genre.

This view contradicts that of Roberta Pearson, who claims that science fiction and fantasy require actors 'to suit their interpretations to the oft-times larger-than-life nature of the text' (2010: 182). Perceiving a 'general distinction between acting in science fiction/fantasy and a realist drama' (181), Pearson cites *Star Trek* (NBC, 1966–69) as an example of television wherein 'the epic quality of some science fiction or fantasy programmes ... requires the greater intensity of a theatrical performance mode' (181), as opposed to the 'cool, low key, realist' performance style she associates with the intimate, close-up nature of most television drama. By way of illustration Pearson quotes from *Star Trek* lead William Shatner's autobiography, in which the actor retrospectively justified his heightened performance:

> There's actually a pretty valid reason for all that scenery chewing ... When you're an actor standing around in a cardboard-and-Christmas-light starship ... you can never be too sure that your scripted lines won't just seem completely ridiculous. It often seemed to me that *without* all of Kirk's emotion, and intensity and high-octane hand-wringing, our villains of the week might have seemed more ridiculous than frightening; the ship's crisis of the week might have seemed a lot less threatening were Kirk not up in arms. [Original emphasis]
> **(Shatner with Kreski 1999: 166–167)**

Shatner's assertion that he adapted his acting style, in effect producing a 'fantastic' performance suited to the unreal nature of the narrative, supports Pearson's drawing of a line between fantasy acting and realistic acting only if we take *Star Trek* as representative of the science fiction/fantasy genre. And herein lies the problem; with a genre that defies the more limited and limiting definitional characteristics of other programme types, no single text can be taken as truly representative. *Star Trek* is *one* example of acting for television science fiction, but cannot be taken as 'typical' telefantasy because, comprised as it is of so many sub-genres, no one representative example can possibly exist.

The potential differences between the depiction of reality/fantasy in a text such as *Star Trek* and the case studies utilised here are highlighted by the diversion between what narratologist

Marie-Laure Ryan has termed the Actual World (AW) and the Textual Actual World (TAW) (1991: 556).[16] Whereas the AW is that in which the viewer exists – the real world – the TAW is the one presented to the viewer in the text. Ryan provides a list of ways in which the TAW resembles or differs from the AW; a comparative exercise that she terms 'accessibility relations' (*ibid.*: 557). While the TAW presented in 'true fiction' contains all the same elements (physical, chronological, taxonomic, logical, linguistic, etc.) as the AW, science fiction and fantasy differ – or can differ – in a number of respects. For example, Ryan states that a science fiction TAW, even when observing the physical compatibility of natural laws, can differ chronologically; *Star Trek*'s temporal setting in the future means that the AW viewer is unable 'to contemplate the entire history of [its] TAW' (*ibid.*). The alien species endemic to *Star Trek*'s TAW are another differentiating element, Vulcans and Klingons not being part of our AW. Were it the purpose of this book to examine a 'fantastic' style of acting – which could perhaps be termed studio and location '*un*realism' – it would be fascinating to examine the development of the non-AW, futuristic cultures and scenarios presented and refined by a franchise such as *Star Trek* over its long television run. However, that is not our objective here; instead, *The Changing Spaces of Television Acting* focuses specifically on UK telefantasy case studies whose TAWs would have been perfectly accessible to their original viewers – at least until the fantastic intrudes upon them. If Bernard Quatermass's role as head of Britain's first manned space flight seems improbable to modern viewers, it is presented as credible and accepted within the TAW, while the characters initially introduced in *Doctor Who* and *Survivors* all have AW jobs (schoolteachers, housewives and office workers) and characteristics. It is only when a non-AW element enters the narrative of each that true disjunction occurs, and the texts enter the realm of the fantastic.[17] Were the acting of all science fiction characters heightened in the way that Shatner suggests is inevitable, whatever seemingly fantastic events occurred could only be perceived as endemic to the TAW, and therefore lose their effect of otherness.[18] However, the fantastic event, when it arrives, must be presented in such a way that the viewer can accept it as taking place within the TAW; too great a disjunction would simply result in ridicule. Overall, the text must possess a degree of verisimilitude, defined by Steve Neale as that which is '"probable", "plausible" or "likely"' (2000: 32). What is accepted as 'probable' can be dependent on genre, yet 'all fiction to some extent involves what has traditionally been called "suspension of disbelief", by virtue of the fact that its agents and events are, by definition, unreal. In actual fact, while disbelief may well be involved, it is often knowledge and judgement that the spectator is required to suspend' (Neale 1990: 163).

For Catherine Johnson, socio-cultural verisimilitude is particularly important in rendering credible the worlds into which the fantastic intrudes:

> When depicting an alien landing on Earth, socio-cultural verisimilitude is essential to make the Earth seem plausible and believable despite the presence of an alien being. While these genres may represent fictional worlds that challenge culturally accepted notions of 'reality', they are also crucially engaged with explaining the rules that govern their particular fictional world, a process that is only possible through generic and socio-cultural verisimilitude.
>
> (2005: 4)

That *The Quatermass Experiment* achieves this despite the comparative crudity (when viewed today) of its special effects is a testament to the realism of its cast's acting: 'While giant vegetable aliens and spacecraft confound the socio-cultural verisimilitude of the 1950s viewer, the serial work[s] hard narratively and stylistically to reinforce the plausibility and believability of such fantastic elements' (*ibid.*: 27).

As always, it is important to place these programmes in historical context. At the time *The Quatermass Experiment* was transmitted there had been relatively few science fiction productions on British television;[19] there was, therefore, no established television performance mode for actors to imitate. Further *Quatermass* serials and *A for Andromeda* (BBC, 1961) aside, things had changed little by the time *Doctor Who* began a decade later, and as will be shown in Chapter 2 the programme's early serials display a similar commitment to verisimilitude. Such was the latter series' longevity that, over the course of its initial twenty-six-year transmission, a number of performance styles evolved over different periods, often associated with particular production teams (Tulloch and Alvarado

1983: 247–248). Guest actors joining the programme for a particular serial might well have styled their performance to fit with what they had already seen of transmitted episodes and so associated, even subconsciously, with a 'house style'. The selection of opening or early episodes as case studies therefore avoids the possible inclusion of any such series-specific style.

While some generically specific television dramas, produced to target certain audience segments, might well engender a particular performance style, the nebulous nature of science fiction in effect precludes such an overt influence. The common link between the episodes focused upon here, of the 'fantastic' intruding into the 'real' world, requires an acting style (for the human characters, at least) that grounds each case study, as far as possible, in contemporaneous realism. As such they provide robust models from which to extrapolate historically representative examples of television acting, offering a valuable window into the developing world of small screen performance. Rather than providing a study of 'fantastic' acting, this book utilises telefantasy case studies to trace the historical development of UK television acting as a whole.

In order to examine these texts a combination of methodologies is employed, comprised primarily of historical research, textual analysis and reception studies. The potential of textual analysis is well summarised by Charles Affron when he states that a screen performance is 'wedded to the text in a way it can never be on the stage. In its relationship to the viewer, the screen performance is indistinguishable from the text it is expressing' (1977: 5). Archive television programmes thus provide examples not only of acting style, but of the times in which they were produced. However, in the absence of contextualising information such analysis risks, to paraphrase Victor Turner, only partially understanding – and hence appreciating – the text it seeks to unpack: 'What we are looking for here is not so much the traditional preoccupation with text alone but text in context … [It is] necessary to do some homework on the history … of the "worlds" which encompass the dramatic traditions we are considering' (1986: 28). As Catherine Johnson points out: 'A programme that appears to be badly paced and poorly executed to contemporary eyes may well be understood as innovative when placed within its context of production and reception' (2007: 61). Johnson therefore recommends seeking out historical reviews to help 'challenge our initial subjective response to an old television programme and provide part of the interpretive context through which we evaluate its function' (*ibid.*).

To this end, historical research here takes two forms: archival, sourcing original production material from the BBC's archives; and specially conducted interviews, putting specific questions to personnel involved in case studies and contemporaneous industry practitioners. The latter is not limited to actors, but also includes directors and producers able to offer insights into the environments in which performances were created. Such original interviews have helped form the basis for several recent television case studies, including Brett Mills' *The Sitcom* (2009) and Roberta Pearson and Maire Messenger Davies' *Star Trek and American Television* (2014). However, performance studies has usually kept interview materials separate from textual analysis, with the former either gathered into historical compendiums[20] or published as original collections.[21] These works are notable for their focus on Hollywood, and television acting is generally less discussed than stage and film.[22] While the interviews conducted for this book allow for specific focus on relevant issues, it is important to consider the potentially complicating issue of memory, whether this takes the form of inaccuracies engendered by the passage of time, or individuals' desire to best represent (and perhaps enhance) personal associations with programmes since acclaimed as landmark productions. As Kerwin Lee Klein highlights, while history is objective 'in the coldest, hardest sense of the word, memory is subjective in the warmest, most inviting sense' (2000: 130). What some might call hindsight can also distort recollection, and Nicola King has pointed out the paradox of knowing and not knowing when relating personal histories: 'any autobiographical narrator ... in the present moment of the narration, possesses the knowledge that she did not have "then", in the moment of the experience' (2000: 2): With specific regard to television history, John Caughie has cautioned against rose-tinted recollections of the so-called Golden Age in the 1960s and 1970s: 'Nostalgia creates a past without rough edges which only exist in fantasy and desire' (2000a: 57). Amy Holdsworth also points out that what is remembered as 'golden' relates directly to the youth of the commentator during the period being recalled (2011: 121); interestingly, though many of the industry subjects featured here are reviewing their early careers in television, most are at pains to provide as de-romanticised a picture as possible. Nevertheless, any potential exaggerations or unwitting inaccuracies are balanced by the inclusion, wherever possible, of archive materials; immutable production records uninfluenced by the passage of time. The inclusion of reception indicators also provides a valuable index of the times in which these programmes were produced, Viewer Research Reports, *Radio Times* correspondence and press reviews demonstrating the extent to which the performances given were acceptable to contemporaneous audiences, and thus indicating their representativeness. While, for the more recent productions, Viewer Reports are no longer available, internet sites such as *Digital Spy* provide a similar barometer of what comprises acceptably realist performance. *Doctor Who* in particular has developed an active fan culture, and while Henry Jenkins (1992) has highlighted the ways in which such groups can shape discourses around television texts, Paul Rixon (2011) more recently pointing out the role played by the internet in these activities, fan responses will not be focused upon specifically here, if only for the reason that commercial magazines and fanzines do not necessarily represent a 'general' audience. In addition, as *The Quatermass Experiment* and *Survivors* arguably do not possess a fan following equal to that enjoyed by *Doctor Who*, examining fan reaction as an example of performance reception might risk skewing focus in favour of the latter.

The book is divided into five chapters. The first examines early studio realism in 'Contact has been Established', the debut episode of *The Quatermass Experiment* from 1953. Chapter 2 then illustrates the extent to which a greater uniformity of scale in terms of physical and vocal projection had emerged by the time of *Doctor Who*'s first episode, 'An Unearthly Child', in 1963. Chapter 3 examines nascent location realism in the 1970s, contrasting scenes from *Survivors*' largely studio-based debut, 'The Fourth Horseman', with the later 'Law and Order', produced entirely on location using OB. Chapter 4 then moves to the location realism which predominated in the 2000s via the modern versions of *Doctor Who* and *Survivors*, while the 2005 re-mount of *The Quatermass Experiment* forms the foundation of Chapter 5, which examines the revival of interest in live drama in the 2000s, and the potential for studio realism's return.

The resulting journey is a fascinating and not always predictable one. We begin six decades in the past, investigating the earliest recorded stages of studio realism in the live era. Though a world aesthetically alien to modern audiences, its complex interplay of determinants must be unpacked and examined if we are to deepen our understanding of the developments that have taken place between then and the location realism of the present day; in brief, the changing spaces of British television acting.

Notes

1 Radio's Val Gielgud had been jointly responsible for sound and vision prior to Barry becoming BBC Television's Head of Drama in 1952.
2 Highlighting the fact that television studies has produced few sustained analyses of performance in serial television (2015: 27), Elliott Logan's examination of Claire Danes' performance as Carrie Mathison in *Homeland* (Showtime, 2011–) is simultaneously limited by his focus on a particular format, rather than television acting per se.
3 Jeremy Butler (2010) similarly considers performance as part of television's *mise-en-scène*, though his focus is on the United States. Butler earlier became one of the first academics to examine television acting when he discussed the impact of re-casting in '"I'm Not a Doctor, But I Play One on TV"' (1991).
4 Cooke has since challenged Jacobs' assumption that this was a 'live' performance, contending that Cushing probably pre-recorded the entire sequence on film (2013: 23–25).
5 Jacobs admits instead to the 'visual pleasure of seeing a skilled actor like Cushing in control of his performance' (2000: 151).
6 This recalls Vsevolod Pudovkin's observation on the unsuitability of Constantin Stanislavski's techniques for the stage, citing an example in which the latter's attempt to convey 'a series of thoughts and emotions' while seated on a bench during a theatre performance was 'lost on the audience because of the distance between. In close-up, however, the public would have been able to follow on the screen all the fine plays of eyes and features and thus take in everything Stanislavski wished to impart' (1953: 116).

7   Most notably *An Actor Prepares* (1934), *Building a Character* (1949) and *Creating a Role* (1961), all translated by Elizabeth Reynolds Hapgood.
8   In *The Intimate Screen* (2000), Jason Jacobs provides ample evidence to support his assertion that 'the development of television drama is not a story of the steady emancipation from theatrical values toward the cinematic, but one where producers were able to choose from a range of stylistic features' (117).
9   Each 'real' voice is of course unique, the strength or breadth of an individual's accent being dependent upon a range of variables impossible to categorise in a work of this scope. The subjectivity of individual responses to the credibility of actors' accents makes a comprehensive argument impossible to construct; rather, this work is concerned with overall historical trends concerning both the use and the acceptability of voice.
10 By this time the use of two videotape editing machines, working in unison, as opposed to the single machine used in the 1960s meant that editing became 'as flexible as film' (Sutton 1982: 124).
11 Rehearsed and performed in segments that are recorded separately, possibly not in story order.
12 Although considered part of the *Doctor Who* canon, the 1996 'television movie' is not included here as it was not solely a UK production.
13 In modern terms, the original version of *Doctor Who* would be better understood as a continuing series of serials.
14 This was not the case for the earlier iterations, where separate episodes would be produced on a week-by-week basis; hence the focus here on single episodes of *The Quatermass Experiment* and *Doctor Who*. Had *Survivors*' production model not altered mid-run, one episode of this series would also have sufficed for the purpose of analysis.
15 The OB process had, however, been used for stand-alone productions, having debuted four years earlier on *A Midsummer Night's Dream* (BBC, 1971) (Smart 2010: 313–314).
16 Although Ryan is writing from a literary perspective, her analytical framework can equally be applied to television.
17 It should be noted that the case studies selected represent, in terms of fantasy narratives, what Farah Mendlesohn terms 'the intrusion fantasy', in which 'the fantastic enters the fictional world' (2008: 1). Other narrative models listed by Mendlesohn include the portal-quest, the immersive (of which *Star Trek* would be an example) and the liminal. A study of telefantasy acting could perhaps compare and contrast examples of each, though that extends beyond the remit of this book.
18 This does not apply to characters that are not part of the 'real' TAW into which they intrude. There is no reason that an actor playing the 'fantastic' character of the Doctor in *Doctor Who* cannot

give a 'heightened' performance, as the Doctor manifestly does not belong to the world of twentieth or twenty-first century Earth. Captain Kirk and the crew of the *Enterprise*, conversely, *can* be seen to belong to their twenty-third century environment.

19 Interestingly, although producer Rudolph Cartier referred to *The Quatermass Experiment* as 'a science fiction serial' in private correspondence, writing to an Air Ministry official that he was 'anxious to lift [it] above the level of strip-cartoons' (BBC WAC T5/418, Letter to C. Moodie Esq.), the programme was ultimately listed as 'a thriller in six parts' in the *Radio Times*.

20 Examples include *Actors on Acting: The Theories, Techniques and Practices of the World's Great Actors, Told in Their Own Words* (Cole and Krich Chinoy 1970) and *Playing to the Camera: Film Actors Discuss Their Craft* (Cardullo et al. 1998).

21 Collections include Carole Zucker's *Figures of Light: Actors and Directors Illuminate the Art of Film Acting* (1995) and *In the Company of Actors: Reflections on the Craft of Acting* (1999a), Joanmarie Kalter's *Actors on Acting: Performing in Theatre and Film Today* (1979), and *The Player* (1962), by Helen and Lillian Ross.

22 Exceptions include Carole Zucker's 'An Interview with Ian Richardson: Making Friends with the Camera' (1999b), which features some interesting reflections on the actor's need for awareness of the lens being used (162), and Max Sexton's 'Philip Jackson: The Craft of Acting' (2015).

1
Scaling down in early studio realism

In the early 1950s, theatre still provided a starting point for the majority of actors working for the BBC, and the processes of live television drama in some ways resembled those of the stage. Movements were carefully planned and lines learnt through repetition in rehearsal rooms before transferring to the studio on the day of broadcast; the performance, once begun, could not be interrupted if an actor 'dried' or even died,[1] replicating and arguably amplifying the pressures of stage work. However, to assume that this similarity in conditions resulted in a purely stage-derived mode of performance would be overly simplistic. Originally launched in Britain in 1936, television was no longer a new medium, and despite the seven-year hiatus imposed by the Second World War, by 1953 it would have been possible for many actors to have accumulated up to a decade of small screen experience. While the absence of archive examples makes a comprehensive assessment of earlier acting style impossible, it is highly unlikely that the developments demonstrated already to have taken place by Jason Jacobs in *The Intimate Screen* had no impact on performance. In his book, Jacobs employs detailed analyses of camera scripts and studio plans on early BBC productions to challenge the view of television drama as 'photographed plays', identifying two screen trends which distinguished it from theatre: the intimate, utilising close-ups as a device to focus on actor expressions and reactions impossible to read on the stage (2000: 116–125), and the expansive, exemplified by the use of pre-filmed inserts (*ibid.*: 125–132). Frequently cited as a pioneer of the latter is Rudolph Cartier, the Austrian émigré whose 1953 production *The Quatermass Experiment* provides this chapter's focus.

Prime among the various determinants of television acting that can be seen at work in *The Quatermass Experiment* is actor experience, and scenes from the opening episode, 'Contact has been Established', illustrate the extent to which certain actors with a greater length (and breadth) of experience had already begun to adapt in terms of vocal projection and physical gesture, while many of their colleagues remained fixed in more stage-derived codes. As always, however, there were a number of other factors at play, not least the exigencies of studio technology and its production processes.

Background

Britain in the summer of 1953 was dominated by the coronation of Queen Elizabeth II, the first such event to be fully televised,[2] and arguably the earliest occasion on which the medium united the country in celebration.[3] The number of television licences held in the United Kingdom swelled to 2,142,452 (Briggs 1979: 240), and in July agreement was announced between the government and the BBC for plans to make television available 'to ninety per cent of the population within a period of eighteen months' ('BBC to Extend Television at Once' 1953: 3). 1953 ultimately became the year in which the manufacture of television sets overtook radio, and by 1955 there would be more viewers than listeners (Crisell 1997: 75).

This, then, was the spirit of national jubilation and technological optimism into which *The Quatermass Experiment* emerged when 'Contact has been Established' was broadcast at 8.15 p.m. on Saturday 18 July. In stark contrast to the twenty-four-hour, multi-channel environment of today, British television of the time was monopolised by the licence fee-funded British Broadcasting Corporation, independent television not arriving until 1955. The amount of programming offered was limited, weekday transmissions not usually commencing until 3.15 p.m. Single dramas dominated, the Sunday evening play forming the centrepiece of the weekly schedule; adaptations of existing stage and literary vehicles still outnumbered works written specifically for television. As nearly all television was live, these Sunday dramas would be performed again on Thursday evenings by the same cast.[4] Serials, however, were not usually re-mounted in this way; a fact that seems to have been the source of discontent for some viewers, Henry Burrows of Derby lamenting: 'I wonder whether other viewers share my feelings that serial plays should have each episode repeated ... It leaves a great feeling of frustration when one missed the last episode of any production' (1953: 35). An alternative to the re-grouping of casts was the nascent telerecording process. However, the poor quality of early telerecording was another cause for complaint, Mrs G. Furness of Huddersfield writing: 'I have found it very disappointing when, having praised a programme to my husband, he has sat back to see the telerecording and – alas! – has seen a much poorer edition' (1953: 32).

The Quatermass Experiment was an early example of the adult serial form, for which Mr Burrows's letter suggests there was already a growing audience. It was also significant in that it was written specifically for television, and became one of the first serials – as opposed to plays – to experiment with telerecording. Although filmed transcripts of *The Quatermass Experiment* were abandoned after the second instalment due to technical problems,[5] the telerecording of serials became more common in subsequent years, live repeat performances ultimately giving way to recordings of the previous month's Sunday plays (Jacobs 2000: 115). These various innovations all took place under BBC Television's first Head of Drama, Michael Barry, who sought to create more original works for the medium. Expanding the existing Script Department, Barry also established the post of Staff Writer, whose first incumbent, Nigel Kneale, wrote *The Quatermass Experiment*. Barry also took on new producer/directors[6] from the world of film and theatre, rather than radio; foremost among these was Rudolph Cartier, who had previously worked as a scriptwriter and producer in Germany, Britain and the United States. Cartier and Kneale first met while working on the adaptation *Arrow to the Heart* (BBC, 1952), and found much common ground, each regarding television up to this point as too slow-paced and reliant on dialogue. Kneale later recalled: 'People were still baffled ... I watched sad radio men trying to turn it into illustrated radio ... and disappointed men from films despairing at time and space that confounded their too-loose scripts' (1959: 86). Kneale and Cartier were also critical of what they saw as an over-dependence on close-ups, which the latter argued should be used sparingly: 'Music at continuous *fortissimo* would make dull listening. The television producer cannot afford to let the visual impact of the close-up be blunted by frequent use ... My practice is to save it until the final dramatic scene' (cited in 'The Man Who Put 1984 Over on Television' 1958: 14). Both men believed in 'opening up' television via the inclusion of pre-filmed 'insert' material, providing 'a useful extension of the story beyond the cramped studio sets' (Kneale 1959: 87).[7]

If, then, we take Cartier's 'expansive' mode of programme-making as representing the latest stage in the development of British television drama, to what extent did the performances of his casts reflect this – if at all?

Actor experience

Although the technological and production constraints imposed by live transmission were, as will be seen, considerable, arguably the prime influence on television acting in the early 1950s was the experience possessed by players. In terms of duration, the careers of the various performers in *The Quatermass Experience* spanned five decades; twenty-five-year-old Moray Watson was the youngest member of the cast, while Katie Johnson was, at seventy-four, the most senior in years. However, this does not necessarily signify that the actors who had been working longest were best adapted to the screen; *type* of experience was also a significant factor. While theatre remained the predominant field of employment, repertory providing the most common starting point for actors,[8] the British film industry was also increasing in significance, as reflected in the 1948 agreement reached between actors' union Equity and the British Film Producers' Association (Sanderson 1984: 284). Although radio had, since the 1920s, provided actors with 'an attractive range of work' (*ibid.*: 223), the amount of experience it offered was initially limited, drama only comprising four per cent of its output until the 1940s (*ibid.*). Experience acquired in each medium presented unique advantages and disadvantages to an actor working in television. According to Alvin Rakoff, who began his BBC directing career in 1953, the fact that the majority arrived from the theatre meant that 'you suddenly had to teach them how to scale down' (2011). While vocal projection was still necessary for the studio boom microphones, it was no longer of the type required to reach audience members seated at the back of an auditorium; a fact to which actors with a grounding in film and radio would be better acclimatised. In addition, the close-ups employed for television transferred the audience's focus from the body – which on the stage provided the actor with a very visible signifying tool in terms of posture, movement and gesture – to the face, clearly visible only to the front few rows of the theatre. Even in mid-shot, the television actor's capacity for body movement and gesture was limited by the relative immobility of the cameras and the size of the frame; viewers in 1953 would have been watching on screens varying in size from eight to fifteen inches.[9] Such considerations required significant adjustments on the part of the stage actor: 'You had to tell [them] [to] what scale and level they could pitch their performance; you were virtually teaching them about a new medium, and with some actors it was almost impossible' (*ibid.*). Actors arriving from weekly repertory, however, had the advantage of being inured to the fast turnaround of learning lines and maintaining continuity of performance when events conspired against them. This was a habit that actors working primarily in film, for which repeated takes would be the norm, or radio, where there was no necessity to block movements, might well have fallen out of. According to Rakoff, film actors, while 'aware they weren't pitching it up to the gallery', were also used to the single camera catering to their moves: 'The director ... could also help them by his immediacy next to the camera on the floor with the actors. But television acting was different; the only immediacy was in the rehearsal room' (*ibid.*). Once a television production transferred to the studio, actors were physically separated from their director, left to the mercies of the cameramen, sound and lighting technicians, and floor manager. Clearly any actor with extensive experience in one medium alone faced various challenges when transferring to television, primarily 'reducing the size of the performance, still trying to keep it emotional, still trying to keep it real, [with] more than one camera' (*ibid.*).

Variety of experience, then, would seem to have been of the utmost importance to television work, and in this respect lead actor Reginald Tate was one of the better equipped members of the cast. Having studied at Leeds College of Music and Drama after the First World War, he went on to four years in repertory before moving to the West End; the typical career trajectory for an actor of the period. Tate made an early start in television, appearing as Stanhope in a November 1937 production of *Journey's End*, and worked regularly in film throughout the 1940s. During the run of *The Quatermass Experiment* he was also playing Mr Rochester on the radio in a Sunday evening Home Service adaptation of *Jane Eyre*. At fifty-six he was a veteran of television drama, with numerous plays to his credit, and the opening sequence from 'Contact has been Established' demonstrates the extent to which his performance already exhibited several traits of studio realism.

The scene begins in the control room of the British Experimental Rocket Group, headed by Professor Bernard Quatermass (Tate). Contact was lost with the first manned space rocket over fifty-seven hours earlier, and Quatermass's team – Judith Carroon (Isabel Dean), whose husband Victor is one of the missing astronauts, and technicians John Paterson (Hugh Kelly) and Peter Hunt (Moray Watson) – are anxiously awaiting news from the tracking station in Tarooma, Australia.

The bulk of the dialogue is between Quatermass and Judith, although the Professor also has a telephone conference with ministry man Blaker (W. Thorp Devereux). The staging reflects this; Judith and Quatermass are seated centrally at a desk downstage, while Paterson and Marsh are positioned at a second desk behind them, raised on a rostrum. The action is covered by three cameras: camera one is locked off on Blaker in a separate partition, while cameras two and four[10] manoeuvre between the left and right of the set, alternately focusing on Judith and Quatermass's desk and that of Paterson and Marsh behind. Director Rudolph Cartier maintains his policy of employing remarkably few extreme close-ups; although Tate is given a number of tracking shots when Quatermass moves around the set, the other actors remain seated throughout.

In Stanislavskian terms, the scene is divided into distinct units. At the outset, Quatermass and his crew are awaiting transmission from Tarooma; when the announcement comes, it brings no news of the rocket. Quatermass then castigates himself for having allowed Judith to stay on the team following her wedding to Victor, at the same time attempting to reassure her that all may not be lost. He then takes a phone call from Blaker, whose attempt to obtain some kind of reassurance from Quatermass is interrupted by a second call from Tarooma. The news that a faint signal from the rocket has been detected sparks the team into action, and Judith hurriedly calculates the ship's trajectory. This sudden rush of excitement is replaced by an uneasy stillness as Quatermass realises that the crew have travelled much further into space than ought to have been possible.

Examples of Tate having reduced his performance from the scale that would be required for theatre, in keeping with studio realism, include the actor's avoidance of physical gesture to 'play' Quatermass's beats or convey his mood changes. Those gestures that he does use seem involuntary – though it is of course entirely possible that they were thoroughly rehearsed bits of 'business' – such as when, after reproving himself for having increased Judith's emotional upset, he briefly rubs his nose between thumb and forefinger. This is swiftly followed by the only moment at which Tate employs an overt gesture, wagging an admonishing finger at Judith after advising her to have faith in her husband and his crewmate's bravery and ingenuity, and urging her to get some sleep. The fact that this finger-wagging is one of the few 'performed' elements in Tate's characterisation is indicative that the character of Quatermass is adopting a stance – that of mildly reproving/comforting patriarch – in which he is not entirely comfortable; his telephone conversation with Blaker later in the scene makes it clear that he himself is far from certain that the rocket crew have survived.

Tate also keeps facial expressions to a minimum, limiting himself to the occasional slight frown and momentarily raising his eyes heavenward when he takes Blaker's hectoring phone call. He avoids projecting vocally except when using the speaker system to communicate with Tarooma, and switches to a softer, lower register both when reproaching himself and attempting to comfort Judith. At these points the actor is still audible, despite being quite low in the studio soundscape; Tate's extensive experience of working in television allows him to gauge the acceptable level to which he can lower his voice for the boom microphone.

Tate is only one member of the cast, however, and there are indications in his colleagues' performances that such scaling down was not uniform. As the only other actor to feature in the 1947 and 1952 editions of *Who's Who in the Theatre* (Parker), Isabel Dean could be considered second to Tate in 'star' status. Like him she had worked in repertory before embarking on a screen career, playing a handful of supporting parts in film, radio and television from 1948; in the year prior to *The Quatermass Experiment* she had graduated to a more substantial role in Dennis Vance's *The Man with the Gun* (BBC, 1952). Her screen experience could therefore be seen as relatively limited in comparison with Tate's, and there are several moments where traits of stage-derived acting are apparent in her performance. For example, Dean employs a number of physical gestures and postures to convey Judith's changing moods and reactions, despite being somewhat limited by the fact that she remains seated throughout the scene. Whereas Tate is able to express Quatermass's restlessness by roving between his own desk and the workspace of Paterson and Marsh, leaning over his two younger colleagues in excitement at the news of the rocket's re-emergence, Dean is restricted to the upper body and head. In the opening tracking shot she is shown sitting rigidly to attention, staring straight ahead and not focusing on the scientific apparatus in front of her.

When Tarooma announce 'No trace has been reported or received', there is a cutaway from Quatermass to a medium close-up of Judith, initially gazing into space (Figure 1.1). On the line, 'Repeat: no trace' Judith slowly lowers her head (Figure 1.2) in a movement indicative of grief or sorrow.

This wordless display visibly conveys greater emotion than has been shown by Quatermass or the technicians (at this point the audience is not aware of Judith's increased emotional connection through her marriage to Victor), and is more redolent of stage gesture, designed to transmit meaning to a large, physically present audience. Compared with Tate's less explicit use of his body, Dean's movements seem more rehearsed, and calculated to produce an effect that is amplified by the fact that Cartier repeatedly cuts to her for reaction shots. This is seen more clearly when Judith and Quatermass discuss the unknown fate of the astronauts. The camera favours Dean throughout the sequence; although Quatermass

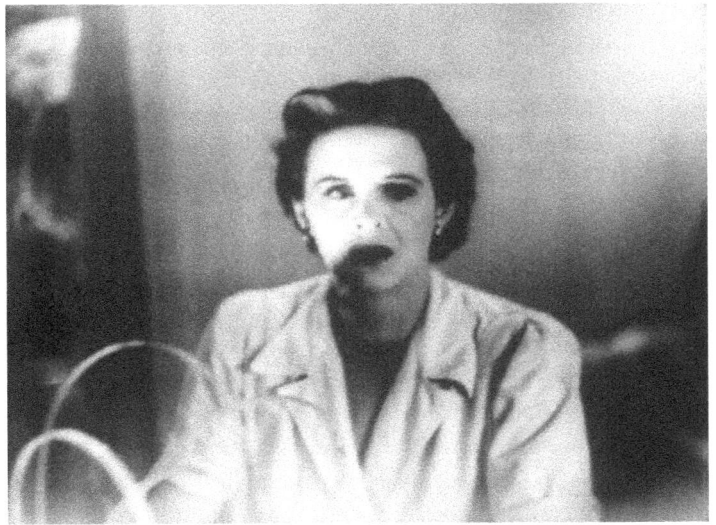

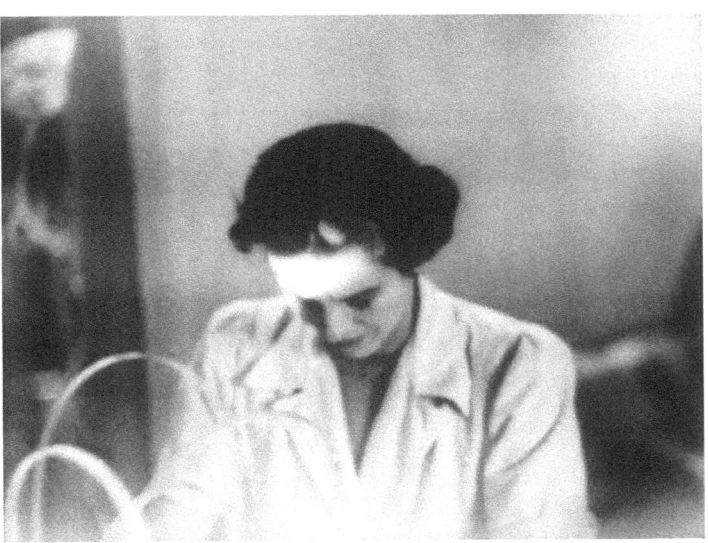

Figures 1.1 and 1.2 Isabel Dean in *The Quatermass Experiment*: 'Contact has been Established'

responds verbally to Judith's observations and questions, his body remains facing forward towards his console as he busies himself with his work, and his face is occasionally out of frame. As Judith, Dean pays little attention to her own equipment, again staring 'off-stage' to the left as she ponders what has become of the crew: 'If they were in a plane and it was hopelessly overdue we'd know that they're dead, but in that thing we just don't know.' On the following line, 'They may still be alive', Dean swerves her upper body and head towards Tate, though not to the extent that she is actually facing him. Dean is limited here by the blocking and camera positions, but this 'swerve', either away from or towards other characters at moments of dramatic tension, becomes a trope that is repeated throughout the first and second episodes.

Later in the same conversation Judith is fingering the apparatus on her desk – without actually operating it – while musing on the randomness of the possible defect that might have taken the crew off-course: 'Those tiny marks on the plastic; they seemed so precise and certain at first. Then they come closer and closer until you see they're only rough scratches.' Although these remarks are ostensibly addressed to Quatermass, the medium-shot framing of Judith alone creates the impression of a stage soliloquy, until she again swerves her body to the right, this time completing her turn to actually face Quatermass, as Judith asks: 'Could it have been like that with our calculations?' At this point Cartier cuts to the camera right of Tate, with both actors in shot.

The swerve is partially repeated while Quatermass is on the telephone to Blaker. Despite the fact that, as Blaker is on a private line to Quatermass, he should not be audible to the control room crew, Cartier cuts away to Judith as the minister asks: 'Frankly, is there any chance for their survival?' Dean here again performs a quarter-turn right (Figure 1.3), mouth half-open in anticipation, as she awaits Quatermass's comfortless response: 'Well, equally frankly I don't ...' As Quatermass cuts himself short, aware that he is being overheard, Dean returns to her former tense, frozen posture.

Dean favours body and head movements over facial expression to convey her character's beats; when she does use the latter, it is to underpin emotion. The relief of discovering the rocket's signal on the line, 'A trace, thank God!' is reinforced by lowered eyelids and visible relaxation of the body (Figure 1.4).

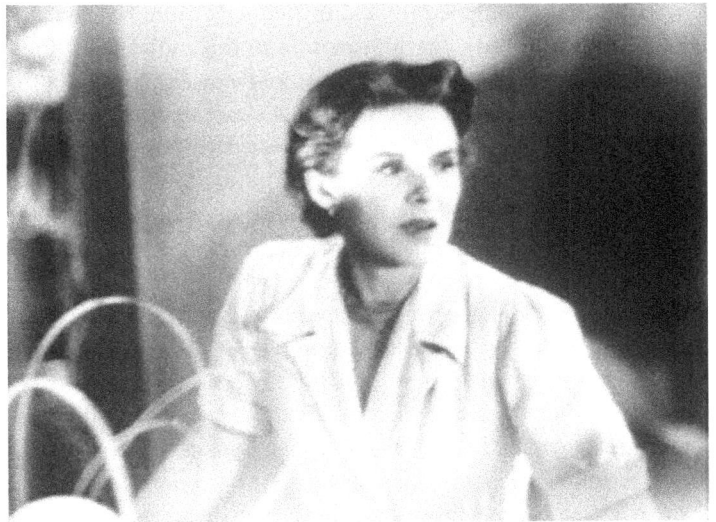

Figures 1.3 and 1.4 Isabel Dean in *The Quatermass Experiment*: 'Contact has been Established'

Such stage-derived postures and movements could be seen as a means of clearly conveying information to the audience on their tiny television screens; Reginald Tate does not employ any such signifiers, though this could be due to the fact that he is allowed greater mobility. Given her physically restricted position, Dean's gesture-based performance might also have been the result of specific direction by Cartier rather than personal actor choice; ascertaining which elements of performance derive from actor or director is always problematic, especially when the participants in question are no longer alive. However, the extent and type of an actor's experience are also conditioning factors in how they react to such direction; it seems reasonable to argue that a less experienced television actor is more likely to seek or 'take' direction than one accustomed to the medium. One possible way to establish how much of a performance is driven by an actor's personal approach is to compare the same performer in different roles. In *Acting in the Cinema* James Naremore considers how actor 'idiolects' can inform performance (1988: 65), and a brief examination of Reginald Tate and Isabel Dean's work in other productions may help demonstrate that their performances in *The Quatermass Experiment* were as much the product of their own acting styles at that time as Cartier's direction, which will be considered later in this chapter.

Due to Tate's untimely death from a heart attack in 1955, the choice of comparative case studies is limited; one of the few extant examples of his television work is a performance as Leblanc in *It is Midnight, Dr. Schweitzer* (BBC, 1953), the earliest full-length BBC play to be preserved in its entirety. As a comparative example of Tate's acting, this text is complicated by the fact that it too was directed by Rudolph Cartier. It is therefore possible that certain similar aspects of the actor's performance were the result of working for the same director, though as already seen in 'Contact has been Established', Cartier's direction certainly did not result in a uniformity of approach among his cast. Transmitted just five months before *The Quatermass Experiment*, *It is Midnight, Dr. Schweitzer* is a world removed from its successor in terms of content and execution. A single adaptation rather than an original serial, the 100-minute drama is the type of dialogue-driven play that Cartier and Kneale (who did not contribute to the script) averred they wished to avoid. Set in the French colony of Gabon on the eve of the First World War, the play deals with the events leading up to the arrest of Dr Albert Schweitzer (Andre Morell), an Alsatian, by civilian governor Leblanc, who is also competing with district military commander Lieuvin (Tom Fleming) for the affections of Schweitzer's nurse, Marie (Greta Gynt). Most of Leblanc's scenes centre round emotional or moral conflicts with Lieuvin or Schweitzer, but where Fleming and Morell raise their voices and gesticulate to convey their characters' viewpoints, Tate employs much the same economy of gesture and voice as can be seen in *The Quatermass Experiment*. This is exemplified by the moment, towards the end of the play, when Leblanc learns that Marie has chosen Lieuvin over him, and that – to compound his defeat – his rival has taken the moral high ground, choosing to fight at the front rather than remain in Gabon and usurp Leblanc's command, as is his right. When Marie delivers this news, Tate turns away from her to face the camera, allowing the viewers – but not the nurse – to witness Leblanc's reaction in close-up. Tate employs a subtle series of facial expressions to convey the until now restrained Leblanc's inner turmoil. First biting his lip in an indication of distress, he then purses his mouth before it slackens and briefly gapes open for a slight intake of breath. Tate then clamps his lips together again momentarily before delivering the line: 'I'm insulted by his generosity. It means he doesn't fear me in the least.'

Tate's performance here, utilising the mouth alone to convey his character's emotional state, indicates that he was already well aware of the effect that minimal adjustments in facial expression could have on the small screen; the same scaled down approach informs his work as Quatermass.

While Tate's work could be seen as the culmination of a decade's screen experience, Isabel Dean's role as Judith Carroon came comparatively early in her television career. However, she continued to work regularly in the medium until her death in 1997. Analysis of her performance in *I, Claudius* (BBC, 1976) shows that, even at a remove of two decades, certain of the physical mannerisms she displayed in 'Contact has been Established' were still present, but that increased experience had informed and modified her deployment of them. In the episode 'Queen of Heaven' Dean plays Lollia, a noblewoman who reveals to her dinner guests how she surrendered herself to the sexual depravities of the emperor Tiberius in order to save her daughter from the same fate. As Lollia recounts her tale, Dean employs the same stare 'off' that can be seen in 'Contact has been Established', only occasionally making eye contact with her husband, Titus (Edward Jewesbury), and their guests.

While in 'Contact has been Established' this stare is used in moments of reverie and reflection, in 'Queen of Heaven' it indicates Lollia's recollection of her experiences at the hands of the Emperor. Dean here alternates the stare with brief moments of eye contact with the other cast members, indicative of Lollia switching between the then (remembering what has happened to her) and now (recounting it). While the same technique had earlier produced a dislocating effect during Judith's conversation with Quatermass, Dean here employs it to suggest distraction of mind – Lollia forcing herself to re-live the horrific events of her abuse – and so heighten the dramatic tension of the scene.

The extent to which Dean's performance is informed by her increased television experience can also be seen at the moment in which she employs a scaled down version of the 'swerve' (Figure 1.5), twisting her head away from the imploring Titus as Lollia recalls the room into which she was led for Tiberius's pleasure. This is followed by another stare 'off' (Figure 1.6), Lollia avoiding eye contact with Titus as she continues her story.

The fact that Dean employed the same physical tropes in productions for different directors at a distance of over twenty years suggests that they represent aspects of her particular actor idiolect, which she learned to employ to greater effect as her television career developed.

Clearly studio realism in the early 1950s was as yet far from uniform, but while less televisually experienced performers such as Dean would learn to adapt, there were also actors working regularly in television who simply failed to fit the mould. This fact is highlighted by the unfavourable comparison made by Nigel Kneale aficionado Mark Gatiss between Tate and his *Quatermass II* (BBC, 1955) successor, John Robinson; an established actor with a similar pedigree in theatre, film, radio and television: '[Tate] is terrific ... You can only imagine what it would have been like if he'd survived. Whereas John Robinson; who knows which provincial rep

Figures 1.5 and 1.6 Isabel Dean and Edward Jewesbury in *I, Claudius*: 'The Queen of Heaven'

company he is projecting for? He's from another time, [yet] actually he's contemporaneous with Reginald Tate' (Gatiss 2011).

Gatiss's remarks highlight the perils of associating performance style with one factor alone. Several other determinants were at play with regard to the acting seen in *The Quatermass Experiment*, not least the mode of production employed.

Production process and technology

Although the processes of live television in certain ways replicated those of theatre, they were additionally complicated by a number of technological factors. A major feature of *The Quatermass Experiment* was its use of pre-filmed inserts, the first of which took place on Thursday 2 and Friday 3 July; more than a week before rehearsals began for the opening episode on 13 July (BBC WAC T5/418 – Memo from Daphne Martin to Transport Manager, 9 July 1953). This pattern of location filming taking place prior to rehearsals and studio recording dated back to the 1930s, and would indeed remain in place for several decades, creating the unfortunate (for the actor) template of being forced to produce a characterisation on film, without a prior preparation period, to which they were then obliged to adhere in the subsequent rehearsal and studio sessions. For Moray Watson, whose first television work this was, the experience must have come in stark contrast to the rehearsal and performance routine of the West End. In this sequence, Quatermass and Peter Marsh enter the crashed rocket to discover that two of the crew are missing; only their empty spacesuits remain. As Marsh, Watson holds his hands frozen in the same position after he lets an empty suit slip from his fingers (Figure 1.7), turning his face towards Quatermass as the camera pans slowly to the right.

In the transmitted version this moment of slowly dawning horror is underscored by eerie incidental music. Given the lack of rehearsals – a process diametrically opposed to the rigorous preparation of the theatre – this moment is notable for its initial lack of dialogue and simplicity of performance. Watson's slightly stylised dropping of the empty suit is suggestive of a directorial decision by Cartier; a simple gesture that allows the audience to register both a key narrative event (the disappearance of the crew members) and its implications (Marsh's incomprehension and perhaps horror).

Figure 1.7 Moray Watson in *The Quatermass Experiment*: 'Contact has been Established'

These are subsequently made explicit in a brief exchange of dialogue between Quatermass and Marsh before the latter exits the rocket, but such performance decisions would have been arrived at rapidly, on the film set, in contrast with the more extensively rehearsed studio scenes that followed.

Following pre-filming, production on *The Quatermass Experiment* settled into a pattern that more closely resembled theatre practice; for each of the six episodes rehearsals took place Monday to Friday, from 10 a.m. to 5 p.m., at the Student Movement House, 103 Gower Street (*ibid.*).[11] In 1982 Shaun Sutton, an experienced television director and former Head of Drama, emphasised the link that still existed to theatre in rehearsal terms:

> The process of rehearsing actors on television is basically no different ... it is the same building of lines into scenes, scenes into sequences, sequences into plays. Most actors like to know their 'moves', their theatrical business, before they put down their scripts. ... they must be made secure in the mechanics of the production. This leaves them free to get on with their performances, which, after all, is what they are there for ... The wise TV director,

having plotted a scene mechanically, will then run it again and again until everyone in it is not only comfortable, but understands precisely what the scene is about.

(1982: 112)

One difference between stage rehearsal and television, however, was the extent to which the director was framing the action to the tiny television screen, rather than a theatre auditorium. Michael Barry, who hailed from a repertory theatre background, later described the mystification he felt, upon his arrival at the BBC, witnessing Dallas Bower's rehearsals for the thirty-minute play *The Beautiful One* (BBC, 1938):

> Although they had reached an advanced stage, the producer was not detached. He was on his feet close to – it seemed at times in among – the actors. The [director] develops a faculty that allows him to perceive, through the patchwork of rehearsal, the rhythmic pattern of movements that will emerge in performance. This is a sense as necessary as a pair of spectacles with special lenses. But all that I saw was Dallas Bower, bustling here and there, moving before, behind and in among the actors. He would touch an elbow to adjust a stance, or whisper, close to an ear, so as not to interrupt the action. He mounted a chair in order to look downwards, or knelt and looked up. Sometimes he would raise both hands before his face and quiz what was going on through the aperture formed by the tips of his extended forefingers and thumbs.

(Barry 1992: 12)

The performance that evolved from these rehearsals would only be transferred to the studio on the day of transmission. Although the relocation of BBC drama to its newly refurbished Lime Grove studios, acquired from Rank in 1949, was already well underway, *The Quatermass Experiment* was transmitted from the old Studio A at Alexandra Palace. Every Saturday morning the cast would assemble at Broadcasting House in Portland Place, West London, at 8.55 a.m., to be transported by coach to north London; technical rehearsals would then begin at around 10.30 a.m. (BBC WAC T5/418 – Memo from Daphne Martin to Transport Manager, 9 July 1953). A crucial difference here between television and theatre is that, whereas in repertory a performance would then be repeated throughout the week while rehearsals for the subsequent production took place during the day, live television meant that the week's rehearsals resulted, in the case of *The Quatermass Experiment*, in just one evening performance.[12] This singularity of performance, combined with the fact that it would be seen by a far greater audience than could possibly attend a theatre, arguably exerted vastly increased pressure on the stage actor, particularly on the day of broadcast. This would be the first time that the cast worked on the actual studio sets, represented at the Gower Street rooms by various layouts of coloured floor tape, and in the presence of cameras, lights and microphone booms. While the director would have been physically present among the cast in rehearsals, on broadcast day he was seated in the gallery, accessible only via a ladder and separated from the rest of the studio by a plate glass screen. Notes would be relayed via the studio manager, who, like the camera and sound crews, would wear headphones to receive directorial instructions spoken into a microphone from the gallery.

Michael Barry later provided a detailed description of the typical events of transmission day in his memoir *From the Palace to the Grove* (1992). The first rehearsal on Saturday morning would see the cast replicating the blocking which had been carefully worked out at Gower Street for the camera, lighting and sound crews. During the first technical rehearsal the director would talk his crews through the pre-planned set-ups, making any adjustments that were necessary in terms of positioning. This procedure, which was clearly conducted for the benefit of the technicians rather than the cast, lasted until noon. Following lunch a second, afternoon run-through took place between one o'clock and 6.45 p.m.:

> Everyone was now more practised. The progress quickened and the production began, magically, to come to life ... When all that time permitted had been accomplished, the studio was made ready for the evening performance. In place of the time that might have allowed more to be achieved, a bond had been created. The engineers respected a [director] who knew his job and did not waste their time. The [director] appreciated colleagues who ... had given their interest and enthusiasm and made his efforts especial to them for the day. The actors saw, with relief, intermediaries who had striven to reduce the harassment of the preparations and provide them with an environment in which to perform.
>
> **(*ibid.*: 14–15)**

Following the second technical rehearsal, the cast and crew would break for supper before reassembling in their starting positions around twenty minutes before transmission. Writing in a somewhat romantic vein, Barry stressed the bond that had by now formed among the company:

> A feeling of buoyancy, if the preparation has gone well, struggles with a nagging concern about the problems to be faced. Some feel a security, born of past success, others seek confidence by being assertive. The inexperienced either withdraw into themselves, or assume a sort of heightened normality. Whichever mask is affected, all of those who share the stress become more closely drawn together.
>
> **(Ibid.: 15)**

It is perhaps significant that many years had elapsed between the events described here and Barry's account of them, written in 1988, and he paints a somewhat idealised picture of actor/director camaraderie, evocative of the theatrical troupe. Peter Cushing, who would star in Cartier and Kneale's *Nineteen Eighty-Four* the following year, provided a grimmer reflection on live television when recalling his 1951 small screen debut:

> Decorating the wall was a large silent clock, the second hand speeding inexorably towards the fatal hour. When it arrived, a sign above flashed 'VISION ON'. My head went numb, as if it had suddenly come into contact with a plank of wood, and my voice seemed to be coming from somewhere else, far, far away – like the view seen through the wrong end of a pair of binoculars.
>
> **(1986: 112)**

For Cushing, television was an isolating and unforgiving medium:

> When a mistake is made in filming, the director 'cuts' and the scene is shot again until you get it right, and in the theatre you can usually cover up anything that goes wrong. But not on television. In that confinement there was no escape, those cameras with lenses like probing microscopes picked up everything that happened as it happened, as if you were a goldfish in a glass bowl.
>
> **(Ibid.: 119)**

Cushing's autobiographies (like Barry's memoir, written with several decades' hindsight) provide several humorous accounts of the exigencies of live television. For example, the actor recalls having to 'dash like a mad thing' along the corridors of Alexandra Palace during *Pride and Prejudice* (BBC, 1952), 'trusting it was odds-on that I'd make my entrance on cue, after tugging open the massive sound-proof door, and enter the correct set, trying to look cool, calm and collected' (1986: 124). In the theatre, such exertions would usually be unnecessary provided the actor was in the wings well in advance of their cue.

Another notable quirk of live television was a technical device known as the 'cut-key':

> At rehearsals for a play to be televised, the assistant floor manager, usually a girl, followed the action with great concentration, making a special note of pauses in the dialogue, so that when the play was being transmitted, she would instantly be aware that an actor had 'dried'. If any untoward 'Macready'[13] (to use the old pro's expression for forgetting one's lines) occurred she would press a button, which cut off all sound from the viewers' sets, quickly prompt the unfortunate victim, release the button, and, with any luck, the action would continue as rehearsed. It was up to the actor Not to Panic – just to stand where he was, looking completely unruffled and at peace with the world. Those quite ghastly breaks in continuity took but a few seconds, but they seemed like eternity to the paralysed performer.
>
> **(Cushing 1988: 20)**

According to Alvin Rakoff, the cut-key's intended function of concealing actor error from the viewers at home was not entirely successful: 'If that was used ... it was a different sound. So if you were sitting at home, this hubbub of electric noises, electronic noises, suddenly went dead, and all the studio sound suddenly went dead – so the audience knew something was wrong' (2011).

Whereas in the theatre an actor's 'dry' could perhaps be covered by an ad lib, in the carefully prepared terrain of live transmission such a cover-up would only add to the confusion, as Moray Watson explains:

> It was very dangerous to ad lib; if you ad libbed then the cameras were all over the place and you thought, 'Oh, God! Where am I? He's saying this, and I should be ...' On the whole, we were only encouraged to ad lib if we could hold our position, and just for a line or two, perhaps while the cut-key was being held. I can say this now because it won't happen again: it was never used on me!
>
> **(2010)**

One of the greatest disparities between live television and stage was the absence of a physical audience, as Michael Barry, himself a RADA-trained actor with extensive theatre experience, evocatively described:

> The nearer that a theatre production comes to performance, the greater in a sense is the human detachment of the actors from the technical process. Their independence grows, until, like a ship launches from its stocks into the sea, the players and audience are alone, separated, held in suspense but face to face and in communion. ... When a television play enters the studio for camera rehearsal and live transmission ... instead of the palpable mystery that is an audience, the players are face to face with a grey anonymity.
>
> **(Barry 1992: 13)**

Peter Cushing, a veteran of live television, claimed never to have lost his terror that 'the audience was the largest you would ever play to, and at the same time, the smallest, consisting mainly of family groups in their sitting rooms' (1986: 119). Again, Cushing was writing here several decades after the event, and it is possible that the actor was exaggerating his sense of unease to entertain his readers, but a contemporaneous interview for the *TV Annual for 1955* makes it clear that Cushing was well aware of having tailored his performance to the small screen:

> Television is so intimate a medium, and so 'quiet' – it is like acting in a small room – that you dare not let up for one moment. You are, as it were, under microscopic attention; whereas the greater size of the stage does allow you now and then to take it less intensely. This means that in TV absolute concentration is needed, and really hard thinking has to go into your part during rehearsal.
>
> **(1955: 63–64)**

Cushing's remarks, which emphasise the importance of the theatrical tradition of rehearsal with regard to emerging studio realism, are those of a stage actor who has adapted to the small screen. While it would seem reasonable to assume that younger actors, in whom the tropes of stage acting were less ingrained, would be better suited to television acting, Michael Barry claimed otherwise: 'I recall few occasions on which the necessary changes of attitude or customary skills were not quickly grasped. And interestingly the older and established players often showed the most curiosity to the new approach that television required' (1992: 33).

Aside of scaling down in terms of physical and vocal projection, an element as basic as 'hitting their marks' to be in frame or focus for a particular shot, allowing for the limited mobility of the studio cameras, was integral to the new skills that television actors had to acquire. As Bruce Norman points out:

> [Actors] needed to be aware of which camera was taking the picture, which might well be taking the close-up, be in exactly the right prearranged position to deliver a particular line as well as delivering it in a natural but, for them as stage performers, wholly *un*natural way. Here was a whole new technique of acting – a technique different from stage, different from film, different from radio. [Original emphasis]
>
> **(Norman 1984: 159)**

Clearly, acting for a live drama involved much more than providing a theatre performance that would simply be captured and relayed by the three or four cameras in the studio. According to Alvin Rakoff, this is a common misconception: 'It's very difficult to explain to younger people ... because it was a multi-set layout, and the cameras moved from set to set. And now people say television drama in those days, they think it was all on a big proscenium arch, and you just shot the stage play. But it was filming on heavy, big cameras, usually three or four in the studio' (2011).

At Alexandra Palace, Rudolph Cartier had four Emitron cameras and two boom microphones at his disposal. The Emitrons dated back to the commencement of BBC Television in 1936, and were fitted with a standard 30-degree lens possessing a narrow field of focus of around ten feet; although the cameras could also take a narrower-angled 75-degree lens, time had to be allowed for it to be fitted (Barry 1992: 22), and the viewfinder was upside down. As Alvin Rakoff explains, the Emitron's limitations meant that cameras 'couldn't get very close to the actors ... One camera was put on bicycle wheels; it must still be in existence in some museum somewhere. And so the cameras that moved were limited; everything was far away'. Given that these weighty machines had to be 'dollied' by hand (*ibid*.: 31), it is a tribute to the skill of Cartier's camera operators that the various tracking shots he employs in 'Contact has been Established' are so smooth. However, in an environment such as this, where actors were more mobile than cameras, it was clearly the former who would have to adapt to the latter. An actor's ability to position themselves correctly thus became much more important than would be the case in the theatre: 'You see actors on the stage and they miss the spot, which means that only half their head is lit, but you've still got some light shining off them. In television you needed actors who could fairly accurately hit their marks without showing it; that's always the real trick' (Rakoff 2011).

The importance of actor positioning is illustrated by a later sequence, after Quatermass and his crew are able to bring the rocket down. While waiting for the crashed vessel to cool sufficiently to gain entry, a reluctant Quatermass and then Judith Carroon are interviewed by a BBC reporter (Pat McGrath). This scene is particularly notable for the way in which Cartier overcomes the Emitron's lack of mobility, as Catherine Johnson has observed, by keeping the camera still and moving the actor (2005: 26). Rather than cutting between the interviewer and his subjects with two cameras in close-up, Cartier keeps them in a single medium two-shot. When the interview with Quatermass concludes, Tate exits to the right, behind McGrath; Isabel Dean then enters from the left. When this interview is over, Dean exits in the same direction.

Such a sequence illustrates the extent to which early studio realism was compromised by technological limitations, but the actors' performances – in particular the distraction and impatience exhibited by Tate as Quatermass, seldom making direct eye contact with his interlocutor – accommodate the potentially static and frontal nature of the sequence. Credit for this must of course also be given to the person whose role it was to choreograph all such on- (and off-) screen movement: director Rudolph Cartier.

Direction

As can be seen, television direction was at this time divided between elements of the theatre director, an immediate presence working closely with actors in the rehearsal rooms, and the technician, planning camera moves prior to entering the studio, and separated from the cast on the day of transmission. At this point in time direction for studio television bore little resemblance to film, due to the fact that editing took place during the performance rather than in post-production; the vision mixer would cut between cameras in real time according to the director's carefully prepared plan. Although several BBC television directors, including George More O'Ferrall and Michael Barry, had begun their careers in the theatre, by now the Corporation was also recruiting from film, and had begun training its own directors specifically for the small screen. In 1953 ex-journalist Alvin Rakoff, newly arrived from Canada, was at twenty-six the youngest BBC director to graduate from the training course:

> The course was six weeks of lectures, and then I think six weeks of practicality. You went in the studio and then did various jobs. Not all of them; you couldn't take the camera, and you couldn't take the sound boom, but you did the floor manager's job, the writing, the directing in the gallery – as much in the studio as could be done. There was hardly any filming done. Filming was almost like a dirty word and a number of us – directors with myself included – changed that, but there was no single camera use at all.
>
> **(Rakoff 2011)**

As with acting, directing for television was an art form that depended on experience as much as training. Even the processes laid down in the BBC's three-month course could mutate and give way to new procedures, in particular the initial method of blocking and planning camera moves in advance of rehearsal:

> When I was being trained at the BBC, the director could originally plan every shot, every camera move, everything, before rehearsals started. He could be an absolute technician to that extent, and very good directors like Julian Amyes and Ian Atkins and suchlike worked that way. Other people like Rudolph Cartier did it totally the other way. You came, you planned, you visualised what you wanted as a director ... but you waited till the evolution ... You had to give the actors their moves in the first three days ... and then you finalise[d] it with the cameras at a later stage, during the last week of rehearsal. So those were the two techniques, and the second one won out eventually, because it was just easier.
>
> **(Ibid.)**

For Rakoff, the switch to this more organic mode of technical planning came as the result of a last-minute request from Michael Barry: 'Somebody had become ill, and he needed a play in four weeks to be mounted on the air, and he said, "Will you do it for me?" And I was so grateful to him, he'd been the guiding hand for me; I mean, he'd given me my first break, so I had to reciprocate with this favour' (*ibid.*). With less preparation time than he was accustomed to, Rakoff abandoned his usual pre-planning of camera moves:

> I arrived on the first day of rehearsal, and I remember I had a stage manager [who] was always with me, and while we were blocking it with the actors she said, 'I missed the move you just gave to so-and-so,' And she looked at my script, and usually I had all my moves and everything written down, and there was nothing on it. And her face went white, and she suddenly realised I was winging it; I was just so tired, I didn't have time to think. I was thinking in visual terms, visualising while I was staging it.
>
> **(Ibid.)**

The fact that the production in question, *Waiting for Gillian* (BBC, 1954), won a clutch of awards convinced Rakoff that directors

> could improvise to a large extent, as long as you had, as I did on *Waiting for Gillian*, actors who were television actors: Ann Crawford, who'd done a lot of primarily screen, very little theatre; and Patrick Barr, who of course was a stalwart of television because ... he could hit his marks and he could convey the lines; and they were very useful qualities to have for a young director.
>
> **(Ibid.)**

From Rakoff's comments it would seem that increased familiarity with the technical demands of television, both in front of and behind the camera, meant that specific styles both of directing and acting were simultaneously evolving and cross-fertilising, again demonstrating the intersection of factors that influenced studio realism's development. Rakoff's reference to 'television actors' implies that a breed of actor was gradually emerging that understood and responded to the television environment; early practitioners of studio realism.

However, though others such as Don Taylor (1990) have defended live studio as a unique directorial art form, for Rakoff its exigencies ultimately represented a compromise:

> There are no pros; there are only cons ... It was tough for the actors, tough for the technicians, tough for everybody; things could go

> wrong ... You could lose a camera in the middle of a play; what do you do then? ... Essentially the director in the gallery in the days of live was a chess player, making sure that he had the whole chess board in position ... The logistics were horrific, and very little to do with creating the right performance or telling the story, because you were so busy with technical logistics. So I say there are no pros, and I repeat that there are no pros.
>
> **(2011)**

Each director of course has their own approach and style, even when trained by the same organisation. According to Shaun Sutton, the good television director 'cherishes his cast, bolsters its morale [and] calms its astonishing insecurities' (Sutton 1982: 112). Moray Watson, however, recalls Rudolph Cartier as being like 'those directors in the early Hollywood films, who wore britches ... always sort of cracking whips. He was ruthless' (2010). Tensions occasionally ran high in rehearsals, when it was essential that actors rid themselves of pre-transmission nerves:

> Isabel [Dean] has this wonderful line to her husband: 'Good luck, darling, and don't forget to bring something back!' Well, because we were all tired, and everything – the idea of bringing back like a piece of Brighton rock or something – we were all corpsing, and Rudolph was absolutely furious [adopting accent]: 'Vot are you all laughing at? There is nothing funny! I don't understand why you are all laughing!' And we did it again, and still two or three people went, and he got even angrier; I think it was partly because we were tired, and it was the end of the day, and you get a bit weak.
>
> **(Ibid.)**

Watson presents an image of Cartier as an exacting taskmaster, but it should be borne in mind that there was a difference between the atmosphere in rehearsals at Gower Street and that in the studio on the day of transmission, when technical requirements were paramount. Nigel Kneale claimed that, as a visual technician, Cartier won the respect and admiration of his actors: 'He would select them very, very carefully, and once he had done that he would then give them all the confidence they needed ... They knew that he would get a wonderful performance from them, and that they would look very good on the screen, that every effort they put in would show. Naturally it aroused a lot of enthusiasm; they just loved Rudi' (Kneale 2005).

Kneale's remarks suggest that, under Cartier, actors would be free to create their own performances as long as they were in accordance with the director's visual plan; a viewpoint with which Moray Watson concurs: 'He was responsible for grouping us, indeed. He left characterisation up to us, but ... he did direct our movement' (2011). Watson, who describes himself as an actor whose performances are created from 'instinct', admits that Cartier allowed his cast this creative leeway, although 'I think he would have corrected me – if he had time, anyway – if it was going to spoil his shot' (*ibid.*).

An example of the ways in which the director's role was dictated by considerations both of studio space and technological requirements is provided by a later sequence in 'Contact has been Established', based at the site where the rocket has landed. This ambitious set, comprising the crashed rocket and the remains of a house, was the largest of four[14] erected in the sixty- by thirty-foot Studio A. As described by Michael Barry, the studio space:

> seemed to shrink alarmingly as the scenery was erected. The [director] first faced this problem on paper, when he plotted his production on a ground plan of the studio. The skill lay in contriving the most convincing backgrounds in the minimum area, [and] also had to take account of the intervening space that would be required to manoeuvre the cameras and microphones. Also, importantly in live production, the movement of the actors had to be studied, as well as the need to change their clothes as they went from set to set. Unless this was all meticulously planned and drilled beforehand, the studio rehearsals would be chaos.
>
> **(Barry 1992: 61–62)**

Once again, the importance of actors hitting marks was paramount. However, the crash set's depth and lack of width result in some extremely frontal groupings; in order to provide the audience with necessary visual information, Cartier is forced to position his cast so that they act outwards towards the 'fourth wall', creating a stage-bound effect missing from the earlier control room scene. An example of this is provided by the arrival first of Len Matthews (Van Boolen) and then his wife (Iris Ballard), who discover that the rocket has demolished most of their neighbour Miss Wilde's (Katie Johnson) house, leaving her stranded on the upper floor. When a policeman (Neil Wilson) also arrives on the scene, he and Len effect a rescue, despite Mrs Matthews's exhortations to abandon the old lady for fear that they will set off what she believes to a bomb.[15]

The scene features a great reliance by the cast on gesture to convey environment and scale. On arriving at the site, Boolen raises his arm to shield himself from the heat being given off by the crashed rocket; recordings of a dog barking and a baby crying, augmented by several shouts off-set, add to the sense of confusion, though there is little visible activity. When Mrs Matthews arrives she clutches at her husband's arm in anxiety before tugging at it in an attempt to drag him away from the danger. Len gestures upwards and behind when he realises Miss Wilde's plight (Figure 1.8), pushing his wife away when she tries to stop him.

The police constable then arrives and attempts to approach the rocket, only to be restrained by Matthews, who again gesticulates towards the trapped Miss Wilde. The policeman then moves downstage, and there is a cut to a camera positioned on the right as he instructs an unseen crowd, located beyond the fourth wall, to stay back, before returning to assist in the rescue attempt.

Figure 1.8 Van Boolen and Iris Ballard in *The Quatermass Experiment*: 'Contact has been Established'

Figures 1.9 and 1.10 Iris Ballard in *The Quatermass Experiment*: 'Contact has been Established'

Mrs Matthews now moves downstage, facing outwards as she cries: 'Len, Len! She's dead, she must be!' (Figure 1.9) As Len is now positioned behind his wife, this creates a somewhat dislocating effect; the character seems to be addressing her exhortation either to herself or some unseen audience rather than her husband. This is reinforced on Iris Ballard's line, 'It's going to go off! It's going to go off!' (Figure 1.10); Cartier again cuts to the camera on the right, with Ballard now directing her lines 'off' to the left, again beyond the fourth wall, before hurriedly exiting to the right.

The problems here of creating a convincing exterior location on a studio set compound the gesture-based, frontal performance of the actors, contributing to the impression of a staged environment. This could be due to the unnatural blocking required by the exigencies of limited studio space, or the cast's relative inexperience with regard to television work; of the three, only Neil Wilson had previously played a substantial role, as cockney trader Henry Smithers in Alvin Rakoff's production of *The Emperor Jones* (BBC, 1953). Both Wilson and Boolen would go on to have extensive television careers, Cartier employing the latter in *Nineteen Eighty-Four*, *Quatermass and the Pit* (BBC, 1958–59) and *Mother Courage and Her Children* (BBC, 1959). Interestingly, Boolen's performance as the truck driver who discovers an alien skull in *Quatermass and the Pit* sees him continue his reliance on gestural acting, as when pointing out that the skull is fossilised, and shrugging in response to his work-mates' query of what to do with it (Figure 1.11). When the site foreman arrives, Boolen again uses gestures to reinforce what he is saying, prodding him on the line, 'Listen, this could mean something good for all of us!' and rubbing his fingers together to indicate the financial possibilities of his find.

Five years after *The Quatermass Experiment*, Boolen was still employing the same types of posture and gesture that would be used to indicate character and situation in the theatre; further evidence that stage-derived performance codes continued to co-exist alongside studio realism, even as the latter became more established.

Director Rudolph Cartier was striving to 'open up' television drama via the use of filmed inserts, yet the crash site sequence described above demonstrates the extent to which he was constrained by the studio space. The lack of uniformity in the cast's performances ultimately illustrates the degree to which directors relied on individual actors' approaches – which, as already seen, were significantly informed by experience and background. While many actors received their grounding in repertory rather than via

Figure 1.11 Van Boolen in *Quatermass and the Pit*: 'The Halfmen'

formal training, those who had attended drama school would have received virtually no preparation for screen work – a fact that could only exacerbate the lack of an established and appropriate television acting style.

Training

Little formal drama training having been available in the UK prior to the early twentieth century, it might be imagined that the discipline would have developed with all the momentum of a new art movement following the founding in 1904 of Britain's first drama school, the Academy of Dramatic Art.[16] In fact, Sir Herbert Beerbohm-Tree's attempt to emulate the systematised training of the Paris Conservatoire, although followed in 1906 by Elsie Fogerty's Central School of Speech and Drama,[17] had changed remarkably little by the 1950s. One of the factors that had contributed to the founding of such schools was the increased need for vocal projection created by the newer, larger theatres (Sanderson 1984: 33). The emphasis of Beerbohm-Tree's and particularly Fogerty's academies was on voice training, though movement also formed a large part of the curriculum. ADA's 1906 prospectus featured Voice Production and Elocution prominently alongside such disciplines as The Art of Expression, Pantomime, Dancing and Callisthenics, Fencing, and Rehearsals (ADA 1906: 8), while the first year of the Central School combined Deportment, Fencing, Ballet and Rehearsal Class with its various voice courses (Susi 2006: 23). From 1908 ADA also introduced the codified movement training of Francois Delsarte[18] (ADA 1908: 7), though this had fallen out of favour by the mid-1920s.

RADA and Central were joined in 1926 by the Webber Douglas Academy, and in 1938 by the London Academy of Music and Dramatic Art (LAMDA); each had evolved from singing or music academies, and the emphasis was again on voice. In light of the radical developments taking place across the Atlantic in the wake of Constantin Stanislavski's publications,[19] the training provided in Britain remained largely focused on the representation of character via external technique. Both Joan Littlewood and Uta Hagen, who later went on to adapt and augment key elements of Stanislavski's theories in their own work, attended RADA in the 1930s. Hagen described her studies as being 'at best academic, stressing the training of voice, speech and movement, but I knew there was something wrong with being lined up against the barre to recite the speeches of Rosalind or Gertrude in unison with twenty others, with the same gestures and inflections' (1991: xviii–xix). Upon her arrival at the Academy, Littlewood found herself surrounded by 'debs or rich Americans acquiring an English accent' (Littlewood 1994: 68), quickly concluding that – her first exposure to the work of Rudolf Laban aside – 'Academy was a waste of time' (*ibid.*: 69).

When Moray Watson attended the Webber Douglas academy between 1949 and 1951, training remained focused on voice and movement:

> [Academy founder] W. Johnstone Douglas did voice training. I think we called it our diction class, and we went to him for half an hour regularly ... We had sword-fighting, dancing. We had a wonderful woman called Thea Tucker to teach us dancing, all the period dances – the pavane, things like that ... And then we had individual directors ... generally from the West End; not directors, they were mostly actors who wanted to do it.
>
> **(2010)**

Since the first days of RADA and Central, student productions had been directed by professionals coming in from the outside. Whether these were established directors or, as Watson suggests, West End actors branching out, it is possible that visiting directors were simply passing on the techniques and styles to which they themselves had been exposed and continued to practise in their own careers. The opportunity for new ideas to permeate the training was therefore limited, even though Watson and his contemporaries were aware of the new acting theories emerging from abroad: 'The students had all heard of Stanislavski, but it was never talked about' (*ibid.*).

This initial resistance to Stanislavski's teachings in Britain is also evidenced in a 1946 article by Michael Redgrave, which outlined his colleagues' reactions to *An Actor Prepares*: 'Quite a few have, I know, read it and have found it immensely stimulating. Other actors have read it, or partly read it, and find it fairly frustrating. Some others again say that they have read it when what they mean is that they have always meant to read it' (cited in Cole and Krich Chinoy 1970: 404).

One exception to this seeming embargo on Stanislavski, however, was the Bristol Old Vic School, founded in 1946. Kenneth Cope, who attended in the early 1950s, recalls the Russian's work playing a prominent part in the training, alongside more traditional areas:

> One thing I remember vividly [from *An Actor Prepares*] was, Stanislavski was giving a class and the carpenter dropped some nails on the floor, and he asked the class to notice that; how he did it, because he was an artisan, a tradesperson. And I've never forgotten that, because he acts totally, utterly natural, and [Stanislavski] said it's very important – particularly when you have to project yourself in the theatre, on the stage, because you're larger than life, basically – because you've got to make it real, as well. So I was impressed, and yeah, we did a lot of Stanislavski.
>
> (2011)

Nevertheless, the Bristol Old Vic School seems to have been the exception rather than the rule, and the Stanislavski techniques employed there would have arrived too late to have informed the majority of the cast in *The Quatermass Experiment*. While, as Michael Redgrave suggests, it is possible that a more studio realist performer such as Reginald Tate would have arrived at the

Russian's works through personal investigation or word of mouth, such a claim is difficult to sustain via analysis. It should also be remembered that many actors working in theatre, film and television at this time did not receive their training at drama school, repertory being an equally acceptable route into the profession. Comparatively few of the cast of *The Quatermass Experiment* received formal training; Isabel Dean had started as a scenic artist at Cheltenham rep in 1937 before moving into acting two years later (Parker 1947: 490), while in an interview with the *Radio Times* Ian Colin (Chief Inspector Lomax) cheerfully admitted to having entered the profession for a bet, after being challenged to audition for the part of Raleigh in *Journey's End* by an actress whose party he was attending: 'Luckily in the scene I was asked to do Raleigh was in a state of nervous tension ... so was I and I suppose the producer mistook my genuine nerves for acting' ('Actor for a Bet' 1953: 13). Colin then '[learned] the business in various repertory companies' (*ibid.*). However, even though each of the cast had come into the profession via differing routes, they would have been exposed to the same repertoire of plays and rehearsal and performance processes.

Those actors attending drama schools were taught to project and enunciate clearly in Standard English; regional accents would be eradicated, and only re-employed if required for roles. As Moray Watson recounts:

> Up till then everybody had to get rid of their dialect, whether they were from the north, Wales, Norfolk, everywhere; which of course in a way feels terrible now ... I'm afraid, as a public schoolboy, they didn't have to get rid of anything, you know ... I had to project and breathe and all that, but there was nothing to get rid of because I was – what do they call it now, RP?
>
> **(2010)**

The same standard mode of speaking would be expected of actors working in repertory, regardless of whether they had been formally trained or not. When a role required a particular accent, however, repertory actors would also need to adopt dialects not their own. This was an area for which training was not always provided, even at the larger academies:[20] 'We weren't specifically taught dialect. If we had to do dialect it was really up to us, and whether we had a good ear ... I don't ever remember having a specific dialect coach' (*ibid*.).

The tracking room scene features actors universally employing Received Pronunciation. By his own admission, this was Moray Watson's real voice, and comparison with Reginald Tate's previous performance in *It is Midnight, Dr. Schweitzer* and Isabel Dean's later ones in *I, Claudius* and *Inspector Morse* (ITV, 1987–2000) suggests that these were the voices they usually employed for professional purposes.[21] As Tate hailed from Yorkshire and Dean from Staffordshire it is entirely possible that these were adopted voices, but the point is moot; what is significant is that such Received Pronunciation is what contemporary audiences expected from authority figures such as Quatermass, and characters belonging to an 'elite' profession, e.g. scientists. While the vowels of the British Experimental Rocket Group team might seem overly polished to modern viewers, their pronunciation is typical of the accepted performance mode of the time; it would be dangerous to judge its acting styles according to received modes of speech which have since become socially outdated.

By contrast, the opening scene at the crash site introduces characters coded as being of a different social class, namely Mr and Mrs Matthews and their neighbour, the genteel Miss Wilde. Katie Johnson's portrayal of the latter, concerned solely with the welfare of her cat, Henry, has verisimilitude. While it is impossible to state definitively that Johnson is playing with her real voice, comparison with her best-known performance as the similarly dithering Mrs Wilberforce in *The Ladykillers* (1955) two years later implies that this is the case. As Len Matthews, Van Boolen employs the same East End accent which he would later use in both *Nineteen Eighty-Four* and *Quatermass and the Pit*. Combined with the fact that Boolen went on to play an assortment of proletarian characters on television, including a night watchman, peasant and soldier, this would seem to suggest that his working class accent was either his real or recovered voice, though it is also possible that it was a mimicked or put on voice perceived as possessing verisimilitude by both directors and audiences of the day. Like Boolen, Iris Ballard uses an East End accent, and her delivery of lines such as 'Oh my Gawd [God]' is in accordance with Kneale's specified spelling in the script;[22] possibly intended as an attempt to provide comic relief after the tension of the control room scenes. I have only been able to access one other of Ballard's screen appearances, the semi-documentary nursing drama *Life in Her Hands* (1951).[23] In her brief, un-credited performance as Nurse Soper, Ballard has just three lines, delivered in the same Standard English practised by the rest of the cast. This suggests that Ballard's East End accent in 'Contact had been Established' was an example of putting on. However, while several of the performances in the episode were criticised for lacking realism in a BBC Viewer Research Report, Ballard's was not among them, and the question of accent was never raised. This suggests that, in terms of voice work, *The Quatermass Experiment* was providing audiences with what they expected and were presumably accustomed to: a depiction of accents in which the comparative inauthenticity (by modern standards) of put on accents was as acceptable as the verisimilitude of real or recovered voice.

Although, as has been seen, most British drama training had not changed significantly by the 1950s, some new ideas had slowly begun to filter through. The movement theories of Rudolf Laban were being taught at RADA by Anny Fligg as early as 1933, when Joan Littlewood was in attendance (Holdsworth 2006: 51). Laban specialised in the use of different movements (pressing, flicking, wringing, dabbing, punching, floating, slashing and gliding) employing varying degrees of gentleness, flexibility and suddenness to express different 'shades' of meaning (Laban 1960: 100). Having arrived in England in 1937, Laban established his Art of Movement Guild eight years later, and a Studio was also set up in Manchester in 1946. It is therefore possible that some actors working in television by the 1950s would have been aware of the Hungarian's theories, and employed them in their work. From this perspective it is interesting to consider the third scene in 'Contact has been Established', which takes place between Quatermass and Blaker in the former's office. As Blaker, W. Thorp Devereux employs conventional gestural signifiers to convey character beats, such as raising the fingers of the right hand to the chin to signify feigned understanding, attempting to cover his confusion when Quatermass discusses the rocket separation procedure. This contrasts sharply with Tate's use of his hands while explaining the separation process; clasping a model of the rocket with both hands, he lightly raises the forefinger of his left and taps against the casing while calculating the combined weight of the rocket sections. Whereas Tate's body stance here is relaxed and loose, Devereux adopts a fixed, rigid posture, right hand on hip, indicative of paying close attention.

In Laban's terminology, Tate employs a variety of dabbing, gliding and floating gestures, while Devereux is restricted to thrusting and pressing, his jabbing finger permanently extended. It is impossible to know whether Tate studied Laban's work, but as one of the few cast members to have attended drama school it is entirely possible. If Devereux, however, was aware of the technique, there is little indication that he consciously applied it; his pointed finger, arm held unnaturally rigid and close to the body, is employed at various points in the scene to question (Figure 1.12), indicate (Figure 1.13) and affirm (Figure 1.14), without variation.

By way of contrast, when Tate uses his forefinger to demonstrate the rocket's planned circuit of the earth, he glides and dabs appropriately for demonstration and emphasis (Figure 1.15).

Laban's theories would later feature in the curricula of most drama schools in Britain, and this scene between Tate and Devereux illustrates the potential influence on performance of the type of training offered. As has already been seen, however, drama schools were typically still secondary to repertory as part of an actor's learning process, making official drama training arguably the least relevant determinant of studio realism in this period.

Reception

What emerges from the extant BBC Viewer Research Reports for the opening and closing episodes of *The Quatermass Experiment* is the extent to which Reginald Tate's studio realist performance found favour with viewers, while various of his colleagues' did not. The survey for 'Contact has been Established' reported that 'viewers liked Reginald Tate' (BBC WAC R9/7/8 – 'A Viewer Research Report', Week 29 1953), while feedback on the final episode included the comment that 'there was some criticism of supporting and "bit" parts – some said that an "unnatural" impression was created, others that no sense of tension was conveyed' (BBC WAC R9/7/8 – 'A Viewer Research Report', Week 34 1953). Characters singled out as 'exaggerated and unreal' in the first episode included

Figures 1.12–1.13 Reginald Tate and W. Thorp Devereux in *The Quatermass Experiment*: 'Contact has been Established'

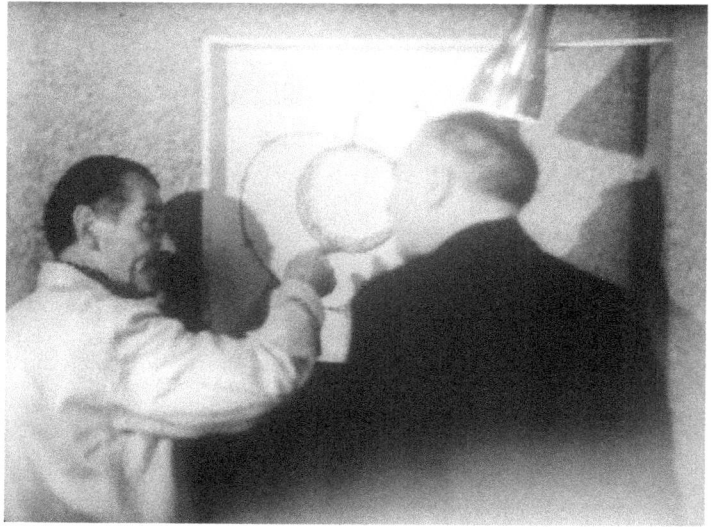

Figure 1.14–1.15 Reginald Tate and W. Thorp Devereux in *The Quatermass Experiment*: 'Contact has been Established'

Denis Wyndham's drunk – a 'very phoney reveller' (*ibid.*) according to a mechanic who participated in the survey – and various of the reporters at the crash site, with one real-life member of that profession querying: 'Why must your "journalists" always be either hard-boiled beyond endurance or imbecilic?' (*ibid.*).

The sequence that struck viewers as so lacking in realism occurs in the latter half of the episode. Quatermass's team have arrived, and are waiting for the rocket to cool sufficiently to gain entry. Peter Marsh is attempting to answer journalists' questions while monitoring the signal being transmitted from inside the capsule, but is disturbed by a drunk (Wyndham) brandishing a football rattle, who admonishes him for being 'too modest' and urges him to take the credit for having planned the entire operation. This character is then apprehended by Neil Wilson's policeman.

The perils of portraying drunkards have been outlined in various acting guides (see Hagen 1991: 178–180), but Wyndham's slurred delivery and stage-derived staggering were evidently regarded as broad even in 1953. What viewers objected to most, however, was that the character's intrusion damaged the credibility of the scenario:

> Viewers said that, had such a thing really happened, the area would have been 'cordoned off' by the police and 'drunks', reporters and miscellaneous members of the public kept off. Several made the point that, where a plot was itself fantastic, it was essential that it should happen against a completely convincing background, and that all the minor incidents should seem probable and authentic.
> **(BBC WAC R9/7/8 – 'A Viewer Research Report', Week 34 1953)**

Representing the 'hard-boiled' journalist is James Fullalove (Paul Whitsun-Jones), who would become a regular character in both *The Quatermass Experiment* and its second sequel, *Quatermass and the Pit*.[24] Although one of the first to scent a story, Fullalove initially displays sardonic detachment from proceedings coupled with a notable disdain for his fellow journalists. Whitsun-Jones adopts a series of physical postures to underpin his character's attitudes, leaning forward slightly, his right hand on his cane, the left behind his back, as he compares the anticipation of the gathered scientists and pressmen to the excitement of a child playing pass the parcel. This assumed pose is indicative of Fullalove himself playing a role, perhaps attempting to goad Quatermass – at whom he shoots a sidelong glance to observe his reaction – into some kind of revelation.

When the capsule is subsequently opened, and Marsh blurts out the fact that – Victor Carroon (Duncan Lamont) aside – the rocket is empty, it is Fullalove alone of the journalists who realises the import of his outburst, tapping a rival reporter on the chest as he informs him: 'As a matter of interest, this happens to be news!' It is perhaps understandable that a real life journalist might take offence at this depiction of the only capable member of his profession on the screen; Whitsun-Jones's performance is one of the more overtly stage-derived in the episode, and as such rang false for many: 'Can it be that newspapermen are like this and do not know it, or could it be that the television drama department ought to come to terms with reality?' ('Saturday Serial' 1953: 3).

Such criticism shows that concepts of what was acceptably 'realistic' in performance on British television were already shifting, the *Manchester Guardian*'s critic lamenting that 'the producers should persuade the detectives, scientists and journalists not to shout at each other too much. Television, like sound broadcasting, exaggerates every tone' ('Bards and Beauties' 1953: 3). By contrast, viewers considered the more studio realist Reginald Tate 'particularly impressive'[25] (BBC WAC R9/7/8 – 'A Viewer Research Report', Week 34 1953). Evidence of Tate's personal input is provided by comparison between the camera script (BBC WAC The Quatermass Experiment/Contact has been Established/BBC/18/07/1953) for the episode and the dialogue as transmitted. There are numerous examples of Tate re-wording his lines, either to simplify them[26] or to add verisimilitude to exchanges with other characters. During the scene in Quatermass's office, Tate twice adjusts or adds to the script to create the impression of spontaneous conversation. As written by Kneale, Quatermass's line, 'Our only chance of saving them is to attempt separation by remote control' is simply followed by Blaker's query: 'Separation?' In the transmitted version, Tate adds the line 'And if we don't ...', allowing Devereux to seemingly interrupt him mid-stream. Conversely, on Blaker's line, 'Sounds simple. Much too simple to accept. My committee ...' Quatermass is scripted to interrupt with: 'It wasn't.' As played on-screen, Devereux delivers a slight variant: 'It sounds simple enough'; Tate immediately talks across him, ad-libbing: 'It wasn't. It wasn't simple.' Tiny touches such as this underpin Tate's performance; the fact that it was so well received at the time would seem to indicate that there was already a growing audience for the scaled down studio realism that Tate represented.

Conclusion

Although studio realism in the early 1950s had begun to distinguish itself from more ostensive, stage-derived performance codes, it was not yet well established. Reginald Tate's performance displays various facets of a studio realist model, most notably the limited projection of voice, which is maintained at the level required by the sound equipment, and a lack of reliance on gesture to signify emotion. However, Tate was working alongside performers such as Isabel Dean, who had yet to scale down her use of body, and Van Boolen, who would continue to successfully employ the same gestural acting style on television for several years. Each of these seems to have been equally acceptable to contemporary audiences, and while there was criticism of what critics perceived as Paul Whitsun-Jones and Denis Wyndham's more stereotyped performances, the equally stage-derived playing of Iris Ballard passed without comment. This was clearly a period in which a plenitude of acting styles was being employed, with varying degrees of cultural acceptance.

Contributory factors were equally varied. While the range and depth of actor experience could, as in Tate's case, result in a studio realist mode of playing, which was notably reduced from the projection required for stage work, actor training and working practices typically remained rooted in the theatre. However, increased familiarity with the technology of television production on the part of both actors and directors – the latter now being trained specifically for the medium – meant that the 'scaling down' process, though far from universal, had begun. Change would, however, be gradual, and did not always follow predictable patterns.

Notes

1 This was famously the case in the 1958 *Armchair Theatre* (ITV, 1956–74) episode 'Underground', in which the cast were forced to continue their performance after actor Gareth Jones suffered a fatal heart attack mid-way through transmission.

2 The fledgling BBC Television Service had broadcast part of the procession following George VI's coronation in 1937.
3 Asa Briggs later reported that '53 per cent of the population – over 19 million – viewed the procession to the Abbey, and 56 per cent – over 20 million – viewed the Coronation Service' (1979: 466).
4 Until 1948 the repeat performances had been given on Tuesday afternoons; the only time at which the actors working predominantly in the theatre had been available (Jacobs 2000: 84). The switch to Thursdays indicates that television was emerging as a medium in its own right, rather than something that theatre actors could 'fit in' between stage engagements.
5 The quality of this recording was marred by an insect appearing on the telefilm monitor midway through the episode, where it remained for several scenes.
6 The BBC preferred the term 'producer' to 'director' to describe whoever was responsible for the direction of a programme or play (Barry 1992: 11). The term 'director' has been used here to refer to the individual who would be understood as such today.
7 Pointing out that the use of filmed inserts in fact dates back to the 1930s, Jason Jacobs contends that Cartier was important for the innovative ways he used film 'to increase mobility and overcome spatial limitations' rather than for having introduced it personally (2000: 131).
8 Although, as reported by Michael Sanderson, repertory would soon come under threat from television, in the late 1940s 'the touring and repertory companies were fairly flourishing' (1984: 277).
9 At this time nine and fourteen inches were the standard screen sizes in Britain. Sets ranged from Bakelite or wooden table-tops to walnut consoles, though in 1952 Decca had also produced a projection model (Bennett-Levy 2001–13).
10 According to the camera script (BBC WAC The Quatermass Experiment/Contact has been Established/BBC/18/07/1953), camera three was already positioned on the set for Quatermass's office, which would be used in the third scene.
11 The BBC also had rooms at Paddington Street. In late July Cartier had requested that, due to the serial's 'semi scientific subject', rehearsals be conducted 'within easy reach of the British Museum Reading Room and University', but the Gower Street booking remained unaltered (BBC WAC T5/418 – Memo from Rudolph Cartier to Mrs Betty Bulling, 27 May 1953).
12 As already seen, some productions would receive two performances, as with the Thursday repeat performances of Sunday evening plays.
13 Named after nineteenth-century actor William Macready, who 'had a habit of pausing inordinately during a speech, to produce some dramatic effect' (Cushing 1988: 20).
14 Other sets included the tracking room, Quatermass's office, and the newsroom, plus a small section for Blaker's office and the newsreader's desk.

15 The scene features several coded Cold War references, with the majority of the locals assuming that the rocket is a missile or explosive of some kind: 'They've finally dropped one!'
16 The Academy was later granted a Royal Charter to become RADA in 1920.
17 The school became the Royal Central School of Speech and Drama from 2012.
18 Though Delsarte's ideas on performance, which centred on using physical posture as a means of representing emotion, have since been derided for their 'pantomimic' nature, his original intention had been to provide a means of performance which correctly mirrored nature (Delaumosne et al. 1893: 384–529).
19 This primarily took the form of the 'Method', as taught by Lee Strasberg at the Group Theatre and later the Actors Studio in New York. However, Richard A. Blum (1984), Richard Hornby (1992) and Robert Barton (2009) have all highlighted the differences between this and Stanislavski's 'system', making the case that the Method was in fact an abstraction of just one of Stanislavski's manifold theories – that of 'emotion memory' – and is not wholly representative of his work.
20 Although Phonetics were first taught at RADA in 1926 (RADA 1926: 11), this subject was to disappear and reappear on the syllabus several times over the next four decades.
21 I have been unable to locate copies of other work by Hugh Kelly or W. Thorp Devereux.
22 Kneale's intended pronunciation is also signified by the use of 'yer' for 'your' and a dropped aitch on "ere' (here) (BBC WAC The Quatermass Experiment/Contact has been Established/BBC/18/07/1953).
23 The BFI's database credits Ballard as having also previously appeared in an episode of children's serial *Five Children and It* (BBC, 1951); there is no record of any television work subsequent to *The Quatermass Experiment*.
24 In the latter Fullalove is portrayed by Brian Worth.
25 The reports cited were based on 292 and 320 completed questionnaires respectively, for episodes that were watched by 3.4 million and 5 million; the extent to which the reactions they present are representative of the total audience is therefore open to question. However, the many positive comments in the reports would seem to be borne out by the increase in viewers of nearly 50 per cent over the course of the serial's transmission.
26 'I'm going to try to re-establish control' becomes 'Let's try and regain control', while Tate replaces the line 'It is possible there will be some danger' with 'Now, there may be some danger'.

2
Refining studio realism

By the early 1960s, television was more established in both reach and form, yet despite significant technological shifts its production processes remained largely unchanged. Actor experience had increased, yet an analysis of studio realism during this period as the result solely of actors' increased familiarity with the medium is complicated by external factors; primarily, the advent in British television and film of social realism. Though frequently linked with a particular 'type' or sub-genre of television drama, e.g. the work of director Ken Loach and Tony Garnett for *The Wednesday Play* (BBC, 1964–70) and later *Play for Today* (BBC, 1970–84), social realism in fact had far wider implications in terms of small screen performance, its influence extending by osmosis into all areas of television drama.

Pre-recorded 'as live', *Doctor Who*'s opening episode 'An Unearthly Child' can be taken as representative of the latest production process. However, as will be seen, this differed remarkably little from the live era in terms of performance pressures. What is notable, however, is the extent to which a greater uniformity of scale had begun to emerge in terms of vocal and gestural projection on the part of actors; a marked refinement of studio realism when compared to the performances examined in *The Quatermass Experiment*. The determining factors behind this change, and their resulting manifestation on screen, will now be examined via a selection of scenes from 'An Unearthly Child'.

Background

Much had altered in Britain since *The Quatermass Experiment*. A few months before that serial's transmission, Joan Littlewood's Theatre Workshop, with its training combination of Stanislavski and Laban, had made a permanent home at the Theatre Royal, Stratford East. Littlewood's pioneering work inspired the opening in 1961 of East 15, the first UK drama school to base its curriculum on Stanislavski's theories.[1] Elsewhere, George Devine's Royal Court production of John Osborne's 1956 play *Look Back in Anger* symbolised a new era for the British stage. Although in recent years authors such as Dan Rebellato (1999) have challenged the view that this production single-handedly transformed the theatrical landscape, its success was indicative of a shift away from established writing and performance styles. Though American Method acting had not yet found its way to British drama schools, its influence could be seen in the cinema via films such as *A Streetcar Named Desire* (1951) and *On the Waterfront* (1954), directed by Actors Studio founder Elia Kazan. This current of change carried over into British film in the early 1960s via 'new wave' directors including Lindsay Anderson, Karel Reisz and Tony Richardson. Britain's social climate was also changing. John Caughie has outlined how a sense of national disillusionment following the humiliation of the Suez Crisis, combined with the increased politicisation of the BBC's Oxbridge intake, and a more liberal regime under Director General Hugh Carleton Greene (1960–69), contributed to (without being solely responsible for) British television's supposed 'Golden Age'; 'like all Golden Ages ... rooted in the transformations and transitions of the culture' (2000a: 87).

The arrival of independent television in 1955,[2] while providing a direct challenge to the BBC's small screen monopoly, had simultaneously expanded the amount of drama being produced. While it has often been assumed that the launch of ITV also led to a further increase in set ownership, which by 1963 had risen to 13.6 million (BARB 2016),[3] independent television was more significant for providing an 'expansion of choice itself' (Turnock 2007: 115). Despite the success and popularity of commercial television, the BBC was awarded the licence for a third national television channel following the Pilkington Committee's recommendations in 1962, and 1964 would see the launch of BBC2, creating yet another source of television drama. The BBC's burgeoning television empire was consolidated by the opening in June 1960 of its Television Centre at White City,[4] and this growth went hand in hand with new technological developments, videotape having been introduced two years before. Although difficult and costly to edit, this new technology meant it was now possible to pre-record much of the Corporation's drama output, sounding the death knell for live drama.

For actors, television's expansion provided ever-increasing opportunities for employment, coupled with a degree of stability and continuity in terms of working practice; despite the new innovations, the BBC's rehearsal and studio processes remained largely unaltered. Until now the small screen had not always seemed a viable – or respectable – career path to stage actors, its negative impact upon regional theatre companies[5] often engendering a sense of resentment on the part of ex-rep actors forced to turn to television (Sanderson 1984: 280). However, for many the medium's expanded reach offered an attractive alternative to treading the boards. It was this that ultimately swayed a reluctant Moray Watson when he was offered a regular role in the BBC soap *Compact* (1962–65): 'I remember my agent [saying]: "You've been in the theatre playing to between three or four hundred, perhaps, and a thousand people, in theatres. If this soap takes off, you'll be suddenly playing twice a week to between five and ten million"' (Watson 2010). For many, the previous stigma of working in television was clearly no longer a barrier, and the small screen had become temptingly lucrative.[6]

Meanwhile, there was major upheaval in the BBC's Drama Department following the arrival of Sydney Newman in December 1962. Fresh from revitalising ABC's live anthology series *Armchair Theatre*, Toronto-born Newman had been one of the first producers to introduce social realist themes to British television drama, drawing audiences of over twelve million. Many saw BBC Controller Kenneth Adam's decision to employ Newman as an indication of the perceived need to compete with commercial television on its own terms, at least stylistically: 'The overall policy... was essentially to beat the commercial network at its own game, while still preserving those qualities deemed essential to the BBC in its public service role ... If ITV drama was upfront and brash, the BBC would be [up] fronter [sic] and brasher' (Taylor 1990: 102–103).

Newman set about reorganising both BBC drama's internal organisation[7] and output, aiming for a broader, more populist appeal.[8] However, broader circumstances should be borne in mind in order to avoid employing a model of 'history as being driven by "great men"' (Bignell 2005a: 59). To accord Newman full credit for changes at the BBC in the 1960s would be to ignore the various social and technological developments already taking place (and examined elsewhere in this chapter), not to mention the influence of Hugh Carleton Greene, already three years into his modernising reign as Director General. However, significant changes were clearly taking place within the Corporation, of which *Doctor Who* is a prime example. One of the earliest commissions by the new Drama Department, the programme is representative of Newman's desire to eschew the children's classic serial in favour of something more experimental. However, moves were in fact already afoot to create such a science fiction series prior to his arrival.[9] Gestating out of meetings in the first half of 1963, *Doctor Who* was envisaged to run for fifty-two weeks (BBC WAC T5/647/1 – 'General Notes on Background and Approach', 13 May 1963); in itself a revolutionary commissioning decision. The programme was also unusual in that, although produced as a 'continuing serial' (*ibid.*), it was in fact something of a crossover format, comprising in modern terms a continuing series of self-contained serials. Although ostensibly aimed at a young audience,[10] its cast of characters could appeal to a broad age range,[11] and the flexibility of time travel as a central device allowed for a variety of narrative styles.

Newman invited twenty-seven-year-old Verity Lambert, formerly a production assistant at ABC, to produce, while recently appointed BBC staff director Waris Hussein was chosen to helm the opening serial. Hussein had previously directed episodes of *Compact*, but although he and Lambert were working alongside BBC stalwarts in the form of associate producer Mervyn Pinfield and story editor David Whitaker, the new arrivals were very much seen as untried talent, as Hussein relates: 'This extraordinary thing came up about a Police Box, which nobody wanted to touch; I was the most junior director there, the youngest, and quite a fish out of water, to be honest. [Verity and I] were out to try and prove ourselves' (2011).

The programme was to be entirely pre-recorded using a mix of studio videotape and a limited amount of film recording at Ealing Studios. Transmitted at 5.15 p.m. on Saturday 23 November 1963, against the third instalment of ITV's children's science fiction serial, *Emerald Soup* (ITV, 1963), its impact was somewhat muted due to the nation's shock at the assassination of US President John F. Kennedy the previous day. The decision to repeat 'An Unearthly Child' the following Saturday, immediately before second episode 'The Cave of Skulls', indicates the importance the BBC attached to its 'Adventure in Space and Time'.[12]

As an example of 'as live' videotaped drama, 'An Unearthly Child' offers a useful example of studio realism's production conditions in the early 1960s. It contains several indications that the scaling down process that had begun in *The Quatermass Experiment* was now settling into a greater uniformity of approach; a performance style that would increasingly mark itself as distinct from stage-derived codes as television drama became more established in form. The various factors contributing to the continuing development of studio realism will now be examined.

Actor experience

By 1963, television was coming of age. In 1953 it had only just begun to supplant radio in popularity and remained a poor third to theatre and cinema in terms of employment, with just 505 actors working in 'films for television' (Sanderson 1984: 285). However, by the end of the decade around 1,500 cinemas had closed, and the number of actors employed in television for the year 1958–59 stood at 3,901 (*ibid.*). Although repertory still provided a potential starting point, the system was in decline, and by 1962 there were only fifty to sixty active companies remaining (*ibid.*: 279).

The principal actors in *Doctor Who* reflected this new combination of theatre and screen experience. Cast as lead character the Doctor was William Hartnell, who had trained at Italia Conti's stage school before joining Shakespearean actor manager Sir Frank Benson's touring company in 1925. Hartnell later worked extensively in film, starting as a light comedy lead in many 'quota quickies' of the 1930s before graduating to character roles for the major British studios. Although best known for playing hardened sergeants, 'heavies' or policemen in films such as *The Way Ahead* (1944), *Brighton Rock* (1947) and *Escape* (1948), it was his vulnerable performance as a rugby talent scout in Lindsay Anderson's *This Sporting Life* (1963) which caught Verity Lambert's attention. Hartnell was also well used to the pressures of multi-camera studio, having played CSM Bullimore for two years of the live sitcom *The Army Game* (ITV, 1957–61). Co-stars William Russell and Jacqueline Hill, playing teachers Ian Chesterton and Barbara Wright, also possessed a mix of stage and screen experience. Russell had started in repertory, while Hill trained at RADA before progressing to the West End; however, each had numerous television appearances to their credit, and Russell was particularly well known after starring in *The Adventures of Sir Lancelot* (ITV, 1956–57) and *Nicholas Nickleby* (BBC, 1957). As Susan Foreman, the 'unearthly child' of the first episode's title, Carole Ann Ford possessed the least stage experience, having served her apprenticeship as a walk-on and model in commercials before graduating to supporting roles. It is significant that, although the ages of the principal cast ranged from twenty-three to fifty-five, each had a roughly equivalent amount of television experience in terms of duration, if not type; a marked contrast to the backgrounds of the actors who had appeared in *The Quatermass Experiment* ten years before.

In addition to increased length of television experience, the introduction of pre-recording meant that actors could now watch their own performances at home on television, allowing them to see how well – or poorly – their stage or film styles translated to the small screen; an important contribution to the scaling down process. Although William Hartnell only acquired his first television set at the end of 1958 (Carney 1996: 132), by the time he came to play the Doctor he had evolved his own theories of television acting, which he related to later *Doctor Who* colleague Peter Purves:

> He took me on one side and he said, 'Television's very small, Peter. You won't see these gestures; [there's] no point in doing large gestures.' And he just showed me all these gestures he did around his face ... As far as television is concerned, the shots are always that tight, there's no point in doing something expansive, because it's not going to be seen.
>
> (Purves 2010)

Hartnell's comments could be taken as indicative of the extent to which experienced television actors were now consciously considering the scale of their performances for the small screen. Though Hartnell was attempting to pass on a specific technique to a younger and less experienced colleague, such advice, if misinterpreted, could also have a negative impact. John Gorrie, who directed an early *Doctor Who* serial, explains:

> In those days there were a lot of rather daft myths about television acting: [for example] – I don't subscribe to this at all – that if you didn't blink it was more effective ... I did once work with an actress who I noticed in rehearsal kept her head unnaturally still, and I said to her one day, 'You seem to be a bit stiff in your head.' And she said, 'Oh yes, I do that deliberately, because I've been told that you mustn't move your head on television.' 'I beg your pardon?' I said: 'No, no, just behave naturally; don't worry about it.' There were these sorts of myths in those days.
>
> (2009)

For William Russell, there was little difference between acting for stage and television: 'I honestly don't think that the platform ever disturbs an actor ... I was with a company, and we used to arrive at a church hall, and we used to pin down the cloth; that was where we were, and on that we acted. So I don't think there's any feeling of that [difference]' (Russell 2006a). Russell clearly felt that acting for television was a simple enough matter of instinctive adjustment, not requiring the use of any particular technique. He was, however, careful to attend when Hartnell imparted advice: 'I admired him a great deal as an actor, so I listened to what he had to say, always. And Bill was in his own character: a bit scratchy, and a bit unpredictable; and these things came over, and he used them' (Russell 2006b). This element of Hartnell drawing upon facets of his own personality in performance could be seen as a result of the need to create a consistent characterisation over a long-running series. *Doctor Who* eventually exceeded expectations by running for twenty-six years, and though Hartnell only remained in the lead for the first three of these, the turnaround was intensive, with limited time for preparation. Until 1969 the programme's schedule consisted of one episode produced each week for the greater part of the year,[13] usually less than a month before transmission. Given the pressures actors were under, they became habituated to working without extensive preparation or research, as Russell confirms: 'I had done quite a lot of swashbuckling roles, you might call them, before, and [Ian] was a sort of continuation of that, for me, in a more modern condition. I don't think we ever had time – because the story always came first – to do more than that' (Russell 2003b). Russell was evidently continuing to play a particular 'type' with which audiences readily identified, whereas Hartnell was seeking to get away from his established image: 'He really enjoyed comedy, Bill. He was always looking for moments to be amusing, and I think it was strange for him that he ended up being this very stone-faced sergeant-major so often in British war films later, which wasn't really his character' (Russell 2009b).

Given the difference between Hartnell's approach, combining external technique with his own personality traits, and Russell's more intuitive attitude, it is interesting to compare how their performances mesh on screen in the first encounter between their characters. Intrigued by the otherworldly quality of their pupil Susan Foreman, Ian and Barbara have followed her to the address where she claims to live with her grandfather. They are concerned to see her enter what appears to be a deserted junkyard, but upon following her inside find that she has seemingly vanished. Their curiosity further piqued by the incongruous presence of a Police Box, which is emitting a faint vibration, they attempt to hide when they are disturbed by the entrance of an eccentrically dressed, elderly man; the Doctor. Sensing their presence, he challenges them to explain themselves, but resolutely refuses to open up the Police Box when they voice the suspicion that Susan is locked inside. Ian is about go in search of a policeman when they hear Susan's voice, calling for her grandfather from inside the box.

The sequence is essentially a battle of wills between Ian and the Doctor – Barbara's few attempts to engage directly with the latter are either brusquely rebutted, or ignored entirely – and can be divided into beats, as first one and then the other tries to gain the upper hand. Ian's objective is to make the Doctor unlock the Police Box, while the Doctor's is to persuade the teachers that their suspicions are groundless, and so manipulate them into leaving. There is still a clear lineage in the performance to the theatre, with the space of Studio D employed in much the same way a stage would be utilised; Hartnell makes a perceptible 'entrance' from stage

Figure 2.1 William Russell and William Hartnell in *Doctor Who*: 'An Unearthly Child'

left, announced by a fit of coughing and emphasised in the way he pauses to wave his handkerchief. Easily read physical gestures are used to signify mood or emotion: Russell rubs his hand awkwardly against his neck to represent Ian's discomfiture at being discovered hiding (Figure 2.1), while Hill puts her hand to her throat to signify Barbara's anxiety for Susan (Figure 2.2). However, these are notably scaled down from the broader gestures employed by actors such as Van Boolen and Iris Ballard in 'Contact has been Established'.

When Barbara explains their concern for Susan, the Doctor's reflective line 'One of their pupils; not the police, then' is delivered by Hartnell in the manner of a stage aside, his voice lowered, eyes momentarily glancing off to the right. However, Russell's next line, 'I beg your pardon?' makes it clear that the Doctor's musing is audible to Ian and Barbara. At this point the Doctor clearly selects Ian as the person to convince, Hartnell taking Russell by the elbow and steering him 'downstage', i.e. towards the camera, as he asks: 'Young man, is it reasonable to suppose that anybody would be inside a cupboard like that?' On this line Hartnell points back towards the Police Box (Figure 2.3); a gesture reminiscent of W. Thorp Devereux in 'Contact has been Established'.

Figure 2.2 Jacqueline Hill, William Russell and William Hartnell in *Doctor Who*: 'An Unearthly Child'

Figure 2.3 William Russell, Jacqueline Hill and William Hartnell in *Doctor Who*: 'An Unearthly Child'

Other theatre conventions present in the scene include the (perfectly audible) stage whisper adopted by Russell and Hill as Ian and Barbara debate what to do next, and Hartnell's employment of various bits of 'business', picking up an old picture frame and examining it while attempting to ignore Ian's exhortation to help them locate Susan.

However, the scene also illustrates the extent to which the actors have adapted to television in terms of economy of voice, movement and facial expression. While clarity of speech is still paramount, there is less vocal projection than was the case in *The Quatermass Experiment*. Hartnell addresses much of his dialogue 'outwards', often due to the fact that he is facing away from the other actors, the Doctor refusing to maintain eye contact with the two teachers. Russell and Hill, however, keep their voices at an approximation of a normal conversational level, at least until the scuffle which ends the sequence, when Ian and Barbara hear Susan's voice; an indication that actors had by now learned at what volume they needed to pitch their delivery in order to be picked up by the studio's boom microphones. Whereas in *The Quatermass Experiment* Reginald Tate was in the minority in this respect, it had now clearly become a more standard part of the television actor's skillset.

Hartnell's close-ups showcase an experienced film actor's awareness of the camera's potential for registering the slightest of movements, his performance comprising a combination of physical stillness and subtlety of expression to convey information. During Barbara and Ian's 'whispered' conversation Hartnell is shown facing the camera, occupying the right-hand side of the frame in medium close-up, as the Doctor feigns to be examining a jug while eavesdropping. His eyes dart first up and then quickly left (Figure 2.4) as he reacts to their discussion of how to gain entry to the Police Box, ending with a slight smile playing around his lips as Ian vainly attempts to contact Susan within.

Hartnell employs a similar technique moments later, when the Doctor attempts to goad the teachers into leaving. The Doctor is standing side-on to Ian and Barbara, and Hartnell is now in close-up, looking almost directly into the camera as he urges Ian to carry out his threat to find a policeman. When Ian sarcastically responds: 'While you nip off quietly in the other direction?', Hartnell's eyes narrow and his lips purse; his expression at this point could be read as one of either irritation or malice (Figure 2.5).

Figure 2.4 and 2.5 William Hartnell in *Doctor Who*: 'An Unearthly Child'

However, the manner in which he then closes his eyes as he mutters 'Insulting' suggests that the Doctor regards himself as being in some way superior to his interlocutor; a fleeting impression that is borne out in subsequent scenes. The exchange is punctuated by brief bursts of whinnying laughter on Hartnell's part – later to become a defining trait of his portrayal – as the Doctor makes light of Barbara's anxieties and Ian's attempts at interrogation. It is important to remember that, although the audience are not yet aware of it, the Doctor is in fact a humanoid alien; Hartnell is therefore not attempting to play a sympathetically human character, which accounts for certain of the eccentricities he employs.

As the Doctor's introductory scene, the sequence is choreographed largely around Hartnell, who makes great use of the studio space, usually moving away from either the other characters or the Police Box, while William Russell and Jacqueline Hill remain static. Ian and Barbara, until now the episode's protagonists, are forced into mainly reactive roles, and their attempts to pin the Doctor down are ineffectual.

Although Jacqueline Hill was an experienced actress and a familiar face to television viewers, she had not at this point achieved 'star' status to the same extent as Hartnell and Russell; prior to *Doctor Who* her highest profile recurring role had been in the mystery serial *Joyous Errand* (BBC, 1957). While she is given comparatively little to do in this scene, it is interesting to consider the ways in which the sequence plays on her better known male colleagues' established screen personae. Former Lancelot William Russell is, figuratively at least, still the knight in shining armour, coming to the aid (or so he believes) of a damsel in distress. Hartnell's film reputation for playing 'tough guys' and villains gives his interpretation of the Doctor a possibly sinister edge, but his earlier experience as a comedian also adds a humorous dimension to the way the Doctor toys with Ian and Barbara. Significantly, one of Sydney Newman's objections to the earlier, un-transmitted 'pilot' was the fact that the Doctor was 'not funny enough' (BBC WAC T5/647/1).

Star status aside, what is notable about this scene is that all the leads are pitching their performances equally to the demands of the small screen. The television sets on which this performance would have been seen typically measured from seventeen to twenty-one inches,[14] still requiring a certain scale of physical gesture to be readable to audiences, yet not of the size employed for *The Quatermass Experiment*, when screens were as small as eight inches. Although certain stage-derived traits are present, they have been tailored to the demands of the studio technology; there is a uniformity of scale among the cast, with little of the disparity in breadth of gesture or vocal projection present ten years before. Studio realism had clearly settled into an established form, the requirements of which television actors understood either through experience or observation. However, as ever this was not the sole determinant of television acting; the various other factors which helped shape performances of the time must also be examined lest any conveniently simplistic conclusions be drawn.

External factors

As already mentioned, the advent of social realism in British theatre, film and television was one of the key developments of the late 1950s and early 1960s. While social realism has often been defined as a particular genre of programme-making, it is a term that is both 'politically and historically contingent ... since society evolves and changes so too social realism evolves and changes' (Lay 2002: 8). British society in 1963 had passed through a significant period of adjustment, which must be considered a major factor, alongside actor experience, in the ongoing evolution of studio realism.

It would be difficult to situate *Doctor Who* directly in the social realist canon; in their analysis of 'An Unearthly Child' John Tulloch and Manuel Alvarado focus on the episode's sense of unreality: 'From the very beginning *Doctor Who* established itself as familiar, but different, normal and uncanny' (1983: 16). Focusing on the atypical (for British television of the time) tracking shot of the Totters Lane junkyard which opens the episode, David Butler states:

> The episode doesn't begin by establishing a naturalistic and mundane world before disrupting that ordinariness with the introduction of the extraordinary and impossible ... and neither does it begin with something obviously unreal. Instead, 'An Unearthly Child' develops something that is much more difficult in mainstream film and television: an uncertainty between what is real and unreal.
>
> (2007: 24)

Given that the episode combines a sense both of realism and the fantastic, it is not the aim here to claim it as a social realist text along the lines of a serial such as *Coronation Street* (ITV, 1960–). Rather, it is necessary to consider to what extent the trend towards social realism, which by the time of the programme's launch was well established in film and television, would have affected both actors' approaches to and contemporary audiences' expectations of performance in television drama as a whole. The idea that social realism's extension into British television – identified by Samantha Lay as its 'natural home' (2002: 68) from the mid-1960s onwards[15] – had no impact on acting for the medium in general is untenable, but before examining precisely what that influence might have been on the performances in 'An Unearthly Child', it is necessary to explain the term and briefly trace its development.

Social realism is a form that was variously associated with the visual arts, documentary, theatre and film before being applied to television. It was John Bratby's painting of a kitchen sink that originally gave rise to the term often associated with or substituted for social realism after being appropriated for David Sylvester's 1954 article of that name; the 'kitchen sink drama' most commonly associated with the birth of social realism in the British performing arts is John Osborne's *Look Back in Anger*, first produced at the Royal Court in May 1956. Although Dan Rebellato has dismissed as 'trite' the assumption that 'a new wave of dramatists sprang up in Osborne's wake; planting their colours on British stages, speaking for a generation who had for so long been silent' (1999: 2), the author readily admits that 'change there certainly was' (*ibid.*). The railings of the play's protagonist Jimmy Porter against middle class complacency and the conservatism of mid-1950s Britain chimed with Sydney Newman at least when he saw it upon his arrival in England, the producer determining that this was the kind of socially relevant material that he intended *Armchair Theatre* to present: 'That play ... seemed to Newman the dazzling light on the road to Damascus; more accurately, it summed up what he had come to believe about the drama. He had developed the notion of "agitational contemporaneity", and *Look Back in Anger* confirmed his ideas' (Sendall 1982: 338).

The play's success coincided with a peak in Britain in the popularity of US actors commonly (though not always accurately) associated with the Method style practised at the Actors Studio under Lee Strasberg.[16] Such figures were highly influential on emerging British thespians, as Tony Garnett, who began his television acting career in 1958, recalls:

> Most young male actors of my generation would decide that they were either Marlon Brando or James Dean. Rather dependent on their size [laughter]. So I decided that I was James Dean; Albert [Finney] was, of course, Marlon Brando. So yes, that style of acting in American cinema was very influential on my generation. And you can see it in the films that start coming through, like *Saturday Night and Sunday Morning* (1960).
>
> **(2010)**

Garnett was one of a group of young actors that came to public attention in the early 1960s playing working or lower middle class anti-heroes, often with their own accents. While influenced by the Method stars, their antecedents were also traceable to *Look Back in Anger*; it was the play's original director Tony Richardson, for example, who later produced *Saturday Night and Sunday Morning*, the gritty drama which made a film star out of the young Finney. Other actors successfully playing with their real voices around this time included Tom Courtenay and Alan Bates, the latter of whom had also appeared in the Royal Court production of *Look Back in Anger*. Their success coincided with a revision of policy with regard to Standard English at leading British drama schools,[17] as Christopher Morahan relates:

> Going back to 1956, one of the phenomena of the times was that RADA no longer attempted to eradicate original accents – no longer eradicate Tom Courtenay's or Albert Finney's accents – and also the films actually began to be made about them. You know, *Saturday Night and Sunday Morning*, and so on; remarkable.
>
> **(2010)**

The increase in regional accents was not born of performers alone, however; the same trend was evident in works now being written for the stage: 'Arnold Wesker and his marvellous plays about Jewishness and his time in East Anglia; Peter Nichols celebrating life in Bristol; David Storey in the theatre, writing about his life, his lovely play *Life Class*, which is about his experience in an art school in Yorkshire. In a way, people became proud of where they came from' (*ibid.*).

It is of course advisable to employ caution when retrospectively applying labels or identifying specific 'movements', and it is unlikely that a new style of acting spontaneously evolved to supplant established modes. As Christopher Morahan points out: 'If we saw Kenneth Haigh's performance as Jimmy Porter [today], I would have thought we would probably think it was rather over the top, but certainly that didn't apply to Mary Ure [and] Alan Bates' (*ibid.*). The seeming cultural explosion of the new wave could equally be seen as a matter of chance timing, as Tony Garnett admits:

> I was a very lucky actor, because I was fashionable. You know, I played either a teddy boy or a neurotic CND undergraduate; one with glasses and one without. But the sort of parts available at that time I fitted in with. You know the old saying that if Albert Finney had been a young actor in the 1930s, he would never have got a job, and if Gerald du Maurier had been an actor in the '60s he would never have got a job. You know; you're fashionable or you're not.
>
> **(2010)**

However, this perceived shift in popular culture, once begun, also filtered through to television via producers such as Sydney Newman, who were influenced by what they saw in the theatre and on film. While giving Newman credit for his pioneering work at ABC, Christopher Morahan also highlights the importance at this time of Granada Television, 'who had a superb record in drama; and the bedrock of their product was *Coronation Street*' (2010). Set in a fictional suburb of Manchester, *Coronation Street* featured a predominantly (though not exclusively) northern cast, its use of an authentic working class idiom in stark contrast to its BBC predecessor, *The Grove Family* (BBC, 1954–57), '[which] was actually full of people not playing their class at all. It was an actress called Ruth Dunning ... and she was playing a housewife in a poor, lower middle class London household, and she wasn't that at all' (*ibid.*). *Coronation Street* marked one of the first occasions in which a television programme made a virtue of employing real regional voice as opposed to mimicked or put on accents; a significant development for studio realism. Though not involved in the programme's production, Christopher Morahan was present at an early script conference for the show:

The producer and the script editors sat round and told stories about Salford. When they talked they spoke Salford, they spoke Manchester, so they wrote it. Jack Rosenthal wrote Manchester ... And that became a very important part of English culture, or British culture ... I think in a strange way the country – or the nation – discovered itself, and this is one of the joys of *Coronation Street*.

(Ibid.)

With its employment of demotic northern English, *Coronation Street* is often cited by television historians alongside *Armchair Theatre* as an early example of small screen social realism (Cooke 2003: 33). For Marion Jordan, *Coronation Street*'s representation of class was a key element of the term: 'Characters should be either working-class or of the classes immediately visible to the working classes (shopkeepers, say...)' (1981: 28). Samantha Lay extends this concept further to encompass 'characters who are inextricably linked to place or environment' (2002: 19).

Such considerations would seem to have little direct relevance to *Doctor Who*, but while this chapter does not aim to position the programme as a social realist text, it is necessary to consider what impact such developments had on acting for television drama in general in order to assess how they are represented in the programme. When considering their impact on 'An Unearthly Child' it is best to focus on the work of William Russell and Jacqueline Hill, who as Ian and Barbara were responsible for portraying the human[18] characters with whom the audience was primarily intended to identify. The choice of schoolteachers as the Doctor's companions was a deliberate move on the part of the production team, the original background notes describing their prototypes[19] as 'the characters we know and sympathise with, the ordinary people to whom extraordinary things happen' (BBC WAC T5/647/1 – 'General Notes on Background and Approach', 13 May 1963); and what could be more real and familiar to younger viewers than a school? This is the environment to which Ian and Barbara are 'inextricably linked' – at least before they are plucked away from it by the Doctor and his TARDIS.

For Stephen Lacey, a key element of social realism was its adoption of 'mimetic dramatic methods ... which foregrounded verisimilitude' (2005: 199), and it is the verisimilitudinous presentation of Coal Hill School and its denizens that provides the key to underscoring the strangeness of what follows. The second scene of 'An Unearthly Child' provides a strong example of this. As the end of lesson bell rings, Barbara emerges into the corridor while asking the (off-screen) Susan to wait for her inside the classroom. Before Barbara goes in search of Ian to ask his advice, there is a brief sequence in the corridor. Two teenage girls from Barbara's class pause in mid-shot before the camera, examining a sheet of paper carried by one of them, presumably containing Barbara's grade for her work. Two male pupils pass by behind them, one pausing to peer over the girls' shoulders at the sheet before pulling a comical face and muttering what sounds like 'Ooh, yes!', pretending to join in their discussion. As the male pupil departs, the first girl whispers something inaudible in the ear of the second (Figure 2.6), who smirks before the pair move out of frame.

The entire sequence lasts mere seconds, and does not appear in the script in any form. Whether or not it was included as the result of an innovation by director Waris Hussein is lost in the mists of time, but the same sequence also appears in the pilot version of the episode, and its inclusion demonstrates the production team's

Figure 2.6 Heather Lyons and Mavis Ranson in *Doctor Who*: 'An Unearthly Child'

desire to add verisimilitude and depth to the Coal Hill School environment.

The subsequent scene between Ian and Barbara, in which the latter explains her unease regarding Susan's family situation, has several similar touches, Ian adjusting the Bunsen burner on his desk and then washing his hands in the classroom basin (the closest the episode comes to kitchen sink drama) while listening to Barbara. The likelihood is that these actions were worked out in rehearsal, though Hussein would have had to request a functioning tap from his set designers before these began. However, they help establish – for both the actors and the audience at home – the fact that these are real people through their presentation in an equally grounded and comprehensible environment. This is reinforced by the performances of Jacqueline Hill and William Russell. As in the subsequent junkyard scene already examined, the actors' vocal work is pitched at a conversational level. Movement, both in terms of physical gesture and traversing the set, is kept to a minimum, and centres on Ian and Barbara's respective objectives: she needs to convince him to assist her in investigating Susan's home situation, while he is primarily concerned with tidying his classroom at the end of the working day. There is an absence of the 'performed' gestures that typified the crash site sequences in 'Contact has been Established', limited here to Barbara rolling her eyes in response to Ian's teasing. As the identifiably 'normal' Ian and Barbara, Russell and Hill were required to produce performances that would not be discordant for 1963 audiences in the wake of the 'normality' presented via socially realistic television texts such as *Coronation Street*. The extent to which they succeeded can be evidenced by comparison with their appearances in television productions contemporaneous with *Doctor Who*. In Russell's case this is slightly problematic, as much of his prior BBC work, including *Nicholas Nickleby*, is missing from the archives. However, the earlier *The Adventures of Sir Lancelot* is preserved in its entirety. Made by the independent Sapphire Films for joint broadcast in America, this was an all-film production, and so presents a somewhat different production model from *Doctor Who*. There is, however, little notable difference between Russell's characterisation of Lancelot and Ian, as the actor himself was earlier seen to acknowledge. Each is a man of action when called for, though also possessed of both intellect and humour. There are also remarkable similarities in the relationships between Ian and the Doctor and Lancelot and Merlin (Cyril Smith), the latter revealed in *The Adventures of Sir Lancelot* to be a gifted scientist rather than a magician, whose mystical predictions are entirely dependent on the practical application of his knowledge. In the opening episode, 'The Knight with the Red Plume', Lancelot is initially suspicious of Merlin's accurate prediction of his arrival at court, and then wryly amused when he discovers that it was the result of a mirror-based light-signalling system set up with a lookout. As can be seen below, Russell adopts several of the same facial expressions while interrogating Merlin as he would later use when playing Ian, although as Lancelot his posture is more aggressive, placing his hand intrusively on Merlin's desk, or leaning in towards him from behind (Figure 2.7).

Though Merlin, like the Doctor, attempts to elude Lancelot's questions, seldom making eye contact, his seated position makes it impossible for him to evade his interlocutor as successfully, and his secret is more quickly uncovered. In many ways the subsequent friendly relationship between Lancelot and Merlin mirrors

Figure 2.7 William Russell and Cyril Smith in *The Adventures of Sir Lancelot*: 'The Knight with the Red Plume'

that which gradually develops in *Doctor Who* between Ian and the Doctor; Russell's performance in the later series can therefore be seen as meeting established audience expectations. And while, as an all-film series, *The Adventures of Sir Lancelot* might not be considered representative of studio realism, the fact that much of it is set in constructed interiors rather than real locations somewhat mitigates this consideration.

As with William Russell, few of Jacqueline Hill's earlier television performances have been preserved. However, 'The Trap', a 1962 episode of detective series *Maigret* (BBC, 1960–63), provides a useful opportunity to compare her acting style with that in 'An Unearthly Child'. Like *Doctor Who*, *Maigret* was a multi-camera studio production, though with a much greater amount of filmed location work. As a result, picture output from the 405-line studio cameras was telerecorded rather than videotaped, and subsequently edited entirely on film (*Maigret*: The Classic TV Archive). For the actors, however, this would have had little impact, and Hill's performance as Yvonne Moncin, whose husband Marcel (Aubrey Woods) is under suspicion of having committed a series of murders in Montmartre, offers firm evidence of a style of acting developed to accommodate the television studio that, despite significant differences in characterisation, varies little between *Maigret* and *Doctor Who*.

In the scene where police inspector Maigret (Rupert Davies) arrives to question Marcel over a button from his suit found at the scene of the latest murder, Yvonne attempts to shield her husband from his interrogation, at times prompting or speaking for Marcel. Despite supplying her husband with an alibi, Yvonne is visibly nervous, though it is not yet clear whether she is aware that he is the killer – as later transpires to be the case. Hill conveys this anxiety via small but noticeable gestures, pulling incessantly at a cigarette throughout the first part of the sequence, and nervously tapping the third finger of her left hand against her right arm as Maigret asks Marcel to show him his wardrobe.

This tiny but significant gesture is an example of an actress well used to the studio set-up, aware that it is not necessary to employ overt, expansive gesticulation to signify subtext. At the end of the scene, after Marcel and Maigret have exited, Hill moves towards the camera – as opposed to the camera moving towards or zooming in on her – so that she is in close-up for a shot that conveys her character's distress. Breaking into tears, she slowly lowers her head, sobbing silently before gradually raising it again, a new expression dawning on her face that could be read either as concern for the fate of her delicate husband, or a dawning realisation of his guilt.

The gesture is choreographed to allow the camera – and so the audience – to take in a significant character beat for Yvonne, and demonstrates the experienced television actress's awareness of how to use the close-up to capture and convey a shift in mood or a mental process, similar to that used by Reginald Tate in *It is Midnight, Dr. Schweitzer*. While it would perhaps be problematic to impose a simplistic reading of *Maigret* as a social realist text, it is arguably more clearly grounded in 'reality' than *Doctor Who*. Like *Doctor Who*, however, it was produced at a time when social realism had become an established form on the small screen. The same economy seen in Hill's work on 'The Trap' also informs her performance in 'An Unearthly Child'; a clear indication that the performances of the contemporary 'human' characters in the latter story can be taken in part as representative of a more general television acting style, not particular to science fiction or children's drama.

If Russell and Hill's performances in 'An Unearthly Child' are in no way out of the ordinary for studio drama of the time, the introduction of Carole Ann Ford as Susan is by contrast designed to suggest her character's strangeness, signifying that she does not belong to the 'real' world of Ian and Barbara. Though involved in the typical teenage practice of listening to pop music on a transistor radio, Ford's performance of Susan's behaviour, consisting of a distant gaze to the eyes and twisting, swooping hand gestures in time to the music (Figure 2.8), marks her out as the unearthly child of the title even before the audience has seen her interact with the other characters. As stated in the Introduction, the performance of aliens of course raises problems with regard to discussion of acting style; Ford's performance here might best be categorised as an example of studio *un*realism, in line with Hartnell's subsequent performance in the junkyard scene. While a detailed examination of such 'fantastic' acting styles would doubtless prove fascinating, it is beyond the remit of this book. However, Ford's performance here is notable for the economy with which it signifies Susan's

Figure 2.8 Carole Ann Ford in *Doctor Who*: 'An Unearthly Child'

alien nature, contrasting with the more realist codes employed by William Russell and Jacqueline Hill.

The divide that has often appeared in academic writing between 'serious' television drama, as considered by John Caughie (2000a), and 'popular' entertainment has been highlighted by Catherine Johnson, who identifies the broad characteristics of the former as 'social realist ... challenging and controversial ... politically motivated', while the latter is 'generic ... stylish and playful ... entertaining and popular' (2005: 46). Examples of this are provided in histories such as Lez Cooke's, in which social realism and popular drama are dealt with as separate entities under the same chapter heading (2003: 29–55). According to Johnson, while these oppositions 'are not necessarily misleading in relation to particular programmes or contexts of production ... a failure to think across and beyond these binary oppositions can limit our understanding of the historical development of British television' (Johnson 2005: 46). The same applies when considering television acting. Based on the (admittedly limited) evidence offered in the textual analyses above, it is impossible to assert that the studio realism employed in 'An Unearthly Child' differs significantly from other contemporaneous drama productions – even those more firmly targeting adults. From the outset, the aim of the *Doctor Who* production team was to create and maintain a level of verisimilitude that would convince children and adults of the time alike, as producer Verity Lambert later affirmed: 'The thing for me with all the casting is, what I wanted – and what I suppose what every producer wants all the time – are people who make you believe in them, who are real. And I really do think, looking at the old *Doctor Who*, nobody was sending it up; everybody played it for the truth, and that made it very convincing' (Lambert 2006). Rather than considering it a handicap, the youth of her audience was, for Lambert, an advantage: 'Children know when they're being patronised; more than adults, actually' (Lambert 2008). Lambert therefore approached the series as being, within reason, a production for adults:

> What I tried to do as a producer [was to] make it as if we were making it for adults, although without sex and violence in it ... It was made to a standard that if you were an adult you would enjoy it. I mean, I made it for me, really, and I think everybody else made it to make it work for them, so there's a great sense of reality, really, in the way people play these episodes; they play it for real, and therefore it makes you believe it.
>
> **(Lambert 2003)**

For William Russell, the world of *Doctor Who* was played to be as real to Ian Chesterton as that of Camelot to Sir Lancelot or Victorian England to Nicholas Nickleby: 'I don't think it was any different from any other kind of acting, really. If you create the character and you follow your instinct as an actor, it doesn't really matter whether it's science fiction or Shakespeare or a modern play. I didn't feel any problem there at all' (Russell 2003a).

Although *Doctor Who* as a text exists independently of the social realist canon, it is highly unlikely that its cast were unaware of social realism in the arts, or unaffected by the changes in performance it had begun to bring about.[20] Such factors should therefore be given at least equal import when considering acting for television as the impact of coincident developments behind the cameras, including the advent of videotape pre-recording.

Production process and technology

While major technological advances had been made since *The Quatermass Experiment*, the BBC's production processes remained in many ways comparatively static.[21] The introduction of videotape in 1958 had not eliminated live drama overnight; some productions, such as *Compact*, combined the two, Tuesday's episode being broadcast live and Wednesday's pre-taped. Although it was decided from the outset that *Doctor Who* would be pre-recorded, this did not represent any significant alleviation of pressure on the actors. For the transmitted version of 'An Unearthly Child', the cast were given four days[22] to rehearse the twenty-five-minute episode at the Drill Hall, 239 Uxbridge Road, working from 10.30 a.m. to 5.30 p.m. between Monday 14 and Thursday 17 October (BBC WAC T5/638/1). William Russell recalls Monday rehearsals as typically beginning with a read-through of the script: 'At that time one could say, "Well, I don't think this works", or "I don't think that works." You could make suggestions: "What about if I said this?" but once we'd started there was no time, really, to start messing about with the script' (Russell 2005a). As with 'Contact has been Established', sets would be represented by coloured tape on the rehearsal room floor to enable blocking, prior to the director planning his camera script before moving into the studio. The environment in which the actors were forced to rapidly evolve their performances was not always conducive to the task at hand; Alvin Rakoff remembers that the various church and drill halls used by the BBC at this time usually lacked such luxuries as central heating: 'You'd get one little gas burner which always ran out; everyone was bundled up' (2011).

As with *The Quatermass Experiment*, the subsequent switch to studio would be the first time the actors encountered the actual sets and props with which they would be recording. According to Peter Purves, however, the adjustment was not difficult for an actor used to the theatre:

> The rehearsal period for television is odd because you don't have a great deal to work with. So when you get onto the set is the first time you see it, and it's the first time it begins to feel real ... You have a technical rehearsal in the studio so you do get used to the set very easily and very quickly; it's the same in the theatre. In the theatre you have a little bit longer to acclimatise to it, but in television you've just got to get on with it. But it isn't hard, it isn't a difficult technique to learn; you look at the sets, see what you've got to do, don't fall over it.
>
> **(Purves 2008)**

Studio rehearsals for 'An Unearthly Child' began at Lime Grove at 10.30 a.m. on Friday 18 October and continued throughout the day, VTR[23] beginning at 8.30 p.m. Unfortunately for the production team, the studio they had been allocated was in many ways inadequate for such a technically ambitious programme. In a memo to Sydney Newman dated 12 August 1963, Donald Wilson protested that the imposition of Studio D was 'too crippling a restriction ... A programme such as *Dr Who*, if it is to fulfil our joint purpose, should be mounted in a studio with the most up to date technical equipment available. I can assure you that the programmes will be good, though in TC3, TC4 or Riverside 1 they would be even better'[24] (BBC WAC T5/647/1). In a December memo Verity Lambert lamented the studio's lack of space for sets or dollies, and 'cameras which cannot take either wide angle or zoom lenses' (BBC WAC T5/647/1, 5 December 1963). Director Richard Martin remembers Studio D as 'a long corridor of a studio. Nothing fitted in it; you couldn't get long shots in it' (Martin 2006). For this reason, actors still had to adjust their performances to accommodate the technology: 'You didn't have room; the actors frequently couldn't take you into a scene. The camera went into a scene and then you followed, because you were absolutely pressed against the wall!' (Russell 2009a).

The technical limitations of Studio D were compounded by the fact that the video technology that facilitated the new recording process was also in its primitive, early stages. Electronic editing was unheard of, and although by 1963 BBC producer Duncan Wood had pioneered a method of splicing the Ampex videotape, this was crude, being conducted by hand with a razor blade, and at £100 a reel prohibitively expensive (Turnock 2007: 96).[25] The absence of post-production video editing required compromise and innovation in equal measure. Midway through 'An Unearthly Child' there is a 'flashback' sequence as Barbara and Ian, seated in the latter's car (Figure 2.9), recall classroom incidents in which Susan has displayed both advanced scientific knowledge and a surprising ignorance of everyday facts. Due to the scene being played 'as live', in real time without edits, director Waris Hussein is forced to use the camera in the 'flashback' shots to represent first Barbara and then Ian's physical point of view, pointing directly at Ford's face (Figure 2.10) as she speaks her half of the dialogue without them in shot. Russell and Hill then speak their lines 'off', from the car set,

Figure 2.9 William Russell and Jacqueline Hill in *Doctor Who*: 'An Unearthly Child'

Figure 2.10 Carole Ann Ford in *Doctor Who*: 'An Unearthly Child'

to which Hussein returns when they continue their conversation in the 'present'.

The exigencies of 'as live' recording were clearly little different from those of live. As an actor, Tony Garnett had little fondness for the pressures of either:

> I remember being in a play at the Television Centre – this was live – and I was playing a boy who had a number of girlfriends. And I would be sitting in a scene with a young woman, and we would have a two-hander. So there would be a camera on her – there – and a camera on me – there. And it was written in such a way that hers was the last speech; and as soon as she started her last speech, an AFM[26] would come and just tap my leg, and I would just quietly move away, and she would have her eye-line and go on speaking as though I was still there, and I would run across the studio floor, changing my clothes as I went. And before I got there that scene was over, and another scene had started with another young woman, looking straight ahead of her, and I had to sit in, pick up a drink, and be ready with my line when she'd finished that. That was the kind of nonsense that you were put in for, even after they were able to record.
>
> **(2010)**

This anecdote again illustrates the extent to which acting for television was distinct from stage work, where actors would seldom be required to perform segments of dialogue to a colleague who was no longer physically present. Such pressures, however, clearly had little creative merit for Garnett, who when he later became a producer was one of the pioneers in taking drama out of the studio and onto location. Dismissing the exigencies of evening recording as 'utterly ridiculous' (*ibid.*), Garnett claims that the decision to continue the procedure even after pre-recording had replaced live transmission was taken in order 'to save on cutting the tape, to save on time ... but of course they couldn't say that, so they elevated it into an aesthetic. And the aesthetic was from the theatre, which was: "the performances are better if there's continuity"' (*ibid.*). Actor John Ringham, who first worked on *Doctor Who* in 1964, recalled live television as:

> a nightmare from beginning to end, because for two minutes before [you start] a deathly silence falls on the studio; nobody moves or talks. So the tension builds up and it builds up and it builds up. And then you get the call to start and it becomes panic-stricken. And success is to get from A to Z without disaster; that is

success. Without a boom coming into shot, a microphone, without a camera being in the wrong position, without a door jamming so that you can't get through the thing.

(2002)

Whether there was any difference in terms of quality of performance between live and 'as live' seems to have been a source of some debate. Ringham's comments suggest a tangible sense of relief on the part of actors when the pressures of entirely live performance were lifted slightly, but certain of those behind the cameras at the BBC seemed to have preferred the immediacy of the old system. According to Moray Watson, *Compact*'s producers Hazel Adair and Peter Ling felt that their cast delivered better performances on the Tuesday transmissions:

> Because it was live, and there was the adrenalin, the excitement. We didn't agree with it, because we just said, 'Oh, fuck!' when we dried on the Wednesday, and they hated that because they couldn't show it, and they had to go again. So at the end of the Wednesday recording we all stayed behind and they said, 'Oh, there are three or four re-takes' – not necessarily because people had dried, but for some reason; you know, cameras or microphones getting into shot, things like that. I remember Peter Ling, he just said, 'Up in the gallery we prefer the Tuesday.' ... We felt we were equally good – or bad – on the Wednesday, but they didn't.
>
> (Watson 2010)

As Watson mentions, with videotape pre-recording there was the (expensive) possibility of re-taking a scene if something went drastically wrong, providing a slight alleviation of pressure on the actor. However, the number of edits allowed was limited: 'I think we were allowed to cut the tape in those days four times. I actually have to confess I did exceed that from time to time' (Lambert 2002). Ian Cullen, who appeared in 1964 *Doctor Who* serial 'The Aztecs', points out that, even when re-takes were possible, acting was one of the last factors to be considered:

> At the end of a recording session there was a short period to record the re-takes and put right anything that had gone wrong, and the order of priority was always the technical mistakes first. Camera mistakes had to be corrected; then any sound errors would be corrected if there was a technical mistake. And at the end of the line would be the actors, if they'd fluffed a line, or made a mistake, or

dropped their prop, or done something wrong, or looked a bit stupid, or weren't very good; then they might get a chance. But in the main, actors didn't get a chance to have a re-take, because they always ran out of recording time.

(2002)

On studio days, William Russell felt that the evening recording created a sense of event which was beneficial to the cast: 'I actually rather liked the preparation through the day, the technical things, and then the performance. Because we all – all of us – came up for the performance' (Russell 2005b). Richard Martin had worked as an actor in the days of live television before turning to directing, and so was well aware of the various advantages and disadvantages of both continuity recording and out-of-sequence filming:

> The concept was still, in order to make it cheap, that it was a bastard half-hour between theatre and film. So we were allowed to prepare it, but we were still given the evening, exactly like the theatre, where we gave the performance. What this did was twofold: it excited the actors into a greater degree of concentration and urgency – so it was over to them, it was their show, as it were – and we were rushing about with our cameras to hold up with them. But of course with something as complicated as this it beggared the possibilities, the physical possibilities, because we couldn't do it shot by shot.

(2005)

Martin's comments belie the visual imperative of the director, who would prefer to piece together his cast's performances from different takes, while the actor in him understands the challenges of performing in short segments: 'It is incredibly difficult for any actor to keep the same intensity of performance and emotional level in the shot by shot situation [as] is naturally generated by telling a story in an evening performance' (*ibid.*). However, in light of Tony Garnet's comments regarding the extraordinary physical demands sometimes made by 'in continuity' performance, it is questionable to what extent that procedure 'naturally' assisted the actor in the realisation of narrative; it could equally be argued that out-of sequence recording, or at least continuity recording with breaks between scenes, allowed the cast more time to prepare psychologically, i.e. to 'get into' character. Established BBC procedures had clearly been little affected by the introduction of pre-recording, and directors' preferences for working processes would be dictated by personal experience and training. Despite being produced with the BBC's more antiquated facilities, 'An Unearthly Child' is notable for being very much the product of new blood in this respect.

Direction

Waris Hussein, the twenty-four-year-old director of 'An Unearthly Chid', had applied to the BBC's training course directly upon graduating from Cambridge University, but found the competition stiff: 'There were only, like, five people [employed as directors] from the outside world ... From the time I applied, I hear – and this may not be an accurate number – but there were at least five thousand applications' (2011). The BBC had by now extended its training from three to six months,[27] but the multi-camera studio course was kept entirely separate from single camera: 'The single camera technique was actually allocated to the film department, which was a separate unit which was based at Ealing. We were based out of Television Centre, so there was a big segregation ... The single camera that we used subsequently, which was for exterior filming, basically was telecine inserts' (ibid.).

Hussein's approach to directing *Doctor Who* is notable for attempting at times to emulate a long take, single camera approach,[28] but Hussein believes that the four-camera technique was invaluable in his subsequent career: 'It taught me how to economise on my shooting; it taught me how to develop shots for the single camera that now I have the fluidity to do it with. I also know how to compose a picture very quickly, with the help of my crew. No, I think I was very fortunate' (ibid.).

Such technical expertise was vital to plan and conduct the studio recording sessions, but the job of a television director still comprised elements of the theatre in terms of managing actors in rehearsals: 'You don't only have to know all your techniques about how to use your camera, and how many times you can break tape; you've also got to work psychologically with the actors' (ibid.). However, technical know-how could be an advantage when dealing with the cast, as Hussein learned when challenged by one (unnamed) leading actor:

> He said, 'Oh, I don't think I want to do that. Why can't I move over here?' thereby destroying [the camera plan]; it's like a domino effect … I had to think very quickly on my feet, because this was a test; the moment you show any hesitation or weakness, especially on the first few days, then you're in trouble. So I said, 'Oh, that's great, actually. You'd be walking out of shot, and you can come back in, because there's no wall there.' And that made sense to him; he knew what I was talking about. And the fact that he wasn't going to be in shot, which was a vanity project, you then are actually one step ahead of him; a psychological game.
>
> **(Ibid.)**

However, Hussein emphasises that he found theatre-trained actors, as opposed to those more experienced in film, 'much more flexible in terms of accepting what they're told to do. In film you can have lengthy discussions about something [on the set]; in television you have to sort all that out prior to going into the studio. It's already fixed. You can't suddenly start improvising something that didn't happen in rehearsal' (*ibid.*). According to Hussein, actors were by now adept at scaling their performance: 'All I needed to do with someone who'd learned their craft was to say: "Bring it down; don't push it too much vocally." In theatre you have to push it; in a film, you've got to bring it in, and that's all you needed to do as a director' (*ibid.*).

The closing sequence of 'An Unearthly Child' offers an example of the symbiosis that took place in the studio between actors, director and technicians, being demanding in terms of performance – each of the four main cast members carrying an important share of the narrative – and technically complex in its execution. Following a scuffle outside the Police Box with the Doctor, Barbara and Ian have forced their way inside to discover Susan in an impossibly large, futuristic control room, dominated by a central console (Figure 2.11).

When the teachers question their pupil she explains that they have entered the TARDIS, a dimensionally transcendental craft in which she and the Doctor travel through time and space. Ian and Barbara struggle to grasp what Susan has told them, much to her frustration and the Doctor's condescending amusement. When the Doctor

Figure 2.11 Carole Ann Ford in *Doctor Who*: 'An Unearthly Child'

refuses either to adequately explain himself or to allow the teachers to leave the ship, convinced that they will betray his and Susan's presence to the authorities, Susan tries to persuade him to relent. He replies that if Ian and Barbara are to leave then she must also go with them. However, the Doctor's move to operate the door mechanism is revealed to be a bluff when Susan realises that he is in fact setting the TARDIS in flight. When she tries to stop the Doctor he loses control of the ship, resulting in an extremely turbulent take-off.

The set for the main TARDIS interior was one of three erected in Studio D for the recording, along with the classroom/corridor combination and junkyard, but occupied nearly half the space available. As three cameras had been covering the previous junkyard scene, only one could be pre-positioned in the console room. However, the third of the cameras in the junkyard in fact deserted the scene prior to Ian's scuffle with the Doctor, moving across to the TARDIS set. This was common practice in live and 'as live' studio work, as Waris Hussein explains:

> You've got to have enough time to release one of those cameras to move to the other set. So in your camera script you put: 'Camera three move to position' – and you give them A, B and C positions;

I think it was: 'Move to position C.' And he would then move across, and I'm talking to him on the earphones all the time. It's rather like a pilot landing a plane; I'm in the control room, my assistant is calling the shots.

(Ibid.)

The effect of such manoeuvres on the actors playing in the previous scene can only be imagined: 'It must have felt quite desperate ... to see this loss of concentration and seeing all these people disappearing out of the corner of your eye' (Martin 2005). However, actor Martin Jarvis, who made one of his earliest television appearances in a 1965 *Doctor Who* serial, believes that this was just one of the many adjustments an actor learned to make through experience: 'One side of your brain is continuing the scene or thinking about that; another is seeing that that camera's gone, there's a red light on the one camera, so you know that's still shooting you. But [it was] very exciting' (2005).

The TARDIS interior scene becomes more fluid and visually complex as a greater number of cameras join the set-up, meaning that the actors have to hit their marks precisely to accommodate the carefully planned moves. William Russell and Jacqueline Hill initially remain in the same position so the camera can pan right from Ian (Figure 2.12) to Barbara in mid close-up, requiring Hill to pause momentarily to allow the camera enough to time to reach her before delivering her line (Figure 2.13). Hussein then cuts to a second camera on Hartnell for his line, while the camera that had been on Hill pans left to Russell again as Hussein cuts back to it for his response; the end of the pan can clearly be seen at the start of the shot.

The actors are then positioned in various groupings until Hussein has enough cameras available to shoot around them. For example, when the Doctor moves over to examine his ormulu clock, which is on the left of a mid-shot frame with William Hartnell approaching from the right, William Russell leaves Jacqueline Hill upstage by the TARDIS doors and moves downstage towards Hartnell, so that his face is behind the clock as Ian attempts to elicit an explanation from the Doctor. At the same time, the camera closes in slightly, placing Hartnell and Russell in medium close-up. When the Doctor tires of the exchange, Hartnell turns his back on both Russell and the camera and moves away; Russell then follows him.

Figure 2.12 William Russell in *Doctor Who*: 'An Unearthly Child'. The camera then pans right to...

Figure 2.13 Jacqueline Hill in *Doctor Who*: 'An Unearthly Child'

This is one of several examples of Hussein shooting the backs of actors in an attempt to get away from outward, 'frontal' acting towards the fourth wall; by this point his other cameras are in position, and subsequent shots become increasingly adventurous, even taking in the set's futuristic ceiling piece.

Blocking is still paramount for the actors, however, and given the complexity of Hussein's camera moves there are moments when the slightest error in positioning can spoil a shot, as when Hartnell's head slightly obscures close-ups of Russell and Hill; cost alone would have made a re-take of these shots prohibitive. Other small mistakes are covered through performance. After the Doctor says 'The children of my civilisation would be insulted', in reference to Ian's resentment at being patronised, Hartnell should pause for Russell's interruption: '*Your* civilisation?' However, he jumps ahead, beginning the later line: 'I tolerate this century, but I don't enjoy it.'[29] The error is quickly corrected when Russell speaks his line over Hartnell's mistake, and the latter picks up with the correct response: 'Yes, *my* civilisation; I tolerate this century, but I don't enjoy it'; if anything, the mistake adds verisimilitude to Ian's interruption. Similarly, when Hartnell's scarf falls to the floor as he is unwinding it, he picks it up and drapes it over a chair with barely a break in the delivery of his line. These are the instinctive responses of actors accustomed to having to improvise through mistakes in live performance, as Ian Cullen confirms: 'It would be impossible for them to say: "Sorry, I've forgotten my words," or "Gosh, the prop's broken"; whatever happened – if the studio caught fire – they would carry on to the end of the sequence' (2002).

This scene is also notable for some early examples of William Hartnell putting his advice to Peter Purves into practice, avoiding expansive movements while keeping his hands in shot for a variety of gestures, whether pensive (Figure 2.14), indicating mirth at Ian's lack of comprehension (Figure 2.15), chiding Susan (Figure 2.16), or offering her the choice of leaving in the TARDIS or staying in the twentieth century (Figure 2.17).

Such gesturally economical acting is calculated to fit the frame of Hussein's cameras, and again positioning is a prime consideration on the part of the actor; any improvisations to cover mistakes must fit in with Hussein's meticulously worked out camera plan. At the close of the sequence, the actors again have to adapt their

Figure 2.14 William Hartnell in *Doctor Who*: 'An Unearthly Child'

Figure 2.15 William Russell and William Hartnell in *Doctor Who*: 'An Unearthly Child'

Figure 2.16 Carole Ann Ford and William Hartnell in *Doctor Who*: 'An Unearthly Child'

Figure 2.17 Jacqueline Hill, Carole Ann Ford, William Hartnell and William Russell in *Doctor Who*: 'An Unearthly Child'

movement to the technological limitations of the day; the turbulent take-off is indicated by much shaking of the cameras, while William Russell and Jacqueline Hill simulate the effect of being buffeted, staggering to and fro before Hill collapses into a chair and Russell sinks to the floor.

The TARDIS scene illustrates the fact that, despite the innovations taking place in technological terms, actors were still catering to technical requirements from the moment production entered the studio. A substantial revolution would have to occur in BBC television's production process before the industrial factors that contributed to studio realism altered in any significant way; namely, a shift from the multi-camera process that the studio required to the single camera model typically employed for location work. Such developments will be examined in Chapter 3, but if in 1963 BBC television showed few signs of immediate change, the same could also be said of other, intersecting factors outside the industry. Although by the early 1960s there seemed to be indications at least that British drama training was slowly adapting to suit the needs of the small screen, these proved largely illusory, and the grounding received by the majority of actors remained, for the most part, rooted in traditional theatre practice.

Training

While little innovation had taken place in drama academies in the first half of the century, the early 1960s saw the founding of East 15, inspired by the work of Joan Littlewood's Theatre Workshop, and the Drama Centre London, a breakaway group from the Central School of Speech and Drama. These were the first British schools to provide training based directly on Stanislavski, whose work has been widely cited for its suitability to screen acting. There are indications that it was around this time that acting for television began to receive critical attention as a style distinct from both theatre and film, Tom C. Battin's article 'The Television Actor' appearing in a 1959 edition of *The Southern Speech Journal*. In this piece, Battin makes the case that any actor of ability can work in television, as long as they are prepared to adapt to the specificities of the medium, e.g. avoiding exaggeration of movement to develop 'a naturalness which the intimacy of the medium demands'

(1959: 210). Other recommendations include increased familiarity with the studio microphone, a reduction of volume in terms of vocal projection (*ibid*.: 211), and awareness of camera position and focal length: 'The actor ... must not appear conscious of being surrounded by cameras ... Facial grimaces, distortion of features, physical expressions of any kind other than natural, will be obvious to the TV audience' (*ibid*.: 214). Battin was a US academic, working at the University of Houston, and it is difficult to ascertain how much impact his writing would have had in the UK. However, it is notable that many of the points he makes were already being addressed in the performances seen in 'An Unearthly Child'. It was also at this point that English drama schools such as RADA and Central began to introduce a limited input on acting for the camera. However, these new developments would have had little direct impact on actors already working in British television drama in 1963, and will therefore be examined instead in Chapter 3, which focuses on a later period by which time their effects were more fully felt. These nascent initiatives aside, formal drama training in Britain remained resolutely focused on stage practice, as Roger Lloyd Pack, who attended RADA between 1963 and 1965, confirmed when interviewed:

> We had a lot of voice classes, about speaking Received English, Received Pronunciation. We had Voices and Technique, given by Peter Barkworth; an object [demonstrates with a mug], and picking that up as well as saying a line, and how much attention you gave to that, and how much attention you gave to the line; that sort of thing. We had Restoration classes, and how to do a Restoration bow – which I became pretty good at, and I've never used ever in my career. And the same with swordfights, fencing, which I enjoyed doing; I never had to do that. We had other forms of movement classes with [June] Kemp ... That covers it, really; technique.
>
> (2011)

Lloyd Pack's comments make it clear that much of the grounding given to young actors was less than useful for their future television careers, and the continued focus on voice is interesting in light of Principal John Fernald's encouragement from the mid-1950s of a greater working class intake. As Tony Garnett points out: 'I was at UCL with Tom Courtenay, who went to RADA, and he was a working class lad from Hull, just as I was a working class lad from Birmingham. And Albert [Finney] had been to RADA, so it wasn't quite as class divided and as snobbish as it would be easy to caricature' (2010). However, the increased number of students from regional backgrounds did not mean that Standard English had in any way receded in importance. Lloyd Pack stated that the RADA voice coaches 'were very insistent that we spoke our vowels correctly ... It was sort of the Voice Beautiful at a time when the kitchen sink drama was around, so in a way it was already a little bit out of date' (2011). Although actors like Tom Courtenay and Albert Finney used their real voices in much of their screen work, they were still trained in Received Pronunciation, which remained the accepted way of speaking for roles not specified as deriving from a particular region. While William Russell and Jacqueline Hill, who both hailed from the Midlands, would jokingly adopt 'Brummie' accents when chatting in rehearsals (Russell, cited in Mulkern 2010), they employed their adopted voices of Standard English for their on-screen performances both in *Doctor Who* and *The Adventures of Sir Lancelot* and *Maigret*. Similarly, William Hartnell had acquired a pronounced working class London accent growing up in Camden. Following his year at the Italia Conti academy, Hartnell's unofficial guardian Hugh Blaker decided to enrol him at public school, hopeful that it would smooth away his rough edges; a move of which Conti approved: 'You will be giving him the one thing that he needs for the development of [his] talent – polish and refinement of manner' (cited in Carney 1996: 35). Archive recordings of interviews with Hartnell unearthed in 2009[30] and 2014[31] reveal few traces of his London 'rough edges', Hartnell using an adopted Standard English. The actor was, however, able to draw upon a range of accents in his television and film career; his performances as sergeant majors in films such as *Carry On Sergeant* (1958) feature a (recalled?) working class accent, though he would use Standard English on the rare occasions that he was given roles of officer rank, as in *Heavens Above* (1963). Hartnell's employment of RP, both as the Doctor and for public appearances, illustrates the fact that, though regional accents had become acceptable in social realist film and television, Standard English was still as much the norm for authority figures as it had been ten years earlier with Bernard Quatermass. This is in marked contrast to the real regional accent employed by Christopher Eccleston when the series was re-launched in 2005 – by which time much had changed in both UK drama training and society as a whole.

Reception

Contemporary response to 'An Unearthly Child' was generally positive; the original transmission of the episode was watched by nearly 4.4 million, comprising 9 per cent of the population as opposed to ITV's 8 per cent, and received a Reaction Index of 63; slightly higher than the average for television drama of 62, and just under the norm for children's television of 64 (BBC WAC R9/7/66 – 'An Audience Research Report', Week 48 1963). 124 viewers contributed to the BBC's Audience Research Report,[32] which offered a somewhat muted response to the performances: 'The acting throughout was considered satisfactory, several viewers adding that it was pleasant to see William Hartnell in the somewhat unusual role (for him) of Dr. Who [sic]' (ibid.). Such comments indicate that audiences at this time were prepared to accept actors cast demonstrably against 'type'; something that would change significantly in the decades to come. Broadcast in the children's slot, it is possible that the BBC's sampling of viewers were not judging the acting according to the expectations of 'adult' drama, though the report's comparison of the Reaction Index with the norms for both children's drama and drama in general indicates that the BBC at least did not regard Doctor Who solely as a children's programme. While some viewers regarded it as 'an enjoyable piece of escapism, not to be taken too seriously' (ibid.), others admitted that 'it was ... written imaginatively enough to appeal to adult minds' (ibid.). Viewers' ready acceptance of the cast's performances in a programme containing such strong fantasy elements would seem to demonstrate that they were not doing anything in acting terms that was particularly dissonant. Insofar as these remarks can be taken as representative of overall audience response, the studio realist style seen in 'An Unearthly Child' can be seen as typical – or at the very least not atypical – of contemporaneous television drama, despite the improbability (to certain viewers' minds) of the narrative scenario within which it was performed.

Conclusion

As a case study, 'An Unearthly Child' cautions against imposing too simplistic a reading on the determinants of acting style. The assertion by Alvin Rakoff, husband of Jacqueline Hill, that 'you had people by then, including my wife, who had done a *lot* of television; they knew about television acting, and it would show' (2011), would seem to indicate that increased actor experience was the major influencing factor. 'An Unearthly Child' certainly contains far fewer traces of stage-derived performance than 'Contact has been Established' ten years before. However, the idea that these scaled down performances were the result of actors' acclimatisation to the studio alone is complicated by the major societal shifts that had taken place over the preceding decade, not least the increase in the number of social realist texts on television. Actors of 1963 were likely to have absorbed aspects of this new wave, if only by osmosis. At the same time, other determinants had not influenced studio realism to the extent or in the ways that might have been expected. As seen, the introduction of pre-recording did little to change the BBC's established production process, representing only a slight alleviation of performance pressures on actors; if technology had advanced significantly, production practice had yet to adjust in line with it. Elsewhere, apparent signs of development in drama training ultimately proved misleading; the acceptance of real, regional voice in the social realist films of the late 1950s and early 1960s did not signify that Received Pronunciation had in any way receded in importance, and it continued to form part of the training provided in most academies. In terms of acting approach, the slowly increasing presence of Stanislavski in British schools had little immediate influence on television acting, and those who were at last being coached in his techniques at East 15 and the Drama Centre would not establish themselves on screen for several years.

The opening of Television Centre provided a clear signal that the BBC was heavily invested in studio drama, which would indeed remain the dominant form for the next two decades. The studio realism that largely derived from this production model consisted of an increased awareness on actors' parts of the studio apparatus and familiarity with its function, as evidenced by reduced vocal projection and diminished employment of broad gesture to indicate mood and emphasise dialogue. This style was now more clearly established than in 1953, its parameters understood – whether consciously or otherwise – by performers, production crews and audiences alike. However, in the 1970s significant developments would begin to take place with regard to several determinants that had until now remained relatively static, laying the groundwork for an eventual transformation in the style of British television acting.

Notes

1. Littlewood had no direct association with East 15, however, as later associate Derek Paget confirms: '[East 15] was [founder] Margaret Bury's toy, and Joan didn't particularly like Margaret Bury' (2011).
2. Although the London service was launched in September, the Midlands and North services did not follow until February and May 1956 respectively, and the ITV network was not completed until 1962, when Channel Television went on air (Johnson and Turnock 2005: 19).
3. Of these households, 12.3 million were equipped to receive ITV.
4. Initially much of the Corporation's output was still produced at Lime Grove and the Riverside Studios in Hammersmith.
5. By 1962 there were only 120 provincial theatres in operation in England, as compared with 300 in 1939 (Sanderson 1984: 279).
6. In 1958 the actors' union Equity, having calculated that an actor working on television earned 4d per week per 1,000 viewers compared with £12.10.0d per week per 1,000 audience in the theatre, had negotiated a two-year increase in the basic minimum fee from 7 to 10 guineas. When this expired, a new proposal to replace the existing system with fees based on performances networked in different regions, taking account of the rise of ITV, was only accepted after a five-month strike by Equity (Sanderson 1984: 283).
7. What had previously been separated as the Drama Group and the Script Department were now combined in a single Drama Department, divided into Plays (headed by Michael Bakewell), Series (Elwyn Jones) and Serials (Donald Wilson). All children's drama was now the responsibility of the newly formed department, and the roles of director, producer and script editor were clearly delineated.
8. Newman later stated that he perceived BBC drama output up to this time as 'catering to a highly educated, cultured class ... I felt that the dramas really weren't speaking about common, everyday things' (Newman 2006)

9 Donald Wilson had commissioned two reports, both titled 'Science Fiction', dated March and 25 July 1962 respectively (BBC WAC T5/647/1), on the form such a programme might take, out of which came the recommendation for a series revolving around time travel.
10 In a memo dated 10 October 1963, Donald Wilson specified that 'while being primarily adventure serials for family viewing, [the series] should have a strong appeal for children' (BBC WAC T5/647/1). Producer Verity Lambert later stated that her brief was to produce drama for children aged between eight and fourteen (2003).
11 Jonathan Bignell has noted that the programme's transmission time, between *Grandstand* (BBC, 1958–2007) and *Juke Box Jury* (BBC, 1959–67), meant that it was tasked with 'gather[ing] these different audience constituencies [adult men and teenagers] together at a transitional point in the BBC schedule' (2007a: 44).
12 As it was billed in the *Radio Times*.
13 During Hartnell's tenure, the programme was never off the air for more than seven weeks at a time (Russell 1995: 4, 7 and 10).
14 Nigel Kneale refers to the 21-inch Home Screen in his article written five years before (1959: 86), though 24-inch sets were being manufactured in the United States as early as 1957 (Bennett-Levy 2001–13).
15 John Caughie has highlighted the fact that, after 1963, the new wave in British cinema had come to 'a remarkably abrupt end' (2000a: 58).
16 Marlon Brando, arguably the Hollywood actor of the time most frequently linked with Strasberg's Method, later stated: 'Lee Strasberg tried to take the credit for teaching me how to act. He never taught me anything ... To me he was a tasteless and untalented person. He never taught me acting' (cited in Barton 2009: 155). The Method was in fact more nebulous than is commonly appreciated, separate and distinct versions having been popularised by Stella Adler (*ibid.*: 158–160) and Sanford Meisner (*ibid.*: 160–163) in addition to Strasberg's work.
17 The change in approach was pioneered at RADA by John Fernald, formerly a director at Liverpool, who took over as Principal in 1955; students were still expected to master Standard English as required, but not at the expense of their original voice.
18 Towards the end of the episode Susan is also revealed be an alien.
19 The characters were originally named Cliff and Lola, along with an early version of Susan, Bridget, who is not specified to be the Doctor's granddaughter (BBC WAC T5/647/1 – 'General Notes on Background and Approach', 13 May 1963)
20 The 2009 DVD commentary on 1964 serial 'The Keys of Marinus', for example, at one point turns to a discussion of the impact made at the time by Joan Littlewood's *Oh! What a Lovely War* at Stratford East.

21 The three editions of production manual *The Grammar of Television Production* (Davis 1960, 1966 and 1974) contain virtually the same wording, the only major changes being an additional chapter on recording in the 1966 edition, while the 1974 version covers the introduction of colour broadcasting and improvements in camera design, zoom lenses having replaced lens turrets by this point (1974: 62).

22 It is important to remember that the cast had already recorded an earlier version of the episode on 27 September, for which five days' rehearsal was allocated. Four days became the rehearsal template from this episode onwards (BBC WAC T5/638/1).

23 Video Tape Recording.

24 Newman replied that Wilson had misunderstood his suggestion to 'live with' Studio D, claiming that when he had originally allocated the studio he had believed that it possessed all the technical facilities the programme required (BBC WAC T5/647/1).

25 Douglas McNaughton has challenged commonly held view that this was the sole determinant of in-continuity, evening recording (2014), citing the BBC's 1958 agreement with actors' union Equity, which stated that recordings should last no longer than three times the duration of the transmitted programme (BBC WAC R8/261/1).

26 Assistant Floor Manager.

27 This was the duration of Waris Hussein's training in 1962 (Hussein 2011); in *Days of Vision*, however, Don Taylor reports that his training in early 1960 lasted only six weeks (1990: 14), and that few of those on the course had directorial ambitions, regarding it as 'a kind of perk' (*ibid.*: 9). It is possible that this was a more compressed course offered to those who already had contracts within the BBC, as was the case with Taylor.

28 Watching the opening sequence of the un-broadcast pilot for the DVD commentary, Hussein noted: 'Some of the shots are trying very hard to be fluid and continuous ... Most of the dramas that one did see were fairly limited in their set-ups; they were always drawing rooms, or internal sets' (2006).

29 The published version of the script indicates that this was indeed an error on Hartnell's part, and a pause should have been left for Russell's line, 'Your civilization ...?' (Coburn and McElroy 1988: 48).

30 A short 1967 feature for television magazine programme *Points West*, conducted while the actor was touring in the pantomime *Puss in Boots*.

31 A thirty-five-minute extract from Hartnell's 1965 interview on *Desert Island Discs* (Hartnell 2013).

32 Other contemporary reaction has proved hard to come by; there were few newspaper reviews, the press still being dominated by the news of the Kennedy assassination the previous Friday.

3
The genesis of location realism

By the mid-1970s, studio realism might be expected to have reached its apotheosis, yet it was by no means all-encompassing as a style of television acting, and there were already elements in play that would ultimately come to threaten its primacy as the dominant mode of acting in British television drama. The decade saw the emergence of various factors that would influence actors' work at the Corporation, beginning with the BBC's further investment in its existing rehearsal and recording model via the opening in 1970 of its purpose-built block of eighteen rehearsal rooms[1] in North Acton, known colloquially as the 'Acton Hilton'. However, this reinforcement of the system underpinning studio realism coincided with various developments that would challenge it as a form of television drama acting. The increased manipulability of videotape, combined with a new Equity agreement (McNaughton 2014), introduced the possibility of out-of-sequence studio schedules and post-production editing, meaning that episodes could for the first time be rehearsed and recorded in separate sections. The 'rehearse/record' process, while not immediately replacing 'in continuity' evening recording, became increasingly favoured as the decade progressed. Also, while the cameras used at Television Centre remained cumbersome, the employment on drama productions of lighter-weight Outside Broadcast (or OB) cameras, until this time more usually employed for sports coverage, introduced a faster and cheaper mode of working outside the studio than the single film camera, which itself had significantly increased in use for television drama since the mid-1960s.

Elsewhere, British drama schools were finally producing actors grounded in the work of Stanislavski, whose theories had by the late 1960s even begun to permeate the training offered at more established academies such as RADA. This, combined with schools' first tentative steps towards screen training, meant that actors entering the television industry in the 1970s were equipped with a skillset arguably more diverse than that possessed by those who had preceded them.

The 1975 series of *Survivors* featured two distinct working processes. While the initial six episodes followed the same pre-filming/rehearsal/studio pattern utilised in *The Quatermass Experiment* and *Doctor Who*, from episode seven onwards this was replaced by an all-Outside Broadcast location video model. A new approach was therefore required on the part of actors and directors alike, with much of the performance preparation now taking place on location rather than being perfected beforehand in a separate rehearsal space: the seeds of location realism. This chapter compares scenes from the opening studio episode, 'The Fourth Horseman', and 'Law and Order', the ninth episode of the series and the third to be recorded entirely using OB. The fact that these episodes shared the same director, Pennant Roberts, and many of the same cast provides two stable factors when examining the implications for studio realism of the move to location. Also considered, however, are the ways in which changes in British drama training affected how emerging actors approached working in television drama.

Background

By the 1970s British television had settled into a 'comfortable duopoly' (Peacock 1986: 38) between the BBC and ITV; in January 1975 domestic set ownership stood at 18.6 million, of which only 0.2 million were not equipped to receive the independent channel (BARB 2016). The launch of BBC2 a decade earlier[2] was the most recent act of significant expansion in British television broadcasting, and it would be nearly eight years before a fourth terrestrial channel was created. Educational programmes aside, weekday television was still comparatively limited; on Wednesday 16 April

1975, when 'The Fourth Horseman' was transmitted, scheduling began at 12.30 p.m., with a two-hour gap in the afternoon prior to the commencement of children's programming at 4 p.m. 'The Fourth Horseman' was shown before *The Nine O'Clock News* (BBC, 1970–2000).

Conceived as an exploration of the after-effects of a virus which wipes out 95 per cent of the Earth's population, *Survivors* was based on a format by Terry Nation, who acted as script consultant on the first series and also wrote seven of its thirteen episodes. Formerly a comedy writer, in the 1960s Nation was best known to British television audiences as creator of the Daleks, chief extra-terrestrial antagonists in several *Doctor Who* serials. Although Nation created the outline for the first series of *Survivors* and the central characters, he was forced to share control of the programme with producer and script editor Terence Dudley. While it was Nation who sought out fellow series one writers Clive Exton[3] and Jack Ronder, Dudley was responsible both for employing directors Pennant Roberts, Gerald Blake and Terence Williams and for casting the lead actors (Cross and Priestner 2005: 27–28). Carolyn Seymour, best known for drama *Take Three Girls* (BBC, 1969–71), was chosen to play housewife Abby Grant, while Lucy Fleming, whose television work consisted mainly of period adaptations, took the role of secretary Jenny Richards. Appearing from episode two as engineer Greg Preston was Ian McCulloch, who had played lead or co-starring roles in *The Borderers* (BBC, 1968–69) and *The Search for the Nile* (BBC, 1971). Although McCulloch in particular was supportive of Nation's vision, the latter's relationship with Terence Dudley soon became 'fraught with difficulty' (Bignell and O'Day 2004: 40), and Nation left *Survivors* when series one concluded.

Nevertheless, it was the higher-profile Nation who was featured as series creator in an interview with the *Radio Times* to publicise the programme's launch. Aware of the public's close identification of him with the Daleks, Nation clearly wished to distance *Survivors* from the perceived science fiction element of *Doctor Who*: 'It's not going into the realms of the impossible; it's starting very close to the possible' ('This Week' 1975: 3). Nation was clearly keen from the outset to ground *Survivors* in reality, but the shift in production processes during the series led to distinct alterations in the on-screen representations of the realism he sought to evoke.

Production process and technology

Production on *Survivors* began in late 1974 (Cross and Priestner 2005: 8). In keeping with the established production process for BBC studio drama, location filming took place prior to rehearsals at Acton, commencing with a mute, single camera film sequence for 'The Fourth Horseman' at the London Westway in which Jenny (Lucy Fleming) makes her way to the hospital on foot to seek aid for her ailing flatmate (*ibid.*: 33). The exigencies of single camera filming will be examined in greater detail in Chapter 4, which deals with a period by which it had become the norm for British television drama. However, as with the pre-filmed inserts for *The Quatermass Experiment* in Chapter 1, the most notable aspect of filmed location work in the 1970s is the absence of a prior rehearsal period, as Lucy Fleming recalls: 'It's very odd, and I remember very clearly the first scene I did, which was on the flyover coming down to the Marylebone Road, where there was always a traffic jam, and I don't think I'd met anybody. I'd met the director and the producer, but apart from that it was just: "Oh, we're going to go and film this bit out there"; "Oh, OK"' (2010).[4]

Use of location film had increased since the early 1960s, with largely film-based dramas such as 'Cathy Come Home' (BBC, 1966) becoming more common first on *The Wednesday Play* and then *Play for Today*. The full import of this will be investigated in Chapter 4, but of equal significance for *Survivors* was the expansion over this period of 'insert' material, pre-filmed on location and subsequently 'played in' during the studio recording sessions. Although this practice dated back to the days of live television, the increased ratio of its use as compared with studio video was now beginning to disrupt the established rehearsal and continuity performance template. Whereas 'Contact has been Established' includes forty-two seconds of pre-filmed inserts, and 'An Unearthly Child' a mere twenty-four seconds, 'The Fourth Horseman' features twenty-two minutes and forty-five seconds of location film, against twenty-five minutes and twenty-four seconds of studio videotape.[5] For the actor, this increase in location filming meant that a greater part of their performance had to be given without the full rehearsal accorded to all-studio productions, which were by now becoming increasingly rare. As Tristan De Vere Cole, who directed on the third series of *Survivors,* later described in *A Guide for Actors New to Television,*[6] 'You may be expected to do your final, most intimate scene on film, with a minimum of rehearsal. You will probably have discussions and line rehearsals in the hotel the night before, but even this may not happen if other actors are unavailable, and you may meet your partner for the first time in front of the camera' (1985: 28).

Location filming meant that characterisations created in the earliest part of the production process, before a significant period of preparation and discussion could take place, would have to be adhered to later in the studio for the sake of continuity. Patrick Malahide, who began his television career around this time and later worked on the re-make of *Survivors,* highlights the shortcomings of this process when describing his first television location shoot:

> The director, Donald McWhinnie, came up to me and he said, 'You haven't done this before, have you?' And I said, 'No,' and he said: 'It's very simple. You walk up that hill, and when we say 'Action!' you run down the hill, you run into shot, you say your lines, and we shoot it.' And I thought: 'Oh, OK, fine.' But having shot that for probably a week, perhaps two weeks, to get the exteriors, we would then solemnly sit down in a rehearsal room and have a read-through ... You went into rehearsal and started to investigate the text, some of which you'd already shot, which was psychologically, as a journey, nonsensical ... Often you were stymied by what you'd already done.
>
> **(2011)**

Although Tristan De Vere Cole claimed that actors would seldom be expected to perform on film without some form of rehearsal, he admitted that it was easy for these 'to become orientated towards the camera and sound crews following the action' (1985: 28). According to Denis Lill, who worked on the 1975 *Survivors* episode 'Corn Dolly' and later became a regular, extensive location rehearsal was the exception rather than the rule: 'Obviously, for some of the big set pieces one did have a certain amount of rehearsal time, but it was very much sort of *ad hoc* and *ad lib* and suck it and see, really; just hope that everything turns out all right in the end, and nothing gets spoilt at the chemist's' (2010). Clearly, while location work offered a degree of spontaneity that might be lacking in the rigorously rehearsed studio sessions, actors were still expected to adapt their performances to suit the technological needs of the production crew. Before all-location filming became the norm, single camera location work was also comparatively restricted in terms of *mise-en-scène*, as Pennant Roberts explained: 'It was very difficult then to maintain the same style and technique between the film parts and the video parts. In some ways, then, we directors fell into bad ways, because what you had to do basically was shoot the film as if it was multi-camera; you couldn't be as filmic as you would have liked to have been' (Roberts 2003a). This obligation to 'match' material filmed on location to a later studio shooting plan – which had yet to be devised – was in marked contrast to an all-film production, where directors would have the possibility of piecing together actors' entire performances from different takes in post-production.

Following location filming in December 1974 and January 1975 (Cross and Priestner 2005: 33), the cast and crew relocated to Acton, the BBC's new rehearsal base for its studio drama, comedy and light entertainment output. This building represented a reassuringly stable and familiar environment, fostering a wider communal spirit for the various actors who congregated there. The familial atmosphere also extended to directors, as actor Kevin McNally, who began his television career in the early 1970s, describes:

> There were a whole bunch of them, and you'd work with them a lot, because there was a lot of television work and they had their ensemble of actors that they would always use, like a repertory company, and there was a sense of: 'There's no point in doing this unless we enjoy it.' Not that one was dilettante about the work at all, but there was certainly a sense of 'a life in the theatre', you know, that was transformed into television.
>
> (2010)

McNally's choice of words is interesting in light of the fact that repertory theatre was already in decline by the time he became a professional actor. The Acton Hilton might have been regarded as a form of substitute for the diminishing theatre world by more established actors and directors, who then engendered a continued sense of the stage ensemble in younger generations working more frequently in television. Such a situation might well have militated against any further development by studio realism away from its theatre roots. However, not all actors shared McNally's fondness for Acton. In a contemporary account of rehearsing at 'the Hilton', McNally's *Poldark* (BBC, 1975–77) co-star Robin Ellis described its atmosphere as 'hardly conducive to creative work. All the rooms are identical, their ceilings are low and there is no air. It's rather like working in a high rise block of flats' (Ellis 1978: 29).

Aesthetics aside, the Acton Hilton seems to have been of significance to actors less for its physical characteristics than the extended community that it represented. Roger Lloyd Pack, who appeared in both the original *Survivors* and the later re-make, echoed McNally's view of the rehearsal block as a communal space: 'The Acton Hilton is like a club, and I think actors like meeting there, and it was a sociable thing that you felt part of the production and you had time to build up to the performance' (2011). However, Lloyd Pack was critical of the actual rehearsal process which took place at Acton, contrasting it unfavourably with its theatre equivalent:

> You'd come in and you'd rehearse, rather like you would a play, really, without the same detail; it was much more perfunctory. Because a lot of television writing is too conventional, and it's not so demanding the same way as theatre plays are. So it wasn't so intense, but you would rehearse it, and the moves and that, and timing, and you'd go over it again.
>
> **(Ibid.)**

This view of television rehearsal as a 'perfunctory' process, concentrating on repetitious movement and blocking rather than characterisation and text, is supported by Patrick Malahide: 'The rehearsal in the rehearsal rooms wasn't for performance, it was in order to accommodate this huge deal of running these cameras, which were vast things like baby elephants, and they'd be pushed all around the studios on the ends of cables. So that was a very cumbersome process' (2011). For Malahide, such rehearsal did little to assist actors in preparing for the final studio performance:

> Looking back at the years I've sat in the Acton Hilton, I find an awful lot of it a dreadful waste of time. An awful lot of it was going over and over and over it again; you know, acting to white tape marks on the floor. Whereas as soon as you're in costume and in the real set, it immediately felt fresher and different. The trouble with

television, because it was rehearsed in such a way, you got there and you couldn't change anything. You'd walk into a set and say: 'Oh, I didn't realise that was going to be there. It would be so much more interesting if I was – oh, but we can't, because we've already got the camera there.' So I found it stultifying; I much prefer the freshness of responding immediately to walking onto the set, wherever it is, in character, in costume, and responding to what you find then. I found all the time rehearsing for television that you were kind of second guessing what you would actually find when you got there, and you'd find that you'd made decisions that weren't right, or that you wouldn't have enough flexibility. And I think anything that keeps things flexible and fresh is what makes drama interesting.

(*Ibid.*)

There is a clear dichotomy here between the positing of the Acton Hilton as an extension of the stage ensemble and the major distinction between the type of rehearsals that took place for theatre and television. Lloyd Pack's description of theatre plays requiring more in-depth work on text than material written for television suggests that the read-through that typically took place on the first day of television rehearsals – as established in Chapter 2, the main occasion on which changes to the script would be agreed – would be insufficient for theatre work. Both Lloyd Pack and Malahide suggest that the subsequent rehearsal period at Acton was more concerned with blocking designed to accommodate the – as yet unseen – cameras to be used in the television studio than with character work. While blocking would also be a consideration of stage rehearsals, the implication here seems to be that it does not predominate to the same extent, with character and text accorded a higher priority in stage work. This contradicts the assertion by Shaun Sutton, quoted in Chapter 1, that television rehearsal was 'basically no different' (1982: 112). Sutton's contemporary Tristan De Vere Cole also highlighted this distinction in his advice to television actors:

> You may be expected to wade into a scene with a minimum, if any, of *character motivation* discussion ... You have been cast because the director sees you in that particular role. He believes that you can call on certain qualities – voice, looks, physique, presence, stillness, etc., to convey that person. It is not like working in a repertory company ... The director will expect you to find your *character* comparatively early. [Original emphasis]

(1985: 49–50)

One reason for this shift away from the theatre rehearsal format could be that directors working at the BBC at this time had less of a theatrical background than in the days of Michael Barry and George More O'Ferrall. It is also possible that, as actors were working more frequently in television than on the stage, their own approach to rehearsal was gradually changing. However, the negative actor recollections of the Acton process cited here might well be clouded by the passing of time, and it should be noted that provision was made for additional rehearsal when a production required it, as outlined by BBC director Graeme Harper: 'When I started in the 1980s it was the common thing, there were certain periods of rehearsal depending on the size of the production. So if you [were] doing a two-and-a-half-hour Shakespearean play you probably would have twelve weeks of rehearsal, certainly of preparation and rehearsal; it would be a massive rehearsal period' (2011).

This supports Roger Lloyd Pack's assertion that stage material such as Shakespeare required greater preparation than television scripts,[7] but according to Harper the rehearsal period allocated even for the latter also allowed time for work beyond blocking alone: 'You discussed with the director everything; every aspect of the character, etc.' (*ibid.*). It is possible that Harper, a former actor, valued the discussion process in rehearsals more than directors who did not share his stage background; approaches to rehearsal and recording clearly varied depending on individual directors. Harper, for example, was one of the first at the BBC to direct from the floor when production moved into the studio, rather than remaining separate from the cast in the gallery, thus maintaining the close contact previously established in rehearsals. Louise Jameson, who began her television career in 1971, cites *Survivors* director Pennant Roberts, with whom she later worked on *Doctor Who* and *Tenko* (BBC, 1981–84), as another whose presence on the studio floor could make a significant difference to the performance dynamic: 'For my money the best directors come down on the floor and talk to you personally, so you've got an eye-to-eye, you've got a debate going' (2011). According to Jameson, gallery direction – in which the director's instructions are relayed via the floor manager – for actors represents 'the art of surrender; hit your mark, don't forget your lines, do the best you can' (*ibid.*).

By the mid-1970s, television directors were beginning to challenge the established processes and procedures employed since the inception of live television, as Denis Lill affirms: 'There were new generations of directors who were employed by the BBC. They'd come along and they would say: "This is madness; it's absolutely ludicrous that you should spend all day doing camera rehearsals, then go and have a huge great meal, then turn round and have to do a performance" – because by the time it actually came round to it, you were absolutely knackered' (2010). Such changing attitudes were facilitated by the fact that videotape was now both cheaper and easier to edit. Additionally, the agreement reached in June 1972 between the BBC and actors' union Equity meant that restrictions on recording, previously limited to three times the duration of a programme's broadcast length, were now lifted (BBC WAC T62/122/1, cited in McNaughton 2014: 16–18); this meant that it was possible to tape sequences throughout the day, with breaks for rehearsal. Although studio work would still be preceded by a period at Acton, scenes were no longer recorded in story order, as Denis Lill recalls: 'It just seemed to make more sense that you got into the studio, you rehearsed a particular scene and then you recorded it. Then you'd say: "Right, thank you, that's in the can. Now we'll move on to the next one"' (2010).

To actors emerging into the television medium, the old process of daytime technical rehearsals and evening recording made little sense, as Kevin McNally relates: 'There was a feeling that you did all the work in rehearsals and then you just literally went in and got it on tape, which now seems a bizarre way to work... It was ridiculously counter-productive, in a way; I often wonder why it lasted as long as it did' (2010).

When the rehearse/record process was first employed it seems to have been welcomed by the majority of actors (Alvarado and Buscombe 1978: 215), but its use was dependent on directors' preferred modes of working, as Patrick Malahide confirms: 'My feeling is that it depended on the director, and I think my impression is that if the directors had done any kind of film drama they would come in and do rehearse/record. And I remember thinking: "Thank God for that!" because rehearse/record was so much more efficient ... It seemed gradually to go from one thing to another' (2011).

Although rehearse/record allowed for more flexibility in the studio, meaning that shooting blocks could be arranged according to the sets that were erected in the studio, rather than in strict story order, scenes would still have to be played in their entirety, and editing would take place 'live', the vision mixer cutting between cameras as the performance took place. This distinction continued to mark television studio drama apart from single camera film production, where scenes could be performed in sections and later pieced together in post-production.

Studio work for 'The Fourth Horseman' began with eight hours of camera rehearsal at Television Centre on Tuesday 18 February 1975, starting at 2 p.m. and concluding at 10 p.m. (BBC WAC Survivors/The Fourth Horseman/BBC1/16/04/1975). According to the camera script, another seven hours of camera rehearsal were allocated the following day between 11 a.m. and 6 p.m., with VTR planned from 7.30 to 10 p.m. It is not possible to state whether Pennant Roberts deviated from this plan in favour of an entirely rehearse/record procedure, but breaks were scheduled in the script between different scenes, indicating that the intention was to record them separately rather than continuously.

An early sequence, in which housewife Abby (Carolyn Seymour) is discussing the impact of the virus – the seriousness of which is not yet known – with her businessman husband David (Peter Bowles), provides an example of the way studio realism had by this point been honed to accommodate the exigencies of the multi-camera recording process. In the camera script the opening section, which takes place in the living room, was planned to be covered by two cameras, but in fact only one is used, with a total shot length of one minute and nine seconds. The scene opens with a wide shot of Abby, seated on the sofa to the right of the screen, while David, on the left, pours them both a whisky. The camera then tracks left and pans right as David moves behind Abby to seat himself on an adjacent couch, and gradually closes in on the two characters as they begin to discuss the situation. Despite having to work with that most stage-bound of devices, the drawing room conversation, the actors' performances here are further scaled down from 'An Unearthly Child'. Aware that they are working mainly in long and medium shot, Seymour and Bowles adjust the volume of their voices to a level slightly above that which would normally be used by two people sitting a mere six feet apart, in order for the boom microphone to pick up their dialogue clearly. However, the projection used is not so strong that it seems abnormally loud; the slight additional volume, first seen in nascent form from Reginald Tate in 'Contact had been Established', has by now become a convention of studio realism.

When the action moves into the kitchen (in real time; the set is clearly adjacent, and Bowles can be seen to move from one set into the other) it is covered by three cameras, although the actual sequence of shots used is somewhat simplified from the camera script. In contrast with the single shot used to cover the action in the lounge, the kitchen sequence consists of sixteen shots, of which the longest is fifty-six seconds and the shortest two, with an average of around fourteen seconds. The languid rate of the cuts reflects the relaxed pace of the conversation, and the actors' performances are timed to accommodate both the lengthy expositional material, delivered with the casual familiarity of a couple who have been together for several years, and the limited scope for real time cutting between cameras offered by the size and design of the set. For example, when David pours a drink the camera slowly pans across and down to his hand on the whisky decanter as Abby asks (off-camera): 'How bad do you think it is?' Bowles is forced to delay the delivery of his line while the camera pans back up to his face. The potentially dislocating effect of this slight hesitation is covered by Bowles visibly pausing, as if to consider the question, until his face is once again in shot.

Such technical demands were endemic to multi-camera recording, and the scene is further complicated in that throughout the majority of the sequence Abby/Seymour is actually cooking David's bacon and eggs in real time. Had any mistakes been made, a re-take of the entire scene would have been the only option. Watching the sequence again for the 2003 DVD commentary, Pennant Roberts recalled: 'It was certainly planned that way; whether we did it more than once, I don't know. But certainly it would have been designed to play continuously. With only two and a half hours to record the lot in, including costume changes, then you would try and rehearse to such a degree that you would get it right first time' (Roberts 2003a).

Bowles and Seymour's body language and delivery throughout this scene combine to convey their characters' gradually mounting sense of unease. Seymour's movements are notably enervated, dabbing at David's bacon and eggs in a manner that hints at her character's lack of appetite, her strength already being sapped by the virus with which she is unknowingly infected.

Bowles keeps David's movements fluid and loose, as exampled by his practised pouring of whisky, but is seldom still for long. After seating himself he twice rises, first to obtain the radio and then to re-fill Abby's glass, joining her at the cooker and taking a brief, listless turn at the cooking while she lays the table. His posture alters while vainly seeking a news broadcast, clutching the radio tightly with his left hand and tilting it towards his craned head. Despite such 'performed' moments, Bowles's rigidity suggesting his character's growing tenseness, there are also moments where the actor employs more seemingly spontaneous touches. The slight extension of Bowles's tongue (Figure 3.1), to indicate concealed amusement as David teases Abby over the 'secret mission' their son Peter has entrusted to him regarding her birthday present, was more easily read on modern family-sized television sets than it would have been ten years before.[8] Whether rehearsed or not, this moment is one that seems to emerge from the situation – and David's coy amusement – rather than having been grafted on as a coded signifier in the manner of Iris Ballard and Van Boolen two decades before.

The actors' vocal work complements their physical. Bowles, often belying his character's confident stance with small sighs and half-laughs, only lowers his voice to become intimate and confiding on the closing lines – coinciding with the first time that David and Abby make sustained eye contact – allowing the viewer to understand that his certainty is waning.

Seymour and Bowles's performances are well adapted to studio requirements, representing several key characteristics of studio realism: they are thoroughly rehearsed, with great attention to technical detail and blocking; there is sustained continuity of performance (Seymour noticeably blinks when fat from the frying pan hits her in the eye, but continues undaunted), and there is great clarity to the delivery of lines – with no overlapping dialogue, for example – that is designed to facilitate audience understanding of substantial exposition.

Figure 3.1 Peter Bowles in *Survivors*: 'The Fourth Horseman'

This style of performance had to be adapted when *Survivors* switched to its all-location Outside Broadcast model. Accounts vary as to the reason for this change, but Pennant Roberts later maintained that it had always been the intention to use OB: 'The only Drama Outside Broadcast unit – which was the one we inherited in April – wasn't available to us in January' (*ibid.*). However, the studio would still be used on occasion; 'When greater camera mobility was an absolute priority such as on ... 'Lights of London' in series two, we reverted to the established combination of filmed location sequences and videotaped studio scenes' (Roberts, cited in Cross and Priestner 2005: 9).

As an alternative to film, OB presented both advantages and disadvantages. Of primary importance to *Survivors* was the faster turnaround; in 1979 the average rate of daily OB footage was six minutes, as compared with two-and-a-half minutes for film (Sutton 1982: 99). Video was quicker and easier to edit (De Vere Cole 1985: 44), and as the programme was being made less than three months ahead of transmission this would have been a definite plus. However, while videotape was more suited to location conditions in that it could accept greater variables in lighting and weather (Sutton 1982: 100), the images it produced looked somewhat flat when compared with film, as Shaun Sutton affirmed: 'It is certainly true that tape pictures can be *too* good, unnaturally sharp and precise, with a depth of focus stretching to the horizon. Such perfection can have a false look' [original emphasis] (*ibid.*: 101). In addition, the video unit required greater personnel than film (De Vere Cole 1985: 44), though for Lucy Fleming the sense of the unit as a 'travelling circus' was a bonus: 'The whole thing was like a great caravanserai. Once we arrived at a place, they set up the scene, we rehearsed it and did it; like filming … We used to just arrive at the hotel and they'd say: "Here's your call; you've got to be somewhere at six"' (2010).

Although the new generation of OB Emitron cameras in use by the mid-1970s could be hand-held (Smart 2010: 316), Pennant Roberts later recalled them as having limited mobility: 'All pictures were routed back to the "scanner", and even with 1,000 yards of cable on the wagon, locations had to be easily accessible. Each episode was recorded in 4.5 days, so that a scheduled unit move for the "short" day was tolerable, but time lost in unloading and loading vehicles constituted a powerful disincentive against split-location days' (cited in Cross and Priestner 2005: 8–9).

Roberts and his fellow directors would often be separate from the cast on location, watching from the control room; according to William Smart, this physical separation made OB 'less of an auteur medium for directors than either the studio, where they had greater ability to control and react to events, or film, where they could reshape material in postproduction' (2010: 318). However, on occasion it was possible to set up temporary monitors 'in the field' (Cross and Priestner 2005: 34), where directors and cast could together watch instant playback; another of videotape's advantages over film. Julie Neubert, who played Wendy in the first series, welcomed this opportunity to discuss her performance with the director close at hand: '[He] could point out what was wrong with the scene … I found that very helpful … It was a bit intimidating, but quite a learning experience' (cited in Cross and Priestner 2005: 34).[9]

One immediate effect of the move to OB was the abandonment of rehearsals at Acton when it was realised that blocking would best be conducted on the location at which scenes were to be recorded, as director Pennant Roberts later related: '[actor] Talfryn [Thomas] kept stepping over the rehearsal room tape into the "river". And then I realised that my concern was totally pointless; that once he was on location all would be well' (cited in Cross and Priestner 2005: 31). Although in a 1990s interview Carolyn Seymour recalled still having two days' rehearsal at Acton prior to shooting on location (Marshall 1995?) – and for series two Kevin McNally remembers a few days of 'chatting, not really blocking' before travelling to the shoot (2010) – the bulk of rehearsal was done *in situ*. This was a major change to the studio rehearse/record system, for which full prior rehearsal at Acton was vital. Pennant Roberts found the new system much more satisfactory: 'The actors were able to take the real surroundings into consideration and make constructive suggestions' (cited in Cross and Priestner 2005: 31).[10]

As opposed to the rigorous blocking and repetition of the Acton Hilton, the type and amount of rehearsal on location was dependent on the material to be recorded, as Denis Lill describes:

> It wasn't an officially designated rehearsal period. You know, provided you got a certain number of scenes shot during the day, provided you stuck to the call sheet and worked it all out, but some scenes need more rehearsal than others ... Some scenes you didn't need to rehearse; you just got on a horse and did the stuff. And there were other scenes that might have involved one or more cameras – more than one camera, anyway – which did involve rehearsals, because of course cameras had to know where to cut and what to focus on and the rest of the stuff. Some of them, if they were shooting in small confines, in a very small room, with a lot of characters, a lot of speeches, that sort of stuff obviously needed more rehearsal than others.
>
> (2010)

Lill's comments indicate that, even with OB location, rehearsal was still something primarily necessitated by camera positioning, rather than a process that was intended to benefit performance. However, the pressures of on the spot rehearsal and recording seem to have been a positive factor for the cast, as Lill relates: 'The directors really had to make it up as they went along ... It was quite exciting, but we did establish a pretty good regime of rehearse/record, basically. We would turn up on location, we would run through the scene, then we would record it, and it got down to a pretty effective and pretty efficient organisation' (*ibid*.). Lucy Fleming also appreciated the immediacy of location recording: 'They just pointed the camera at you and you did it, unlike modern filming where it's very much inter-cut and cut and inter-cut ... It led I think to very realistic acting, which I enjoy' (Fleming 2003). Fleming's remark indicates that OB recording retained stronger links with the studio process – where performances of scenes were given in continuity in their entirety – than with the more piecemeal and repetitive film process, while retaining the advantage of being evolved and taking place on site, providing a greater degree of spontaneity than the pre-prepared studio recording.

According to Kevin McNally, who began his television career in 1976, working on location possessed a unique advantage over the studio: 'It was good, actually, because what happened was, you would all go away, as a film group, and you'd get to know each other because you can't go home at night; you have that location filming camaraderie' (2010). Tristan De Vere Cole also emphasised the company spirit that could emerge on location shoots, especially if actors and crew were staying together at the unit hotel: 'You can go through the next day's scenes with fellow actors; and although it is not obligatory to stay up into the small hours, or prop up the bar, you have an opportunity to get to know the cast and crew' (1985: 30–31).

While on studio productions the tight-knit pre-filming rapport described by McNally and De Vere Cole might well have subsequently served to isolate actors who had not been required on location, the OB schedule adopted by *Survivors* from episode seven meant that this sense of community included the entire cast, as Lucy Fleming affirms: 'I think we all bonded so well because there we were, either in the mud or the cold or somewhere, and quite often you'd just go and change in some shed somewhere [laughter]. Quite a lot of the time we were outside, and we always filmed in January, February, March time' (2010).

An early scene from 'Law and Order' illustrates the difference in performance that could result from the shift to location. Abby has by now become the leader of a small group of survivors who have taken refuge in a large country house, where they are beginning to till the land and maintain livestock. In order to facilitate comparison with the kitchen sequence from 'The Fourth Horseman' this is another domestic scene, in which Abby, Jenny and Greg discuss their next move with other members of their community over breakfast. On location it was usual to use two OB cameras (Cross and Priestner 2005: 9); due to the length of the room used the cast are recorded simultaneously in two groups, one seated at either end of the table.

The early section of this scene at least was clearly recorded in continuity, as signified when the wheelchair-bound Vic Thatcher (Terry Scully) moves seamlessly from one camera to the other to corral the community's two children, Lizzie (Tanya Ronder) and John (Stephen Dudley), into attending their morning lessons. The relative immobility of the OB cameras compared with their pedestal-mounted counterparts at Television Centre meant that some longer than average scenes would be recorded in a single take on location (*ibid.*: 34). However, the subsequent use of alternate groupings from different angles, interspersed with medium close-ups, indicates that either the entire scene – or sections of it – were enacted more than once for different camera set-ups.

A later section of the sequence relies on a multi-camera style of recording, when Greg forbids Jenny to risk her life retrieving supplies from a quarry visited in the previous episode. The first part of the discussion is covered by a three-shot of Greg, Jenny and Paul (Chris Tranchell) (Figure 3.2), in which Jenny criticises Greg's authoritarian attitude as sexist, before cutting to a medium close-up of the latter as he irritably responds: 'You're not going, and that's that!' (Figure 3.3). Director Pennant Roberts then cuts to a medium close-up of Lucy Fleming for Jenny's cowed, wordless reaction (Figure 3.4).

With the actors mainly seated throughout, blocking here is minimal compared with the studio kitchen sequence. Instead of painstakingly working their actions out before transferring them to the set, the cast would have run through the scene with the director at the location in which they were going to record, the faster OB turnaround meaning that they had to adapt quickly to the room's layout and furniture. The result is less pre-planned movement for its own sake; as Pennant Roberts later highlighted, with multi-camera recording 'finding reasons to cut between the cameras was sometimes a headache' (Roberts 2003a). Although less dynamic than the studio session, which sought to make use of the

Figure 3.2 Chris Tranchell, Ian McCulloch and Lucy Fleming in *Survivors*: 'Law and Order'

Figure 3.3 Ian McCulloch in *Survivors*: 'Law and Order'

Figure 3.4 Lucy Fleming in *Survivors*: 'Law and Order'

space in as visually engaging a way as possible, this OB sequence offers a less practised performance, providing an arguably more verisimilitudinous depiction of people conducting a conversation in a domestic scenario. The interior OB scenes on this series of *Survivors* are notably more static than their studio counterparts; a later scene from 'Law and Order', in which Wendy, Charmian (Eileen Helmsby) and Emma (Hana Maria Pravda) prepare food for the party, is filmed entirely with a single camera. After an initial close-up of Wendy chopping lettuce, it pulls back to provide a three-shot of the women's brief conversation around the table, offering little of the movement or variety seen in the episode one kitchen scene between Abby and David.

William Smart accounts for such lack of visual interest in OB work as a result of camera crews' 'inexperience in working with multiple angles and set-ups, or dramatic framing and grouping, these techniques not having been needed in their experience of recording sports and events' (2010: 318). As a result, many such scenes were recorded primarily in long-shot (Sutton 1982: 103). This lack of technical experience distinguishes location realism of the 1970s, in which there was less cutting between close-ups, medium and long shots, and therefore less repetition of movement and need to pay attention to continuity of performance, from its 2000s successor, as will be demonstrated in Chapter 4.

One similarity between the breakfast scene and the kitchen sequence is their heavy dependence on dialogue, but there is a notable difference in the level of vocal projection between the two. Whereas in the earlier scene Carolyn Seymour spoke at a volume slightly above the normal conversational level, her voice is less noticeably projected here, and the same applies to the other actors in the scene. This could be a psychological effect of removing the actors from a performance space such as the studio, where they had to pitch their performances to the technological requirements of the site, and into a real location, to which such technology was not endemic. Although boom microphones could be employed for both types of recording, in the studio they would be seen as part of the established technology, whereas on location they would be – like the actors themselves – an addition to the natural environment, to which both actors and technical crew were forced to adapt. Roger Lloyd Pack contrasted the experience of playing an exterior scene on a studio set with a genuine location: 'if you're performing a scene in a garden, sitting [outside], and there are trees and birds, you would I think automatically ... respond differently' (2011). Certainly the somewhat artificial quality of studio sound contrasts sharply with the more natural tones of the location recording. William Smart has highlighted the fact that OB sound recording often utilised radio mikes, providing 'a sense of immediacy', while at the same time 'running the risk of dialogue becoming muffled by simultaneous local sound such as wind, footsteps, or the echo of location interiors' (2010: 34). Such factors mark OB sound recording as distinct from both location film, where sound could be redubbed and post-synched (*ibid.*), and the studio, which provided a more aurally controlled, antiseptic environment.

The importance of performing environs were famously highlighted by Stanislavski; while walking in the grounds of a palace in Kiev he was inspired to enact a scene from his current stage success, *A Month in the Country*, set in just such a locale. However, the performance style that had won plaudits in the theatre fell strangely flat when reproduced in the actual environment it was intended to represent: 'I stopped, because I could not continue my false and theatrical pose. All that I had done seemed untrue to nature, to reality. And it had been said of us that we had developed simplicity to a point of naturalism!' (Stanislavski 1924: 383). Although other determinants are at work with OB recording – the more natural quality of lighting, no longer provided by a battery of overheard lamps, provides a definite contrast with the bright, flat studio palette – Stanislavski's anecdote regarding the perceived artificiality of prepared, projected performance in a real location is relevant to much of the OB work in *Survivors*. Whether consciously or not, several of the cast were clearly beginning to scale down their performances as a result of the move, and have since indicated that the simple fact of working in a real environment, as opposed to the constructed, three-walled sets of the studio, influenced their acting. For Roger Lloyd Pack, location work 'is more likely to bring a truthful performance, in terms of cinematic truth. It's sort of shaping the truth, because a truthful theatre performance wouldn't necessarily read in the cameras' (2011). Lloyd Pack here echoes Stanislavski when he states that 'if you were theatrical out there [on location] it would be rather obvious, and jar in a way that it may not in the studio' (*ibid.*). For Lloyd Pack, working in the studio 'is like a stage; very rarely can they get behind you, or if they do it's a separate take. And it's usually quite a conventional set-up ... it's always rather the same; to me that can get a bit tedious' (*ibid.*). For Lucy Fleming, multi-camera studio's stage antecedents are not a disadvantage, providing 'a continuity, which is lovely. Like theatre; you're telling the story all the way through' (2010). However, the actress also appreciates the benefits of location work: 'You don't have time to get bored or think it through too much; you kind of just do it instinctively and naturally' (*ibid.*). Denis Lill claims that working in a real environment helped actors 'to play down and to set the piece to a much more realistic style. I mean, it was real just to be out in the open air; to be there, on your horse, doing the stuff. And there's no substitute for that; it is the ultimate realism, really' (2010).

Despite the fact that the move by *Survivors* to an all-OB location model was a pioneering one, and so can only be said to represent the very earliest stages of location realism, its changed mode of production was clearly beginning to produce distinct – albeit subtle – effects in the resulting screen performances. It was, however, not only the cast and production crew who were feeling their way into a new mode of working; equally affected by the move to location was the television director, who had to evolve new ways of working away from the rehearsal room and studio.

Direction

Working on OB clearly necessitated a new approach on the part of directors, and by this time the training offered by the BBC was beginning to address the need for both multiple and single camera technique. When Graeme Harper attended the director's course in 1980, six weeks were spent on each (Harper 2011), but according to Harper it was multi-camera which proved most advantageous:

> When you come to do it on your own, to learn the ABC it's far better to do a multi-camera studio course, because you really learn about angles, and what each camera can give you, and how you can cut that together; you learn to edit. And then when you go and do single camera it's not easier; it's just there's something you've already got into your brain. You know how to angle the camera and get all the different angles to make it look attractive and interesting.
>
> **(Ibid.)**

Another sequence from 'The Fourth Horseman', in which the feverish Abby is confined to bed, is useful in illustrating how the studio allowed the director a degree of manipulation that would be difficult to replicate on location. Pennant Roberts conveys the passing of days via a series of mixes and fades between shots of Abby, her bedside clock and the window, changing the lighting from night to day and back again, and ending with a medium shot of her waking in bed to birdsong and daylight. She calls David's name, to no reply. The action then jumps forward in time slightly, with a cut to a medium shot of the door to the kitchen, through which Abby enters, again calling for her husband. The camera continues to track Abby as she moves from right to left into the kitchen. Roberts cuts to a close-up of Abby's bare feet and a broken glass on the kitchen floor (Figure 3.5), which she dropped earlier when she collapsed. Roberts now cuts to a third camera, which is initially focused on a medium shot of Abby's back as she turns (Figure 3.6), and then a focus pull to direct attention to the telephone hanging off the hook in close-up on the right of the screen (Figure 3.7). The next shot is a close-up of stale bread on the table (Figure 3.8), which then pans across mouldy blocks of cheese and up to a medium shot of Abby as she turns to open the fridge (Figure 3.9). There then is a brief close-up of Abby's face turning away in disgust (Figure 3.10).

Figures 3.5–3.6 Carolyn Seymour in *Survivors*: 'The Fourth Horseman'

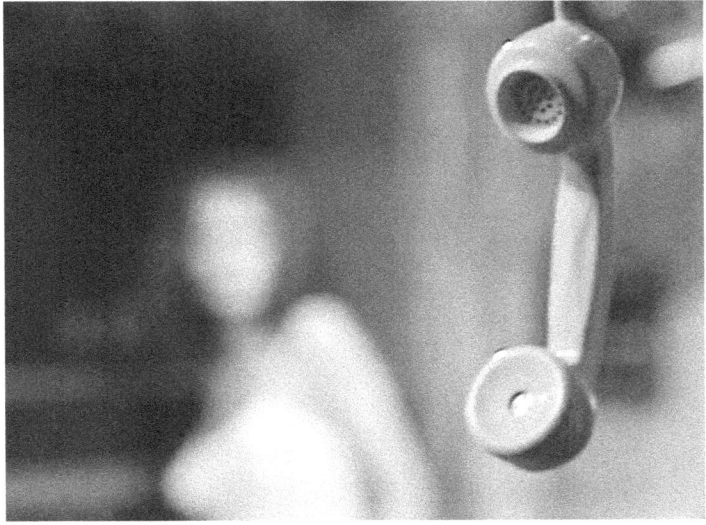

Figures 3.7 Carolyn Seymour in *Survivors*: 'The Fourth Horseman'

Figure 3.8 Shot of the kitchen table in *Survivors*: 'The Fourth Horseman'

Figures 3.9 and 3.10 Carolyn Seymour in *Survivors*: 'The Fourth Horseman'

Roberts now cuts to the longest shot in the sequence. The added sound of a ticking clock informs the viewer that the action has moved to the living room, and the shot begins as a medium-to-long framing of the mirror on the right of the room, above a

Figures 3.11 and 3.12 Carolyn Seymour in *Survivors*: 'The Fourth Horseman'

drinks cabinet. In the mirror the viewer can see Abby approaching the cabinet before she comes into shot, her back to the camera. As Abby reaches down into the cabinet to pull out a bottle of gin and a tumbler, the camera both closes in and changes the angle of approach, revealing more of the background scene reflected in the mirror. David's lifeless body can now clearly be seen slumped, face-down, across the sofa on the other side of the room, providing the audience with the information that he has died before Abby is aware of the fact. It is only as Abby raises the glass to her lips that she sees the reflected image of her husband's dead body in the mirror, and the camera closes in on her reaction (Figure 3.11) as she lowers her glass and begins to turn. In total, this shot lasts twenty-five seconds. The sequence ends with a cut to a second camera positioned in the living room, providing a close-up of Abby's shocked reaction as she completes her turn (Figure 3.12).

This segment is in stark contrast to the earlier kitchen scene between Abby and David. Whereas the first conveyed information through dialogue, this scene is largely silent, relying instead on visual signifiers. Roberts's use of the camera here to represent the passing of time and the revelation, one by one, of indicators that Abby's safe and comfortable world has crumbled (dead phone, rotting food, dead body) is complemented by Carolyn Seymour's performance. Abby's weakness is signified by small, subtle gestures: placing a steadying hand against the fridge before opening it; closing her eyes in revulsion at the state of the fridge's contents; eyes widening only slightly as she catches sight of David's body in the mirror; mouth slackly parted in a silent intake of horrified breath as she turns. Seymour's subtlety of reaction conveys levels of drama and emotion that would be difficult to replicate on the stage, while adapted to Roberts's multi-camera set-up in a way that marks it out as separate from cinema. Although recorded in segments that were then edited together in post-production, these were singular (i.e. the performance was not repeated numerous times for different angles) and semi-continuous. The camera script indicates pauses for make-up and lighting changes during the bedroom sequence, followed by 'run ons'[11] when Abby moves downstairs, and a break in recording after Abby leaves the kitchen. It was not the case that the sequence was played repeatedly for a number of different framings; this would have required the basic replication of the same moves and gestures, while allowing Seymour the comparative luxury of several takes to scale and adjust Abby's reaction upon seeing David's body according to the proximity of the single camera. Instead, Seymour must maintain a 'one off' continuity of performance – as seen earlier, there is not the option of numerous takes due to pressures of time – and has limited opportunity to judge the scale of Abby's reaction to suit the slow zoom of the cumbersome studio camera.

The move to OB would represent a new challenge for directors; neither multi- nor single camera in the purest sense, it required a new combination of the techniques in which they had been trained. But while directing location video for *Survivors* necessitated the adjustment of an established training system, elsewhere actor training was at last showing signs of adapting to the medium of the small screen.

Training

Actors graduating from drama school in the late 1960s and early 1970s were the first to receive grounding in acting for the camera. However, it would be misleading to claim that this training was comprehensive, or that it had in any way supplanted the more established stage-related areas of voice and movement. Although Broadcasting had featured in RADA's training since 1928 (RADA 1928: 12), it was first expanded to include Television Technique in 1959 (RADA 1959: 7). In 1962 a survey of major drama schools discovered that all bar two believed some form of television training was now necessary (Sanderson 1984: 281); in the same year, the Glasgow College of Dramatic Art became the first to incorporate a television studio into its facilities. Roger Lloyd Pack described the camera experience offered by RADA between 1963 and 1965: 'I played *The Caretaker* in one ... I think we went into a little studio somewhere in central London, and recorded it. So we did have some camera technique' (2011). However, the training provided by RADA was limited to a few days' camera work at most; a situation that would change little over the next decade. Louise Jameson attended the Royal Academy between 1969 and 1971: 'I think we had one workshop on camera. Everything was geared towards theatre; everything. But I think that changed pretty soon after I left, I think around '73, '74' (2011). Jameson's impression was that the amount of television input increased soon after her departure, yet Michael Sanderson claims that it was around this time that RADA abandoned screen training altogether due to prohibitive expense: 'Its very high cost – £300 a day for studio rent – outweighed any marginal gain in technique ... The schools believed that, given thorough training in voice and movement, the actor could adjust to the special conditions of television and film studios as long as the basic acting craft was there' (Sanderson 1984: 281–282). If this was the case then Kevin McNally, who completed his studies at RADA in 1974, was one of the last to benefit from the screen training offered in his final term:

> They would hire Thames Television studios and we would work on scenes. And we would go into the studio and we would have them filmed, multi-camera. But what they chose to shoot was extracts from the Restoration plays that we'd just finished, so it was this bizarre amalgam of putting us in front of a camera, doing about the most heightened performance we would ever do. So it wasn't very much help. It was sort of helpful by the time one got a job in television; you sort of knew that you didn't see the director, they were up in a box, you would have a relationship with the floor manager and you probably wouldn't speak to the cameramen very much. So you learned that.
>
> **(2011)**

Clearly the input offered by RADA at least was of limited practical use to students, as McNally observes:

> I wouldn't say that working for a week and then going along to Thames for a day constituted an acting for screen course, but [RADA Principal] Hugh Cruttwell was a reasonably progressive man; he'd been training people for the radio for years, we had quite extensive radio training. There certainly was no attempt to train you for film, but he did know that the multi-camera television was such a bulk of the work that any successful actor would get at the time that he tried to give us a little sniff of it.
>
> **(2010)**

Arguably of more lasting significance in terms of training was the increasing permeation around this time of the Stanislavski system at British schools. However, while the Bristol Old Vic School was featuring Stanislavski by the early 1950s, pinpointing precise dates for his emergence in syllabi elsewhere is problematic. In 1960, RADA Principal John Fernald had acknowledged the existence of both Stanislavski and the Method in the introduction to the Academy's prospectus, though damning them with faint praise: 'Different "systems" of acting ... can lead to many illusions, though the systems themselves, as they go, are sound' (RADA 1960: 4). This less than ringing endorsement suggests that the Russian did not yet feature in the Academy's official syllabus, and it would not be until 1988 that the prospectus advertised 'Stanislavski-based teaching' as part of its training (RADA 1988: 4). Lolly Susi states in her history of Central that the Method (if not pure Stanislavski[12]) had become part of the syllabus there by the early 1960s (2006: 126), but when various of that school's students and staff split away to form the Drama Centre London in 1963, the training offered by Christopher Fettes at the new school exhibited – in the words of Simon Callow, who attended from 1969 – 'absolute fidelity to [Stanislavski's] texts (*not* Lee Strasberg's)' [original emphasis] (1984: 18). Similarly, at East 15, whose opening by Margaret Bury in 1961 was inspired by the Stanislavski- and Laban-based work she had experienced at Joan Littlewood's Theatre Workshop, the training offered initially focused closely on the Russian's work. Actor and drama trainer Trevor Rawlins has conducted his own research into this area: 'I interviewed someone from the first couple of years of East 15, which is early 1960s, and they did actually specifically work through the books, chapter by chapter, at that time' (2011).

However, at other academies the Russian's theories and ideas were often not attributed directly to him, even when they *were* being taught: 'The influence of Stanislavski became so pervasive that people were teaching it whether they knew they were or not, and people were so influenced by it that even if they said they weren't they kind of were' (*ibid.*). Roger Lloyd Pack's recollection of being taught Stanislavski at RADA in the mid-1960s is in direct contrast to the Academy's prospectus for that period: 'We were taught Stanislavski; emotional memory and this sort of thing. And we were very aware of Lee Strasberg, the American approach to it ... I'm sure it was taught as part of the syllabus' (2011). In 1973 Hugh Cruttwell stated: 'We assume that Stanislavski has been absorbed into the mainstream of theatre and doesn't need to be specially taught' (cited in Billington 1973: 3). Louise Jameson, meanwhile, recalls that 'the actual name Stanislavski was rarely used ... People were just picking up the language without really aligning it to

Stanislavski' (2011). Nevertheless, it is clear that the Russian's ideas by now formed a major part of the work done at the Academy: 'We did a lot of work on objectives and obstacles, which is the absolute foundation stone, I think, for any Stanislavski work, and is the basis for all my work since. I think if you get those two things right, if your character knows exactly what they want, and what's in the way, and how you're going to get round that obstacle, that's all you need to know' (*ibid.*).

Given that tutors might not have referenced Stanislavski in class, another potential source of his technique was the visiting directors responsible for coaching students for their final productions, as Kevin McNally highlights:

> It didn't have [Stanislavski] necessarily on the syllabus, but of course these changes happen incrementally. What happened is that, at RADA and the better drama schools, the edge that they had and the attraction they had for actors was that you got to work with professionals. The directors would be professional directors brought in, albeit – as we now know – directors on their uppers, but certainly people who had worked professionally. And of course by 1972 any young person who came to direct at RADA would have been influenced by Stanislavski, and so there was just an innate and general level of Stanislavski – not maybe quite Method – but a more rigorous psychological approach to acting, rather than outward performance.
>
> **(2010)**

Hugh Cruttwell admitted that, with eight to twelve teachers working at the Academy at any one time, 'if you wanted to instil a particular approach to acting, it would be impractical ... There may also be directors working here with whom I'm out of sympathy but whose approach I think the students should learn about. It's a catholic affair' (cited in Billington 1973: 3).

Despite the slow permeation of Stanislavski's work in Britain, there remained lingering suspicion among many, often compounded by the common confusion of the Russian's work with Lee Strasberg's Method, as Denis Lill relates:

> I was aware that there was this Stanislavskian school of acting around, and generally speaking he wasn't particularly well thought of, and his particular style of acting wasn't well thought of, and it seemed to be particularly specialised in the American market,

more so than here. In rep you didn't have time to get down and get all methodical about it; you just simply had to bash it out as best you could ... The Stanislavski 'Method' seemed to involve an awful lot of sitting down and studying it and talking about it, rather than actually getting up and doing it.

(2010)

Of the regular cast for the 1975 series of *Survivors*, Hana Maria Pravda was perhaps most likely to have received 'pure' Stanislavski training, having been instructed by former Moscow Arts Theatre director Aleksei Dikij in Leningrad in 1936. However, Carolyn Seymour had attended Central in the mid-1960s, by which time the Russian's work was beginning to be taught, and Chris Tranchell graduated from the Bristol Old Vic School, where Stanislavski formed a major part of the syllabus. Talfryn Thomas had trained earlier at LAMDA, while Ian McCulloch had no formal training, having acted at university prior to joining the RSC; Lucy Fleming had started in repertory before attending English Stage Company classes at the Royal Court. However, it would be erroneous to assume that Pravda, Seymour and Tranchell alone were exposed to Stanislavski's work; although Lucy Fleming's training did not directly reference Stanislavski, focusing on improvisation, speech, movement and mime (Fleming 2010), the Royal Court's then-artistic director William Gaskill later made it clear that he was as aware of Stanislavski as he was of other theatre practitioners and teachers such as Bertolt Brecht and Laban (Gaskill 1988: 16), whose theories informed his work.

The stance that has often been adopted – either by American authors such as Judith Weston, who dismisses 'outside-in' acting of the type seen in 'British acting and university departments and movie actors of the 1930s and 1940s' (1996: 14), or Richard Hornby, who claims the British as superior to America's 'Strasbergian' actors, particularly in 'classical roles' (1992: 9) – perpetuates the idea that British actors remain unfamiliar with the precepts and practices of the Stanislavski system. This general lack of mention or acknowledgement of Stanislavski's influence on British acting could be explained by the fact that much of the Russian's writing has since come to be seen by British actors as self-evident; a theory endorsed by Roger Lloyd Pack:

> The thing about Stanislavski, in a way maybe I've just assimilated it, but it's sort of a normal thing to do that seems to be a natural given that that's how you approach a part; that you see where you are in the scene, and what your action is, and what your overall motivation is, and where your journey is, and where you're coming from and where you're going to ... A lot of that I instinctively do, and I think you find a lot of actors do. I suppose Stanislavski – maybe before that it wasn't so – but he maybe put it down, and because he's put it down it's become a sort of orthodoxy.
>
> (2011)

Lloyd Pack's description of the Stanislavski system as 'natural' could equally be seen as a testament to the extent to which the Russian's approach has pervaded modern acting, but the fact remains that, though Stanislavski had by the 1970s permeated the consciousness of many British actors, adding another potential approach to interpreting character, drama training in Britain also continued its old focus on movement, text and voice.[13] A picture consequently emerges of British drama schools, in the decade leading up to *Survivors*, attempting for the first time to accommodate the expanding medium of television, without abandoning the traditional methods of stagecraft that had underpinned the syllabi of the more established institutions since the turn of the century. The result was actors who felt equally able to work in television and on the stage, as Louise Jameson states: 'I think if you can do classical theatre you can do just about anything. And if you've done some Stanislavski training within that then you're equipped to work on a soap script or a piece of Greek tragedy' (2011).

The continuing bias towards theatre skills would ensure that the type of acting seen on television from even the most recently trained actors remained rooted in the realism of the constructed performance space; at least until changing production modes began to challenge this way of working, taking the actor away from the artificial construct of the studio and out into real locations.

A scene towards the climax of 'Law and Order', in which most of the series regulars appear, offers an opportunity to consider the impact of formal training. The group are voting on the punishment of Barney, a mentally backward member of the community who they have (wrongly) judged to be guilty of murdering Wendy, a young woman in their group. The suggested options are to either take Barney's life or banish him from the community – the latter being an event he would be unlikely to survive. As *de facto* leader, Abby asks each person to name their preferred mode of punishment in turn, making a written note of their decisions. In the opening shot everyone bar Jenny can be seen in various tense, stiff or subdued postures, while Seymour's nervous toying with a pencil and reluctance to make direct eye contact, seated away from the others, belies Abby's confident manner and calm, level tone of voice.

Director Pennant Roberts cuts between shots of the various community members as they cast their votes, and back to Abby to capture her reaction, gradually building the tension. Greg votes for execution; Tom Price (Talfryn Thomas) – who, as the audience is already aware, is the real culprit – for banishment. Charmian votes for exile, and her former employer Arthur Russell (Michael Gover) for the death penalty. Roberts cuts to a medium shot of Abby as she makes a note of their decisions, before switching to a three-shot of Paul, who votes for death, and Emma and Jenny, who each opt for banishment. Roberts again cuts to a shot of Abby, seemingly dispassionately writing down their judgements, before cutting to Vic Thatcher as he too opts for death. Roberts now cuts to a medium close side-shot of Abby, who visibly gulps before quietly announcing that the vote stands at four-four. Seymour's eyes are clearly already watering as Greg points out that Abby has the casting vote. There is now a medium shot of Emma which pans slowly left to a frontal close-up of Abby as she begins to sob (Figure 3.13); a wordless admission that she is sanctioning Barney's death. It is impossible to discern how Seymour achieved this performance, but she seems to be crying real tears, heightening one of the most dramatic moments of the series thus far.

As an actress trained around the time Stanislavski's ideas were coming to prominence in Britain, it is unlikely that Seymour had not encountered the technique of emotion memory – a means of 'bringing back feelings you have already experienced' (Stanislavski 1934: 168) – though it cannot be stated with any certainty that she is consciously employing it here. Seymour later admitted that she felt little personal rapport with her character's decision:

Figure 3.13 Carolyn Seymour in *Survivors*: 'Law and Order'

> This was terribly difficult for me because I do not believe in capital punishment so it was a very hard story for me to do. I really fought against it. I wanted to stop it because I have a moral objection to capital punishment. I would have banished the man found guilty ... I really didn't want him to be executed. I realise that individual communities had to administer their own justice the best they could, in the absence of law courts and police to enforce the law, but it was absolutely the wrong kind of justice that I would have meted out had I been Abby Grant.
>
> **(Cited in Marshall 1995?)**

The distance between actress and character would seem to indicate the necessity for some form of technique to achieve the emotional pitch reached in this moment, though whether it was acquired and applied as the result of training or a matter of personal inspiration is again difficult to establish.

As Sharon Marie Carnicke cautions: 'attention paid to the actors' use of body and voice offers a more productive avenue for discussion than do alignments of specific acting approaches with performance styles ... No single element is sufficient to account for actors' representation of characters or the performances we see on the screen' (Carnicke 2006: 63). It is not possible to offer Seymour's work in this scene as an example of pure 'Stanislavskian' acting – such models seldom exist – yet it is significant that the training that many actors working in television at this time had received facilitated a more psychological approach to characterisation, as opposed to building character from externals alone such as movement and voice. Seymour's performance here could be seen as evidence of this.

However, not all actors had undergone such training, and as the style of acting seen on television continued to evolve they would have to adapt to the new techniques. Whether through training, experience or instinct, some were more adaptable than others, but even those seemingly least suited to location realism proved able to subjugate their usual processes and methods to the emerging style.

Actor experience

By far the most televisually experienced of the principal cast for the 1975 series, Talfryn Thomas had been playing quirky character roles on the small screen since the late 1950s, his unique physiognomy familiar to viewers from supporting roles in numerous series including *The Avengers* (ITV, 1961–69), *The Saint* (ITV, 1962–69), *The Persuaders!* (ITV, 1971–72) and *Doctor Who*. In 1974 he had a regular role as journalist Private Cheeseman in the popular sitcom *Dad's Army* (BBC, 1968–77), and it is probable that the audience for *Survivors* had greater pre-conceived performance expectations of Thomas than of the three main leads. However, while Tom Price indeed functions largely as comic relief in the early episodes, these associations are shockingly undercut in 'Law and Order' when he drunkenly kills Wendy, and allows the innocent Barney to be executed in his place.

Despite Thomas's extensive television experience, his performance style varied remarkably little whether working in the studio or on film, in drama or in comedy.[14] Figures 3.14, taken from the first episode of the *Doctor Who* serial 'The Green Death', and 3.15, from the *Dad's Army* episode 'My British Buddy' (both made in 1973) illustrate the use Thomas habitually made of his hands to emphasise dialogue; a style of acting that by the mid-1970s was at odds with the more scaled down studio realism exhibited by performers such as Carolyn Seymour and Peter Bowles.

Figure 3.14 Talfryn Thomas in *Doctor Who*: 'The Green Death Episode One'

Figure 3.15 Talfryn Thomas in *Dad's Army*: 'My British Buddy'

The same tropes can be seen in the filmed location scenes from 'The Fourth Horseman', in which the itinerant Tom Price first encounters Lucy. This was Thomas's earliest work on the series, yet his performance here differs little from that given throughout the majority of his episodes. A diverse range of shots are used to frame Thomas and Lucy Fleming in their depictions of the very different characters of Price and Lucy. Fleming's is a more internalised performance, seldom moving or gesturing after Price has commanded her to keep away from his makeshift tent, whereas Thomas employs broader physical gestures, stomping around as he dispenses advice to Lucy and boasts of his skill in catching a rabbit. Director Pennant Roberts employs a greater number of close-ups for Fleming, focusing on her facial expressions to convey mood, with a selection of medium shots and medium close-ups of Thomas to keep his many gesticulations in frame, as exampled by the sweeping gesture he employs on the line 'I'm keeping away from everybody'.

However, these framings also reflect the positioning of Jenny and Price within the narrative. As one of the central characters, whose story has been closely followed thus far in the opening episode, Jenny is a primary point of identification for the audience; she therefore receives a greater number of close-ups. Price, from the perspective of both Jenny and the viewer at home, is a stranger; symbolic of the new, alien environment created by the virus, he is constantly kept at a distance, in medium or long shot.

Although framings here could be seen as dictating the scale of performance, Thomas is in fact simply employing the same broad physicality that characterises his previous work, alongside his slightly stylised intonation. Partly as a result of his prominent Welsh accent, he places particular emphasis on the significant words and syllables in his dialogue, e.g. 'I'm *kee*ping a*way* from them. I'm *kee*ping a*way* from *every*body. I don't want to *catch* their *germs*', stabbing the air with his finger to emphasise Price's advice (Figure 3.16). This performance, reminiscent of W. Thorp Devereux's in *The Quatermass Experiment*, is problematic to situate in either studio or location realism – highlighting once again that these are far from being a simple binary. Every beat is 'acted out' via visual or vocal signifiers; when Jenny admits that she has taken food from a shop, Thomas starts forward, pointing his finger in a

Figure 3.16 Talfryn Thomas in *Survivors*: 'The Fourth Horseman'

gesture that could be read as either accusing or reprimanding, only to falter and half nod as she defensively informs him that she left money on the counter in recompense.

Thomas had very few studio scenes for *Survivors*, the majority of his work taking place on location, but the switch to OB seems initially to have had little effect on his performance. His gestural acting can be seen again in an early sequence from 'Law and Order', in which Price attempts to avoid censure for having allowed the community's pigs to escape by pointing the finger – literally – at fellow resident Arthur Russell. On two occasions Thomas jabs his finger as Price accuses Arthur, firstly of not having staked out the pig pen correctly, and then of hoarding food. He then clasps his hands in a protective or defensive gesture as he waits for Abby's response to his assertion.

The same gestural acting is seen again later in the episode, though in a very different context. Following Abby's casting vote for Barney's death, the remaining men of the group draw lots to decide who will have the responsibility of carrying out the execution. Greg, the last candidate before Price, selects the short straw; signifying the Welshman's relief, Thomas clutches at his chest, his eyes staring ahead at the floor, unfocused (Figure 3.17).

Figure 3.17 Talfryn Thomas in *Survivors*: 'Law and Order'

Such moments are in keeping with Thomas's earlier style, though clearly in a different emotional key. However, in a subsequent scene the actor seems to undergo a shift in style. As Greg departs to shoot Barney, Price is shown alone, seated on his bed, eyes staring upwards and hands clasped tightly before him in a posture almost suggestive of prayer. He then raises his still-clasped fists to his mouth (Figure 3.18); the effect is a stylised but disturbing depiction of Price's guilt, the character sucking at his thumbs in an infantile gesture of self-comfort.

For the moment of Barney's off-screen death, director Pennant Roberts employs a large close-up of Thomas's face, his gazing eyes first blinking in a flinch at the sound of Greg's gun being shot, before closing as he moans and again raises his clenched hands to his mouth to gnaw at them (Figure 3.18).

It is interesting to compare Roberts's use of the camera here with Price's earlier, filmed encounter with Jenny on location in 'The Fourth Horseman'. At that point in the series Price represented the outsider; the character about whom the audience knew least. As a point of viewer identification, Jenny received the close-ups, while Price was kept at a distance, in medium shot. Now

Figure 3.18 Talfryn Thomas in *Survivors*: 'Law and Order'

that the viewer is being asked to question their understanding of and perspective on Price, it is he who receives the close-up shots, resulting in a less projected performance from Talfryn Thomas; an indication of the importance of narrative and direction on acting style.

When Greg returns he is met on the stairs by Abby, who takes him to Price's room. There the Welshman kneels before them to reveal the blood-stained murder weapon, holding it up to them (Figure 3.19) in a silent, supplicant admission of his guilt. The camera closes in on Thomas's face as, like Seymour in the earlier scene, tears stream down it.

These moments depicting Tom Price's belated confession show Thomas performing in a wholly different key to his usual style. Significantly, Clive Exton's script has the usually-verbose Welshman silent in his penitence, forcing Thomas to employ a different performance mode. There are still signs of the actor's habitual reliance on physical gesture in the final shot of the episode (Figure 3.20), rubbing his hands together and whispering an apology to Barney's now abandoned bow and arrow as he begs forgiveness. While such visual signifiers of psychological upset contain

Figures 3.19 and 3.20 Talfryn Thomas in *Survivors*: 'Law and Order'

stage-derived traces, they are nevertheless more contained than the majority of Thomas's performances in the series to date.

Thomas might of course have produced the same performance had 'Law and Order' been recorded entirely at Television Centre, and it would be futile to assert that no actor reached similar heights of emotional realism in the multi-camera era. Whether his comparatively contained performance here was a result of the intensive location rehearsal and performance set-up, or simply a response to the scripted opportunity to display another side to his character, is impossible to state. Although Thomas was working for the same director as on 'The Fourth Horseman', the emotional register required in 'Law and Order' was vastly different. While the use of a close-up in Figure 3.20 militates against Thomas's usual broad gestures, it is interesting to note that the camera script specifies a slightly more physical performance: 'A single, distant shot. Price closes his eyes, moans, and collapses on the bed' (BBC WAC Survivors/Law and Order/BBC1/18/06/1975). As Sharon Marie Carnicke has highlighted, it is extremely limiting to expect actors always to perform in one particular style, and their mode of working can be adapted to suit particular circumstances: 'Single actors adjust their techniques ... within the limits of their skills and anatomies' (2004: 63). There is little evidence from Thomas's work on other programmes that he possessed a particularly broad skillset, though it is equally possible that he was typecast due to his unusual physiognomy, and therefore limited in the emotional range he might be employed to depict. Nonetheless, this more minimal performance in the closing moments of 'Law and Order', while possibly the result of editing and directorial influences, shows that even seemingly inflexible actors could modify and adapt, especially when placed in altered production circumstances.

Reception

Ratings for the first series of *Survivors* began with 7.07 million, peaking at 9.39 million for episode three (Cross and Priestner 2005: 37). The lowest viewing figure was 6.51 million for episode six, and the series ended on 7.58 million (*ibid.*), indicating a reasonably consistent audience for the programme. Critical and audience reaction was mixed, with little indication from viewers' comments that the shift to Outside Broadcast led to a perceived increase in verisimilitude. The Audience Research Report for the first OB episode, 'Starvation', cited 'praise for the acting of the entire cast, only a minority (less than one in five) finding it mediocre' (BBC WAC R9/7/135 – 'An Audience Research Report', Week 23 1975), with child actors Stephen Dudley and Tanya Ronder singled out alongside Talfryn Thomas as 'outstanding'. Thomas's style at this point was still employing the gestural mode that cannot easily be reconciled with either studio realism or location realism; the positive audience reaction demonstrates the breadth of performance styles that were still acceptable for television drama at the time. It is unfortunate that no report exists for 'Law and Order', in which Thomas's altered performance style might have provided a stronger test of audience reaction. However, the same report also concludes that 'all [the actors] were thought to have portrayed the various characters convincingly and well' (*ibid.*), indicating at least that the more scaled down location performance of Carolyn Seymour was not discordant for contemporary audiences.

Elsewhere, negative opinion of performance seemed more related to Terry Nation's scripts. The *Sunday Times* reviewer disparaged the series' 'largely middle class cardboard characters' ('Television' 1975: 32), while Clive James described the programme as 'a desperate struggle by the last half-dozen actors in England to get their mouths around Terry Nation's dialogue before they die of hunger' (1975: 26). Such remarks might indicate that, in the wake of the social realist movement examined in the previous chapter, audiences and critics were beginning to find the 'middle class' Received Pronunciation practised by the majority of the cast a less than credible depiction of contemporary society. However, it is interesting to note that there is slightly greater use of real voice in *Survivors* than in *The Quatermass Experiment* or *Doctor Who*; Talfryn Thomas speaks with his original Welsh accent, and Hana Maria Pravda also employs her original Czech voice. However, the practice of mimicking is also alive and well, as evidenced by Dorset-born Chris Tranchell's cockney Paul Pitman, while New Zealander Denis Lill (who in real life speaks with adopted RP) employs a Welsh accent as Charles Vaughan.

Although one viewer of the series finale complained 'I've seen commuters looking more upset at a strike than these characters were at a catastrophe' (BBC WAC R9/7/136 – 'An Audience Research Report', Week 29 1975) – perhaps suggesting that the slight scaling down of performance resulting from the move to location was, for some, already noticeable – performances were generally well received, with Carolyn Seymour in particular 'linger[ing] in several minds' (*ibid.*). The *Radio Times* contained several letters praising the series' acting alongside other elements, with Andrew Smith of Hull citing 'the fine writing, superb acting, and the professionalism of the directors and crew. The number of "unknowns" in the cast is also refreshing' (1975: 55).

The lack of more focused praise or criticism of the acting in *Survivors* before and after the move to OB complicates a simplistic reading of the acting style resulting from the shift to location. Evidence suggests that actors responded to the location model in different ways, but the less projected performances it engendered in some were appreciated by many viewers, sowing the seeds for a mode of television acting that would gradually come to precedence in the following decades.

Conclusion

The 1975 series of *Survivors* offers several lessons. Although studio realism was by the 1970s an established form, there were notable exceptions who continued to flourish within the system. The fact that Talfryn Thomas continued to work regularly until his death in 1982, despite his largely unvarying performance, demonstrates that there was still room within the parameters of television drama for more stage-derived performers.

The move by *Survivors* to Outside Broadcast location demonstrates once again the multiplicity of the factors affecting small screen acting. Although stagecraft still provided an early grounding for many actors, the decline of repertory meant that television had increased in importance as a medium of employment. Technology and training, the latter until now the more static of determinants, began to combine as changes in the site of drama production necessitated new approaches. The rigorous, thoroughly-blocked rehearsal of studio recording was no longer applicable to the rehearse/record template necessitated by location work, and the increased focus in British drama schools on

Stanislavski's character analysis and self-preparation techniques would provide vital tools for actors as rehearsal time began to decrease. The switch from studio to location resulted in a radical diminution of actor movement designed purely for the sake of visual interest, though this was as much the result of inexperience on the part of camera operators as actors' performance choices. Perhaps more significantly, the moderated vocal projection into which studio realism had by now settled was reduced still further when actors moved into real locations, providing a marked contrast with the antiseptic construct of the three-walled studio sets and their imposing technical paraphernalia.

It is important to remember, however, that the use of OB video on *Survivors* was primarily an economical alternative to the costly and time-intensive single camera film and studio process, and was at the time atypical of BBC series drama. The result can therefore be regarded as location realism in its rawest state, and if this was the genesis of a new form, studio realism remained dominant. The renewed process of scaling down required by increased location work in the 1970s and 1980s[15] was, as ever, an ongoing process, and the routines and habits of studio realism were too established to be abandoned overnight. In the 1990s, however, both studio drama and OB location would become largely obsolescent, and by the mid-2000s, television drama was almost entirely based on a single camera model; the era of location realism.

Notes

1. The original outline for Television Centre included rehearsal rooms, but these were rejected due to cost, 'and also because it would be using available space which might be required either for additional studios or offices' (BBC WAC R37/121/1 – memo from R.A. Florence, Head of Central Services, 31 August 1956).
2. The main channel was re-named BBC1.
3. Credited on screen as M.K. Jeeves.
4. Pennant Roberts in fact recalled Terence Dudley lunching with the three leads and directors at Television Centre restaurant earlier in 1974, prior to the start of production (Cross and Priestner 2005: 8). However, when filming commenced the cast and director had yet to actually work together on scripts.
5. Not including the opening and closing title sequences.

6 This actors' handbook is unique in its focus on UK television acting, most 'how to' guides providing advice on US single camera television. Typical examples include Judith Weston's *Directing Actors: Creating Memorable Performances for Film and Television* (1996), Tony Barr's *Acting for the Camera* (1997), Ian Bernard's *Film and Television Acting* (1998) and Patrick Tucker's *Secrets of Screen Acting* (2014).
7 Susan Willis provides several examples of the comparatively luxurious rehearsal time allocated to the BBC's Shakespeare productions, director Jane Howell taking two hours to outline her vision for *Henry VI-Richard III* before the first day read-through even began (1991: 171).
8 The website of the *South West England Vintage Television Museum*, www.tvmuseum.co.uk/, features several colour television sets manufactured in the 1970s, ranging in size from nineteen to twenty-five inches.
9 Although director Cedric Messina had previously employed OB on several *Play of the Month* productions (Smart 2010: 313–314), *Survivors* is significant for employing OB on an ongoing basis. The lack of availability of an OB crew for the first six episodes is indicative that this was 'a new departure for BBC Drama' (Roberts 2003b).
10 For first few episodes of the second series, rehearsals briefly returned to Acton, but thereafter were conducted entirely on location (Cross and Priestner 2005: 96).
11 The camera continues to record during breaks in performance.
12 It is, however, possible that Susi is making a common and erroneous direct association between the Method and Stanislavski.
13 Kevin McNally received an extensive grounding in movement, period movement, fencing, animal study, Alexander Technique and Standard English, the latter remaining an important part of the syllabus (McNally 2010).
14 There is insufficient space here to investigate the differences between the two genres, but with the presence of a studio audience British sitcom of this time arguably required a more heightened performance style than its drama equivalent.
15 In this period OB was used either for entire serials, such as *The Mayor of Casterbridge* (BBC, 1978), or as a cheaper alternative to film for location work combined with multi-camera studio interiors, as on *Doctor Who* serials from 1986 onwards.

4
The age of location realism

By the time *Doctor Who* and *Survivors* were re-made in the mid to late 2000s, the television drama landscape had been transformed in virtually every respect. The rehearsal room/studio recording template was now the sole domain of situation comedy, and while certain soaps still utilised multi-camera recording, it was no longer accompanied by a prior preparation period. Although constructed sets still played a role, they were to be found on soundstages rather than in the comparatively cramped confines of Television Centre. While in the 1990s film had superseded videotape, HD video was fast becoming the recording medium of choice, and location had finally usurped the studio as the prime site of drama performance. This elimination of its various conditioning factors sounded the death knell for studio realism, yet effects were felt only gradually, with various external factors also at play. While the elimination of rehearsals placed the onus of performance preparation more squarely upon actors, the increased use of Stanislavski's theories in British drama schools, combined with specific training for screen acting, better equipped emerging performers for a working environment in which television was now the most common area of employment.[1] When summarising the demands of television performance in this period, actor Kim Durham concluded that the need for private preparation and flexibility of approach – combined with techniques of concentration and relaxation – were all compatible with 'the broadly Stanislavskian methodology which is the orthodoxy of British stage training' (2002: 93).

This chapter's case studies, *Doctor Who* and *Survivors*, are useful in several respects. Both are representative of the production practices of modern BBC drama in that they are made primarily using a single camera location model, allowing comparisons to be made between location realism in the 2000s and its 1970s forbear. With its large regular cast, *Survivors* is representative of the ensemble drama that now forms the basis of much prime-time drama scheduling, while *Doctor Who* features a greater reliance on CGI, providing an opportunity to examine the challenges to the actor of working on visual effects-driven productions. As the better known of the series, *Doctor Who* has generated a greater quantity of behind-the-scenes material, and sequences have been selected largely on the basis of the production information this makes available. *Survivors* employs a number of sequences loosely adapted from Terry Nation's 1975 storylines; scenes will therefore be used for comparison with the original.

As the determinants of television acting have begun to intersect more closely, the use of sub-headings here is altered slightly to reflect this, with the descending order of relevance employed in previous chapters more loosely applied. As production process to a large extent now dictates the opportunity for direction of actors, these two factors are outlined jointly before proceeding to training and technology, the latter pair having in recent years become more closely intertwined to meet the emerging requirements of the workplace. However, it should be borne in mind that each of these four factors is arguably of equal weight in terms of modern location realism. Actor experience will then be examined, alongside generational differences – which, as will be seen, have significant implications for acting style – before concluding, as always, with reception.

Background

In performance terms, television history provides few conveniently demarcated paradigm shifts. However, with regard to the break-up of the BBC's studio system, one of the most significant events was the passing of the Broadcasting Act of 1990, following which the Corporation was obliged to allocate 25 per cent of its output to independent companies. As a consequence, much of the drama traditionally produced at Television Centre was now made by organisations with no similar investment in studio plant. This was followed in 1993 by the instigation of 'Producer Choice', a policy under which producers could use outside suppliers as opposed to internal departments should they prove more cost-effective. 'In-house' BBC drama production between 1992 and 1995 dropped from 74 per cent to 54 per cent (Born 2005: 134), as the environment that had fostered studio realism disintegrated in a new, market-driven 'culture of entrepreneurism' (*ibid.*: 128).

It should not be assumed, however, that studio drama perished overnight; it had in fact been in decline for much of the 1980s, as all-film production came increasingly into favour. Film inserts had played a part in BBC drama even in the days of live broadcasts, though all-film productions such as *Fabian of Scotland Yard* (BBC, 1954–56) were comparatively rare. Throughout the 1960s the BBC remained resolutely invested in what former Controller of BBC1 Jonathan Powell describes as the '24-four hour machine' of videotaped studio drama (2010), despite competition in terms of overseas sales from commercial rival ITC's filmed productions, such as *The Saint*. The 'documentary dramas' of Ken Loach and Tony Garnett, exemplified by 'Cathy Come Home', pointed a possible alternative, with performances evolved mainly on location for single camera. However, Garnett describes the negotiations required to commission these films as 'the biggest professional battle of my life. They said: "We've just built the Television Centre, and the big studios are there mainly for the drama and big entertainment. We'll let you produce films, and everybody else will want to do it"; which is exactly what happened' (2010). In the 1970s many *Play for Today* entries were made on film, but such anthology series output paled in comparison with Thames Television's Euston Films, whose series successes included *The Sweeney* (ITV, 1975–78) and *Minder* (ITV, 1979–93). Patrick Malahide, a regular in the latter, describes the sense of liberation felt by independent companies not 'hidebound with plant' to the same extent as the BBC: 'Euston Films [said]: "OK, we're going to make this series. Well, what do we need? We're making it about London; we'll make it in London. We don't have to justify what we're doing by using a studio"' (2011).[2]

It was not until the late 1970s that the BBC significantly expanded its filmed output,[3] though by the early 1980s the department was actively preferring celluloid to videotape: 'That argument came around the *Dynasty* (ABC, 1981–89) time; US programmes threatened to swamp the [British] ratings' (Powell 2010). John Ellis agrees that audiences now expected prestige productions to be made entirely on film, 'not least because of expectations created by ... the presence of US mini-series on UK screens' (2005: 50).[4] Until this point, film's expense had caused it to be used sparingly; however, the rising cost of television drama in general meant that studio videotape was now little cheaper (Powell 2010).[5]

By the time the Broadcasting Act came into effect, studio drama had clearly fallen out of favour. When producer Simon Curtis initially opted to use multi-camera videotape for *Performance* (BBC, 1991–95), he was aware that 'the Drama Department at the BBC was determined to become a film department' (cited in Ridgman 1998: 199), admitting that his decision 'went against conventional wisdom' (*ibid.*: 200). The fact that the final productions were made on film would seem to confirm director Christopher Morahan's description of the series as 'the last post for studio drama' (2010).

Rather than heralding the destruction of the studio system, Producer Choice can be taken as an indication that it had already, in essence, been abandoned by the BBC. However, other implications for actors included its effect on the variety of work available. Like multi-camera studio, the single play had been in decline since the 1980s (Gardner and Wyver 1983). The Singles department was increasingly pressurised under Producer Choice, its budgets being among the highest in television (Born 2005: 117). This increased vulnerability coincided with an expansion in episodic series, leading to a situation in which 'long-running series and serials ... dominate[d] the output of major channels' (Bignell *et al.* 2000: 1–2). In an era where programming decisions were more than ever driven by commissioning executives' perception of market demand, the new proliferation of soaps, hospital dramas and crime series[6] meant a reduction in the range of genres – and therefore the variety of roles – available to television actors, and coincided with an increase in the practice of casting to type.

It was into this much-changed television environment that *Doctor Who* and *Survivors* were re-launched in 2005 and 2008 on BBC1, now part of a 24-hour broadcasting landscape of cable, satellite and digital channels. A wider variety of US drama was now more readily available than ever before – which had significant implications for British productions. Robin Nelson has highlighted how shorter and more rapidly intercut narrative 'bytes' (1997: 33) have replaced the lengthier, dialogue-based scenes typical of studio drama, coinciding with the rise of the 'flexi-narrative' (*ibid.*: 77), wherein a number of story strands run across entire series rather than being resolved within the space of a single episode. Each featured prominently in *Doctor Who* and *Survivors*, while the US showrunner model, whereby an executive producer and head writer co-ordinated both series style and overall narrative, also influenced *Doctor Who* executive Russell T Davies. According to Charlie Higson, who had earlier attempted a similar feat on *Randall and Hopkirk (Deceased)* (BBC, 2000–1): '[Russell] went over and worked with the Americans for a long time, seeing how they set up and run these drama series … It's like x number of single episodes, then you do a double episode, and you have your thread that runs all the way through. They really studied it hard, which is probably why they were more successful than we were' (2010).

In addition, Davies faced the challenge of positioning a new version of 'old' television for modern viewers accustomed to all-film drama:

> Hopefully it's less studio-bound; I think that will be the greatest visible change in it, is that it was terribly, terribly confined in sort of three-walled sets. We're doing a lot of film location; like, at least so far maybe about seventy per cent of it is on location. So that makes the whole picture look bigger, more ambitious and more epic; and more modern, frankly. (Davies 2005b)[7]

Survivors showrunner Adrian Hodges was also aware of the need to differentiate his version from the cheap (to modern eyes) OB look of the original: 'We were using 35mm for the first series, and it gives it a very filmic look … There is an enormous difference in that the audience expectation of a BBC drama now, in most cases, is that it will look cinematic' (2011).

The 'cinematic' or 'filmic' production model cited by Hodges is far removed from that of studio realism. By the time *Doctor Who* and *Survivors* went into production,[8] casts faced challenges that would never have arisen on their predecessors; how these affected performance will now be examined via scenes from the opening series of each.

Production process and direction

Modern television drama production has seen a significant shift in the degree of control that both actor and director exert over screen performance. With little or no rehearsal of the type formerly carried out at the Acton Hilton, characterisation is now more than ever the responsibility of the actor, contact time with the director usually being limited to a cast read-through of the script[9] and a brief blocking session on the day of recording. However, the multiple-take nature of single camera recording means that performances can now be pieced together in post-production, mediated by the employment of editing, sound effects and music. While the possibility of additional takes seemingly provides the actor with more flexibility, enabling them to 'try out' different performance ideas and arguably leading to greater spontaneity, the majority of these will be in the form of 'coverage' from different angles, in which the actor will have to replicate the same moves and intonation for the sake of editing continuity. The selection of takes is normally the domain of the director and editor, who thus have the power to mediate – while still being essentially bound to – the performance that the actor provides on the day. This delicate balance of control over the performance ultimately seen on the screen is in marked contrast to the comparatively lengthy process of deliberation and pre-planning which typified the studio era, while advances in technology mean that location realism in the 2000s is in many ways distinct from the nascent form examined in Chapter 3.

Arguably the last recognisable remnant of the old rehearsal process is the modern 'table read'; a group reading of the script which represents the actors' sole opportunity (in production terms) to meet their director[10] and fellow cast members before filming. One notable difference is that table reads are conducted in production 'blocks', i.e. cast regulars will almost certainly be reading scripts back-to-back for two (or even three) separate episodes that do not necessarily follow each other in transmission order, rather than focusing on one particular episode prior to shooting. Also, while a first day rehearsal read-through at the Acton Hilton would usually have been attended by the director and script editor to agree cuts or amendments, the modern-day equivalent is, according to *Doctor Who* director Richard Clark, a much larger affair: 'The read-through is quite a major event. What you'll find is … all the producers of the department, the exec producers, you know, everybody turns up to the read-through, and generally full cast, assuming that it's possible' (2011).

Whether an actor attends the reading is dependent on a number of factors, not least their prominence in the storyline. Andrew Tiernan has appeared in both *Survivors* and *Doctor Who*, but while the character he played in the former recurred over several episodes, requiring regular read-through attendance, his guest appearance in the latter was restricted to a handful of scenes: 'If you are lucky enough to be asked to a read-through it's only really useful for the production people including the writer, producers, make-up and costume. On *Doctor Who* I didn't get a read-through … I met everybody on the first day of filming' (2011). The sense of company represented by the Acton Hilton now applies only to the regular core cast, filming sessions having become a more fragmented experience.

The amount of preparation time allowed for a forty-five- or sixty-minute episodic drama such as *Doctor Who* or *Survivors*[11] is dependent on its place in the production schedule, each episode being allocated an average of two weeks' shooting as one half of a production block. However, additional preparation time is allowed prior to the first block of any new series, as Howard Burch, former executive producer at BBC collaborator Kudos Productions, explains: 'You'd start off with the lead director,[12] and then he would be given that first week of rehearsals. And in our case I think he probably used three out of the five days for rehearsals, and the rehearsal days weren't necessarily that long; you know, they'd probably start at ten, and finish certainly by four' (2011). The fact that so little of the first week is allotted to rehearsal is due to the remainder being taken up with costume fittings, make-up tests and even last-minute location scouting and script changes (*ibid.*). The few days' rehearsal available to the lead director represents their only opportunity to 'get the tone right, to get the chemistry between the actors right, to explore scenes that could be problematic, that might need re-writing, just so you've got that useful window to be able to sort stuff out if there are going to be any problems further down the line' (*ibid.*). Once this is concluded, production becomes an ongoing process in which less preparation time is available, as Richard Clark describes: 'When one person is shooting, another one is prepping, another one is editing; so it's a rolling system, basically. And you know, thirteen episodes of *Doctor Who* is about as many episodes as we can generally do in this country before you're doing a soap' (2011).[13]

Extensive rehearsal is clearly no longer the norm, although showrunners such as Adrian Hodges are sensitive to the need to accommodate actors wherever possible: 'We would use [the read-through] as our opportunity to extend the rehearsal period, and we did, I think, have a day or two, here and there. But basically it would be a case of the director and me working the day before with the actors; the director on the spot, me often by telephone or whatever discussing motivation for them. But it's not enough time' (2011).

In such a situation the onus is on the actor to prepare their characterisation prior to arriving on set, as Roger Lloyd Pack described:

> It's not satisfactory. It means you have to sort of work on a character on your own, and – I've got used to it now – you can tell from the script what sort of character he is. And you sort of know what they want, really, generally speaking, although within what you do [the director] might say: 'A bit less' or 'A bit more.' You will get some notes on what you're doing, but you have to come with a character already prepared ... There's no time for any questions about: 'What do you think my character would do in this situation?'
> (2011)

Survivors regular Phillip Rhys developed a mode of self-direction to provide directors with the performance he believed they wanted:

> As wonderful as these directors are, they literally don't have that time, they don't have the patience to direct you; to take you to the side, have a five-minute dialogue ... The best way to that is to some degree be able to third eye yourself, to be able to be subjective and direct yourself. And a lot of the directors – and a lot of fabulous directors – are coming from an editorial background ... so they've already seen the final stuff edited in their head. So it's how you can contribute to the bigger picture.
> (2011)

This self-help rehearsing ethos extends to collaboration with other actors, to be accommodated in the filming schedule as and when time permits: 'If you want to do it you call up the actor yourself: "Do you want to come to my hotel room? Let's work on stuff", and that's what you do. On the big scenes you do that, the night before, a couple of days before. And we did that, and there was that kind of spirit on the set' (*ibid.*).

These actors are, however, speaking from the perspective of either a series lead or a 'name' guest actor, who might therefore be allowed a certain leeway in their performances. For less established cast members, the type of advance preparation possible is more limited. Kemal Sylvester, who has played supporting roles in series including *Sherlock* (BBC, 2010–) and *Silent Witness* (BBC, 1996–), finds that any prior choices are liable to change on the day:

> It's always a bit iffy about how much you can change from what you did in the audition, because what you did in the audition is presumably what they want. But then again, the amount of stuff that's changed when you get there; I mean, the amount of times that I've got a script, I'm reading it, and I'm thinking, 'Right, he's in the office, and he's being interviewed.' So you kind of do it, and you're sat [*sic*] at the desk, you know, you're learning the lines, and you can't help but get into, you know: 'Maybe if I lean back at that point, and maybe if I put my hand there at that point,' and you get in there, and they say: 'Actually, I think we're going to shoot this walking down the corridor,' and all that stuff that you've now got fixed in your head is just completely wrong. So you need to be prepared to a point, because you're not going to get any kind of chat about it there and then ... The lines could change at any given moment; the blocking is almost guaranteed to change from what you've imagined in your brain.
>
> **(2010)**

Sylvester's comments regarding positioning and gesture indicate a desire for the physical preparation and blocking of studio realism, while the need for flexibility and an immediate response to the performing environment is more indicative of location realism. This need for both preparation and flexibility is also emphasised by *Doctor Who* guest actor Mark Gatiss:

> If you know the script backwards then you've got freedom to improvise, or just relax into it. The danger comes if you don't know it,

and you're scrabbling for the thing; then you're not even thinking about your environment. But then, you could rehearse something till you're blue in the face and then the location falls through, and you would literally have to re-block it in half an hour at the beginning of the day, so you've got to be open to that.

(2011)

Without the period of preparation and planning that helped shape studio realism, actors' performance would now seem to be a combination of that provided at their audition (assuming the part was not a straight offer, bypassing the requirement to read), any notes provided after the read-through (assuming the actor was in attendance), any preparation they choose to conduct – either alone or with fellow cast members, in their own time – and the direction they receive on the day of filming. The latter can, however, be brief. An extract from *Calling the Shots* (2007), Graeme Harper's journal of directing *Doctor Who*, illustrates the pace at which director and cast now work: 'Eight o'clock in the morning, and everyone's on set, waiting with baited [sic] breath. By nine o'clock we are rehearsed, lit and ready to shoot' (42). Due to the limited contact time available, Harper tries where possible to talk to his actors before filming begins, if only in the make-up room (2011). This approach, though not universal, is also shared by fellow *Doctor Who* director Andrew Gunn:

> I always try and either meet with or at least talk on the phone to all the cast ... which I've been told not many directors do ... Even if someone's coming in to do just a few lines for a couple of hours, I will always call them to talk about the story, to talk about the character, to talk about what I expect from them in terms of the level of performance and the style of performance, because there's no point waiting till they turn up on set and then realising that they're thinking in a completely different way. So, it's to make them feel welcome and comfortable and tell them what I want them to do, basically.

(2011)

In terms of actual rehearsal, directors Graeme Harper, Colin Teague and Jamie Payne all state that they typically spend just ten to fifteen minutes alone with their actors, reading and then blocking the scene to be filmed (Harper 2011; Payne 2011; Teague 2011).

This is the cast's sole opportunity to raise any issues about which they are unsure, but is also, according to Harper, a chance for creative input: 'The secret is: let the actor show you something first, before you start stepping in to correct it or change it ... Most actors want that second go; it's something that appeals. If they don't think it'll work, most good actors will still do it ... and you can then both agree whether it's a good thing or not' (2011). When this initial rehearsal is complete, the film crew are called in and the scene is performed again, after which lighting is planned, props are set in place, and filming commences, possibly with the director watching via a monitor in another room (Lawson 2014: 57). This is a microcosm of the process that formerly took place at Acton, and on the rehearse/record schedule at Television Centre, though with the major difference that scenes are unlikely to be played through just once in their entirety, repeated takes for 'coverage' from different angles being the norm.

A segment from documentary series *Doctor Who Confidential* (BBC, 2005–11) illustrates just how rapidly performance choices are evolved between actor and director, and the speed with which they can be abandoned. While rehearsing a scene on the London Embankment for the opening episode, 'Rose', actors Christopher Eccleston (playing the Doctor) and Billie Piper (Rose Tyler) are shown with director Keith Boak discussing how the dialogue should be played when the Doctor's new companion questions him as to the external appearance of his space and time ship the TARDIS, which appears in 'disguise' as a 1950s Police Box. This was the first major dialogue scene the two actors had filmed together (Davies 2005c), and it is interesting to note the extent to which it differs from the final, transmitted version. Eccleston's initial performance choice, made in consultation with Boak, is that the Doctor's reaction to Rose's question is primarily defensive, stating 'I think he knows it's a bad disguise', and encouraging Piper to 'wind me up about it'. It is clear here that Eccleston, the more televisually experienced of the two actors, is taking the initiative, yet these performance choices do not survive to the final edit. In the screened version, Piper's 'winding up' of the Doctor has been replaced by Rose's genuine curiosity and incomprehension, and Eccleston's delivery of the line 'It's a disguise' has mellowed to become more affectionate. Placing his hand lightly on the side of the TARDIS,

Figure 4.1 Christopher Eccleston in *Doctor Who*: 'Rose'

his broad grin no longer signifies the original intention to convey the Doctor's awareness of his ship's inadequacy (Figure 4.1).

It is of course possible that the 'rehearsal' shown in *Doctor Who Confidential* was staged for the documentary's cameras, but if genuine its notable difference from the transmitted version is an example of the speed with which performance ideas can be tried and discarded. Such an approach has closer links with film-making than with traditional studio drama, where the performance would have been evolved and agreed upon in advance of recording. Hollywood actor Jeff Daniels has described the freedom which he believes the film approach allows:

> In film there's no such thing as 'wrong choices.' I spent the first half dozen films I made thinking 'I've got to do it perfectly.' What you see in *Terms of Endearment* (1983), for instance, is an actor who's trying not to make any mistakes. I was aware of everything I did: every hand gesture, every inflection ... but I learned from watching Jack Nicholson to simply walk into the action of the scene and go with whatever happens. He'll set himself up with the basics of the character and the situation, and then he'll just go with it. He's not afraid of making wrong choices. You can always throw away a particular take later.
> **(Cited in Cardullo *et al.* 1998: 249)**

Daniels fails to mention that the multiple-take 'trying out' of different styles ultimately places the choice of performance in the hands of the director and editor, rather than the actor; it is possible that Piper and Eccleston's lines were filmed in a number of different ways, with the final selection left to Keith Boak. Also, the potential for character discussion and re-takes might not be as available to most actors as it is to a 'star' such as Nicholson or leads Eccleston and Piper, the latter pair working to much tighter filming schedules in television than are available in film. Kemal Sylvester's account of working on episodic drama creates the impression of a situation in which supporting actors have significantly less say than regulars: 'You might run the lines but there's no real discussion about how you're going to play it, or anything like that. And a lot of the time, if you're doing stuff with the regulars … they'll just slope off and make their phone calls' (2010). Clearly, the degree of control that actors exert over their performance is dependent upon status, as Julia Dalkin, who has played supporting roles in dramas including *EastEnders* and *A Touch of Frost* (ITV, 1992–2010), affirms: 'If you have no clout, you can't always do it again, because they're already off onto the next scene, or the main actor doesn't want to' (2010). Even more senior actors, such as *Poirot* (ITV, 1989–2013) star Philip Jackson, sometimes 'do not necessarily feel … central to the process. This is more obvious when things are happening quickly on the set and there are pressures to shoot fast. Time is money and the normal tendency is to cram in as much as possible' (cited in Sexton 2015: 125).

One factor that affects all actors is the late arrival of scripts, which according to *Survivors* director Jamie Payne are often not ready until the week before shooting commences (2011). Even then the script provided for the read-through can differ significantly from that used for filming, with last-minute re-writes signified by differently-coloured pages of script, as Andrew Gunn relates: 'An actor can come in, having rehearsed the scene, and be handed a blue page, you know, with a sometimes complete re-write. So you can imagine this, as an actor you've done your prep and you're suddenly handed these pages … You have to adapt very quickly' (2011). Such a situation might, as Robert Barton points out, result in a more spontaneous performance: 'The film actor may have a newly memorized, newly revised script never spoken out loud in front of anyone before the moment the cameras run. It may be fresh but raw' (2009: 208). According to Jamie Payne, however, the revelation of new character information in re-written pages of script can also cause actors to regret performance choices already made and recorded on film: 'Actors are given scenes, and they go: "Oh my God! If I knew [sic] that that was going to happen ... I'd have played that completely differently"' (2011).

On the first year of *Doctor Who* several scenes were either re-written or inserted at the eleventh hour due to episodes under-running, one example being 'The Doctor Dances' (Moffat 2005a). Towards the story's conclusion, Christopher Eccleston was required to deliver a lengthy piece of exposition in which the Doctor explains to Captain Jack (John Barrowman) how the latter's actions have placed the entire human race in danger. The pages for this speech were re-written and handed to the actor just fifteen minutes before filming began (Barrowman 2005), and this brief sequence provides an example of the ways in which actors' performances are dictated – and to an extent compromised – by production pressures. Remaining rooted to the spot, Eccleston adopts a rigid stance, folding his arms to deliver his speech (Figure 4.2) as the camera tracks slowly round him to the left in medium shot, and gradually closes in. Eschewing physical gestures, he relies entirely on his voice, which gradually rises in speed and volume to become more accusing as he makes Jack aware of his culpability.

The physical simplicity of this choice – for what could have been a more 'performed' and dramatic moment of emotional intensity – is a result of necessity, time being of the essence. In this sense it differs from the early location realism of Chapter 3, in that it did not evolve primarily out of the performing environment. Actors in the 1970s were working with a script that could be discussed and amended in advance of the performance, whereas Eccleston was learning his lines very much 'on the spot'. Had the actor requested significant cuts to his dialogue during filming, they would have required approval at a level higher than the director, as Patrick Malahide relates: 'There's the executive producer who has to be rung up, and everybody's on their BlackBerrys. It goes up this, sort of, not a chain of command; it's a chain of indecision. And it goes all the way back up this so-called creative process, and actually prevents creative decisions being made on the floor' (2011).[14] Any such negotiation represents a significant delay to shooting, with film units under increasing pressure to film more pages of script

Figure 4.2 Christopher Eccleston in *Doctor Who*: 'The Doctor Dances'

per day. With ten days typically allocated to a one-hour drama, this means recording around six pages per day, which compares with two pages for a feature film production (Lawson 2014: 24). On a continuing drama such as *Holby City*, as many as thirteen to fifteen pages a day will be shot, while up to thirty pages can be recorded on a soap such as *EastEnders* (ibid.: 25).

It could be argued that the pressures represented by attenuated rehearsal, tight filming schedules and last-minute re-writes lead to a spontaneity of performance that would have been lacking in the more prepared performances of the studio era. In the days of live and 'as live' production, actors had to sustain a performance throughout an entire scene, or even an entire episode. The same was also partially true for early location realism, when the relative inexperience of camera operators meant that longer takes and static framings were more common. However, due to the increased prevalence of post-production editing, actors must now concentrate on replicating the performance decided upon on the day for repeated takes, in order to accommodate various camera angles and framings – which would seem to militate against the spontaneity argued for by Jeff Daniels and Robert Barton. A scene from the opening episode of *Survivors* illustrates the exigencies of the multiple take, and the necessity for – and effects on acting of – repetition of performance. This sequence is adapted directly from original series episode 'The Fourth Horseman', in which Abby (now played by Julie Graham) wakes from her fever to discover husband David's (Shaun Dingwall) lifeless body in the living room. Instead of the dissolves employed in 1975 to signify the passing of time as Abby lay in bed, a caption is used to inform the audience that this scene takes place '3 days later'. Director John Alexander then cuts to an extreme close-up of Abby's eye blinking open (Figure 4.3) – a shot type impossible to replicate in the multi-camera set-up – accompanied by a non-diegetic sound effect akin to a cymbal crash. Alexander then cuts alternately between medium (Figure 4.4) and long shots (Figure 4.5) of Abby sitting up in bed, registering the open curtains and daylight before stumbling to the floor, signifying the character's physical weakness.

Julie Graham would have had to perform these admittedly simple actions at least twice to allow for Alexander's cuts, as when a medium close-up of Graham pulling herself off the floor cuts in continuity to a long shot of her seating herself again on the bed. A single jump cut is then employed as Abby rises and stumbles towards the door, leaning against the frame as she calls David's name. This shot is hand-held, adding to the sense of Abby's disorientation.

Jump cuts are again used when Abby enters the kitchen, and it is notable that Graham here employs a number of hand-based physical signifiers, clasping her brow to indicate confusion (Figure 4.6) and masking her mouth in disgust at the putrefaction of the fridge's contents (Figure 4.7).

Julie Graham's interpretation includes more 'performed' signifiers than Carolyn Seymour's in the original, yet it is possible that such gestures form part of a performance topography; a series of established moves that are easier to replicate in repeated takes than an entirely spontaneous response to the environment, which would then have to be precisely recalled and reproduced. A sequence such as this would have been run through and blocked only very briefly before filming, at which time Graham and Alexander would agree the actions to be performed. That there were at least two takes of this scene is clear from the cut between a head shot of Abby from one angle, opening a kitchen cupboard, and a close-up of her hands from another as she opens a packet of biscuits; the sound of the

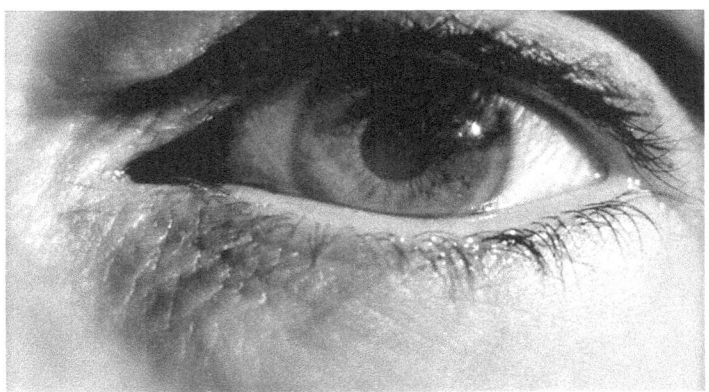

Figures 4.3–4.5 Julie Graham in *Survivors*: 'Episode 1'

Figures 4.6 and 4.7 Julie Graham in *Survivors*: 'Episode 1'

packet rustling, used over both shots, indicates that this is not intended as a jump cut, as employed elsewhere in the scene.

The same topography can be detected when Abby moves into the living room, where the sequence of events departs from that of 'The Fourth Horseman'. A combination of medium shots and close-ups are employed as Abby opens the curtains and turns. Alexander then holds Graham's face in a close-up of her stunned, frozen expression, mouth hanging slightly open (Figure 4.8), followed by a second close-up of David's face in sharp focus to the left of the frame, eyes staring sightlessly (Figure 4.9), with Abby out of focus in the background. Focus is then pulled to bring Abby's figure into relief as she begins to scream, raising her hands to her mouth in horror (Figure 4.10). Her hands then drop as she continues to scream, Alexander cutting to a close-up of Abby's face, mouth wide open (Figure 4.11), her trauma accentuated by doom-laden non-diegetic music on the soundtrack. Whereas in the original the audience was made aware of David's death just before Abby via his corpse's reflection in the mirror, here she notices his body shortly before it is revealed on screen.

The editing and post-production techniques employed detract from the sense of a sustained performance being given, as displayed in the original by Carolyn Seymour. Julie Graham would have had to repeat her movements and reactions for different takes and camera angles, while simultaneously being aware of the impact that the proximity of the camera and the type of lens used would have on the degree of facial expression required. Graham's employment of physical signifiers for her character's beats is indicative of a need to provide visual marker buoys; her awareness that her performance will subsequently be pieced together results in a more noticeable subdivision of moments and actions, like pieces of a jigsaw.

The choices of one actor will of course vary from another; Graham's full-throated scream of horror, for example, represents the inverse of Carolyn Seymour's shocked intake of breath, but is no less valid as a reaction to her character's situation. However, performing for a single camera with post-production editing – as

Figure 4.8 Julie Graham in *Survivors*: 'Episode 1'

Figures 4.9 and 4.10 Julie Graham and Shaun Dingwall in *Survivors*: 'Episode 1'

Figure 4.11 Julie Graham in *Survivors*: 'Episode 1'

opposed to multiple cameras in uninterrupted takes – requires distinct approaches, as several of those interviewed for this book were quick to point out. For some, multi-camera allows the actor increased freedom to focus more on what is happening 'in the moment', rather than remaining constantly aware of the need for repeated performance continuity, as Louise Jameson explains: 'You can click more into your objectives, rather than thinking, "Oh, this is where I pick up the ..."' and having to recreate them' (2011).[15] Single and multi-camera also engender different types of camera awareness, especially as the latter is no longer preceded by painstaking blocking. For Kim Durham, who worked on individual episodes of *EastEnders* and *Inspector Morse* in the late 1990s, the opportunity offered by the former, a multi-camera production, 'to play the entire scene facilitates the imagination and [offers] real stimuli for the generation of a reaction' (2002: 88). By contrast, for the close-up reaction shots of *Inspector Morse*'s single camera model, 'one [has] to create the illusion of the stimulus' (*ibid*.: 92). Having begun her television career in the late 1990s, Julia Dalkin was habituated to single camera filming when she appeared in two 2009 episodes of *EastEnders*, and found the multi-camera process employed on the series invigorating:

> I loved it, and I just thought: 'Why isn't it all like this?' To me it made a lot more sense ... I think you get a better performance out of it ... As far as developing a character, you're finding things – and I'm not talking about going off and doing something totally different, but there are subtleties or things that you would do or find as you're going along. You'll do one thing, and say, 'Oh no, I'd rather do this', or you or the person you're working with does something different. You've got to respond to that; you can't keep doing the rigidity of what you're doing, you're working in a sort of malleable area ... I think the long scenes work really well, because it's like doing a short play.
>
> **(2010)**

Dalkin's reference to finding subtleties *during* the performance, which would be limited to two or three takes (*ibid*.), reflects the lack of rehearsal on such programmes; its 'one-off' nature arguably leads to a greater sense of spontaneity than would be found in filmed performances which require precise replication. It is important to bear in mind here that Dalkin is speaking from the perspective of a guest actor, appearing in a limited run of episodes; regular cast members on such programmes are subject to a punishing production turnaround, which might well limit the options for exploring interpretive possibilities.

Nevertheless, many actors share Dalkin's appreciation of the continuous performance that multi-camera allows, including original *Survivors* actress Lucy Fleming: 'You're not doing it in such short bits and bytes and things, and you don't have to sustain it from different points of view' (2010). Seasoned film and television actor Jason Flemyng also understands the attraction of multi-camera, while pointing out the very different skillsets required: 'Yeah, it is nice; you do get a feeling of continuity through, but it's a different skill. Shooting a [single camera] scene in sections, it's much more detailed and intricate, and sort of a bit more scientific and a bit more technical. You know, you can't be losing yourself in your character ... when you're doing it fifteen or twenty times' (2011). Flemyng's reference to actors 'losing themselves in their character' supports Dalkin's reflections on multi-camera's potential for more involved performance, while emphasising the greater technical awareness required for single camera. However, as a British actor accustomed to working in Hollywood, Flemyng's estimated number of takes is perhaps not applicable to British television drama, as Charlie Higson asserts:

> If you've got enough money you can shoot the scene from every single angle, as many takes as you like, as many fancy camera moves, special effects shots, whatever, and you get to the edit and you've got endless choice. Now, nine times out of ten you don't have the money to get all that ... On British TV you're working with ever tighter budgets, ever shorter shoots, fewer and fewer opportunities to properly go out on location. You're restricted. You've got to work in the edit with what you *did* get.
>
> (2010)

Interviewed by Max Sexton, actor Philip Jackson claims that television directors are under far greater pressure than those working in film: 'TV directors have to cover themselves and shoot every possible angle on a scene to make sure they have options in the editing suite. Film directors have usually planned more carefully' (2015: 126). This question of to what extent directors 'work with what they get' to create a performance in the edit has long been debated in film and performance studies. Most often cited as proof that cutting can mediate an audience's reading of the actor's work is Soviet director Lev Kuleshov's now legendary demonstration for Russian matinee idol Vitold Polonsky:

> Polonsky asserted that there would be an enormous difference between an actor's face when portraying a man sitting in jail longing for freedom and seeing an open cell door, and ... [if] the protagonist was starving and was shown a bowl of soup. The reaction ... would be completely different. We then performed an experiment. We shot two such scenes, exchanged the close-ups ... and it became obvious that the actor's performance[s] ... were rendered completely unnoticeable by montage.
> **(Kuleshov 1974: 192)**

The Kuleshov Effect can be seen as influencing the widely disseminated belief that, 'since film acting is done in bits and pieces, a whole performance can be patched together with tricks and quick fixes' (Weston 1996: 159). However, Kuleshov later sought to dispel the common misconception that he believed actors' performances to be irrelevant (*ibid.*: 209), and authors including Cynthia Baron and Sharon Marie Carnicke have vigorously challenged the assumption that performance is 'created in the editing room' (2008: 1). Several of the actors interviewed here regard the power of the edit in a negative light, Kenneth Cope complaining: 'They can edit and cut it, and cut all your best bits out, which makes me angry ... If you've been in the business a bit of time ... you can put something in – but you can't, basically, because you get shot down if you do – which will make it enhance the thing. And it's not just a laid-on joke, it's something that comes out of the scene that makes it better' (2011).

Suzan Sylvester, who appeared in the *Quatermass Experiment* re-mount but works primarily in the theatre, finds that post-production mediation has often changed her original intention as a performer: 'TV's all about the editing ... What you do a lot of the time on tape can just not be there, or not look the way you thought.

You only need to put a little bit of music over something, or cut it in a certain way, to completely change somebody's intention of what their performance is' (2010).

Phillip Rhys, however, believes that such additions can only enhance his acting, provided the original performance is pitched correctly: 'Less is more; it's the biggest lesson that I still learn with that camera. You cannot lie, you cannot cheat, and when they add the music and they add the score and how they've shot it and your wardrobe is conveying probably already so much' (2011). Rhys's comments suggest that an actor's awareness of the additional textures that will be layered onto their performance in post-production discourage overt projection of emotion for the camera, yet the obverse of this situation is described by director Andrew Gunn, who finds that younger generations are now reluctant to provide him with even a minimal degree of performance:

> I sometimes have to really encourage actors to overplay, because they underplay so much [laughter]. I do have to say: 'I need a reaction from you,' and they say: 'I'm giving you one.' 'Well, the thing is I can't see it; it's so understated that we need a reaction.' And they go: 'Oh, it's a bit soapy to do that,' and you go: 'Well, yes, you might think it is, but if you give me just a little bit more there; just a little bit more in the eyes.' And they're sometimes quite reluctant, particularly the guys [laughter], because they want to look cool, and over-acting is not cool. And you go: 'Well, you're not over-acting; you're just acting. I need something, because I'm going to cut to you in the edit, and I need something in the face that tells me how you feel about what's happened or what's said.' You know; so it can be so understated that it barely registers.
>
> **(2011)**

Gunn's remarks would seem to contradict the Kuleshov Effect, yet it is clear that control over television performance is the province of neither actor nor director alone. For directors and editors to 'work with what they get', they must first be provided with a performance of some kind by the actor, whose offered starting point is subsequently open to moderation via the use of cutting, sound effects and music.

A sequence that appears in both the 1975 and 2008 versions of *Survivors* provides an example of how post-production can modify performance. In 'Gone Away', the third episode of the original series (recorded before the OB production model was adopted), Abby, Greg and Jenny enter a deserted supermarket in search of food. They are unnerved by the sight of a dead body hanging with the sign 'looter' attached as a warning, but Abby and Jenny continue to fill their trolleys, Greg opting to wait outside. When they attempt to exit they are stopped by three armed men who claim to be representatives of the 'provisional government', and tell the survivors that they have no right to the goods in the supermarket. The men force them at gunpoint to unload the goods from their van, until Jenny grabs one of the men's weapons, allowing her, Abby and Greg to escape with their booty intact. The entire sequence consists of both single camera exterior material and multi-camera video for the interior studio set, and lasts eleven minutes and forty-six seconds. As with all episodes of the original series, there is no use of incidental music or post-production sound effects; a result of the limited amount of time available for editing, rather than a creative choice (Cross and Priestner 2005: 36).

In episode two of the 2008 series it is Abby, Greg, Tanya and Naj who make the supermarket expedition, and the latter who discovers the body. As the group attempt to leave they are stopped at gunpoint by Dexter (Anthony Flanagan) and his posse of vigilantes, who force them to abandon their food. Unlike the original, Dexter is not affiliated with a pseudo-political group, and the survivors make no last-minute stand. This sequence is entirely single camera location film, and lasts just two minutes and five seconds; extensive use is made of non-diegetic sound.

An example of music rather than performance being used as a primary signifier is provided by the representation of the corpse's discovery in the two episodes. In 'Gone Away', Abby's sharp intake of breath is accompanied by a close-up of Carolyn Seymour covering her mouth with her hand (Figure 4.12), providing a clear signifier of shock at some (as yet) unseen sight. The camera then cuts to a shot of the dead man's feet, panning swiftly up and pausing on a shot of the sign 'Looter' and the man's dangling arm. Director Terence Williams then cuts to a high angle long shot of Abby, Greg and Jenny's reaction (Figure 4.13), the latter running to the other end of the aisle, covering her mouth and leaning over as if to vomit.

In the re-make, the lead-up to the discovery consists of a series of medium shots of Naj (Chahak Patel) riding his trolley, and a

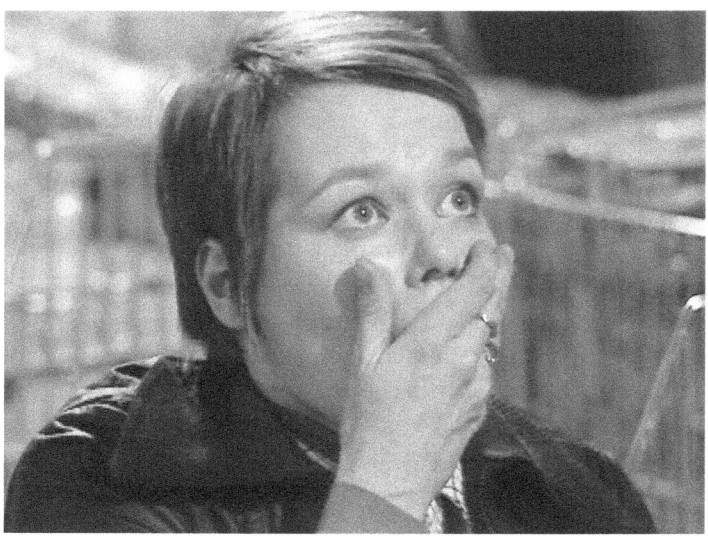

Figure 4.12 Carolyn Seymour in *Survivors*: 'Gone Away'

Figure 4.13 Ian McCulloch, Carolyn Seymour and anonymous actor in *Survivors*: 'Gone Away'

montage of jump cuts of Greg (Paterson Joseph) searching through papers in the supermarket manager's office. This is underpinned by regular, pulsing incidental music in a low register, periodically pierced by chords in a higher pitch. A sense of building menace is thus created that would not necessarily be present if this segment had a purely diegetic soundtrack; although the rapidly-cut shots of Joseph rifling through papers would provide a certain urgency, Chahak Patel's carefree actions are not suggestive of any lurking danger. At the moment Naj notices the corpse, Patel is in medium shot, staring upwards (Figure 4.14). The actor avoids any explicit reaction; instead, the musical pulse that has been building reaches a crescendo, and the revelation of the hanging looter, in a medium shot pan, is accompanied on the soundtrack by a synthesised sound effect similar to a crashing gong. As Greg arrives on the scene, the music becomes more subdued – the aftermath of the shock – continuing in a minor key and underpinned by a scurrying of strings as director Andrew Gunn cuts to a long shot of the dead man from the survivors' perspective (Figure 4.15), reinforcing the horror of the situation.

There is less explicit 'performance' in the later version of the sequence when compared with the original, in which gestures and facial expressions are used to emphasise the characters' reactions. Prior to the discovery of the looter, Abby, Greg and Jenny register their disgust at the presence of rats in the supermarket with

Figure 4.14 Chahak Patel in *Survivors*: 'Episode 2'

Figure 4.15 Julie Graham, anonymous actor, Chahak Patel and Paterson Joseph in *Survivors*: 'Episode 2'

a combination of physical reactions: Carolyn Seymour freezes, arms stiffening in shock, Ian McCulloch wrinkles his nose and grimaces, and Lucy Fleming curls her upper lip slightly as the camera pans left. As real rats were being used in the studio (and can later be seen in shot with the cast), it is possible that such reactions were entirely authentic; however, there are other moments in which physical gestures are used to augment the action. Carolyn Seymour places a hand uneasily on her stomach and Lucy Fleming covers her mouth to suggest Abby and Jenny's biliousness and nausea following sight of the corpse. In a subsequent exterior shot Ian McCulloch drums his fingers on the roof of their car, glancing around nervously and checking his watch to suggest Greg's impatience and unease.

It should not be thought, however, that such overt signifiers are limited purely to studio realism. In the original episode actor Brian Peck combines a calm, even tone as his gun-wielding character attempts to persuade Abby and company to join them, only breaking into a snarl when disarmed and held at gunpoint (Figure 4.16).

In the 2008 version, however, Dexter and his posse are more clearly coded as villains from the outset via their use of facial expression; Annie Lovett and Anthony Flanagan employ sneers to mock and intimidate Greg and Abby (Figure 4.17), making no attempt to mask or justify their actions under any kind of political ideology.

Figure 4.16 Barry Stanton and Brian Peck in *Survivors*: 'Gone Away'

Figure 4.17 Annie Lovett and Anthony Flanagan in *Survivors*: 'Episode 2'

As incidental music is added in post-production, actors usually have little idea at the time of filming how their performances are to be augmented. Given the comments of director Andrew Gunn regarding the need for actors to emote on-screen, it is notable that his use of music is more dramatic in the supermarket section, in which the cast could be said to, in his words, 'underplay' their reaction to the corpse. For the exterior scene with Dexter's mob, in which facial expressions are more clearly projecting character and mood, the score is less obvious, rumbling quietly beneath the dialogue; still sinister, yet less clearly signalling dramatic intent.

It would be erroneous to assume that modern television drama has become entirely dominated by cutting and non-diegetic additions, however. A sequence from *Doctor Who*'s opening episode, 'Rose', shows that the long take survives intact in modern location realism, allowing actors the liberation of comparatively continuous performance. In this scene, the Doctor (Christopher Eccleston) and Rose (Billie Piper) have just survived an attack in the latter's flat by the plastic arm of an alien Auton mannequin. Her curiosity piqued, Rose pursues the Doctor as he exits. The larger part of the ensuing exterior dialogue is covered by a tracking shot lasting one minute and twenty-eight seconds; the longest single take in the episode, and a late addition as a result of the script under-running (Davies 2005c).

It is interesting to compare this sequence with the parallel scene from 'An Unearthly Child' in which William Hartnell's Doctor first encounters Ian and Barbara, illustrating some of the central differences between studio and location realism. The pace of the dialogue here is much faster, with less emphasis on vocal projection. It is now common for actors to wear sensitive radio microphones, meaning that even the minimal need for projection formerly required by the overhead boom microphones is no longer such a consideration.[16] Although physical gestures are still employed, they are – at least on the part of Billie Piper – increasingly scaled down. Even though the actors are appearing in medium long shot for a widescreen frame (increasingly employed for television drama from the 2000s), Piper's hand gestures are kept largely within the lines of her body, used minimally to emphasise certain of her character's lines. When the Doctor initially refuses to answer her questions, she points with her right hand as Rose says: 'I'll go to the police; you said that if I did that I'd get people killed.' This gesture is, however, lacking in vigour, indicating the half-hearted nature of Rose's threat.

Later, Rose gestures lightly with open palms as she questions the Doctor's identity: 'Doctor *what*?', again avoiding expansive gestures. The fact that Rose is trailing behind the Doctor – both physically and in terms of understanding – means that he cannot see these actions. At one point the actress skips lightly as Rose tries to catch up with the Doctor, briefly taking him by the arm in an attempt to foster intimacy and trust on the line, 'Come on, you can tell me'.

In contrast, Eccleston strides jauntily ahead, employing a number of 'performed' gestures reflective both of the Doctor's 'otherness' and the fact that he is, in a sense, giving a performance for Rose's benefit; warning her off while simultaneously stimulating her curiosity. Examples include the brief wave and manic facial expression that he provides as his character confirms his title: 'Just "the Doctor". Hello!' These performance choices are also partly dictated by narrative agency; the need to signify the Doctor as 'other' compared to Rose, the present-day, 'normal' point of identification for viewers.

Towards the end of this sequence the plastic Auton arm that the Doctor carries is employed by both actors as an 'object of attention'; a Strasbergian Method term defined by Sharon Marie Carnicke as something within the frame which will 'direct the viewer's eye to the character's priorities' (2006: 25). Eccleston uses the limb to extend his own gestures, arms held wide open plaintively as he points out that he alone can battle the Auton threat, humans being too concerned with 'chips and telly' to be aware of the 'war' that is being conducted beneath their noses. This line again signals the Doctor's alien-ness, but proves a turning point in the conversation as Rose then reaches across to take possession of the plastic arm, signalling her willingness to listen to the Doctor's tale. This moment of narrative shift – Rose switching from curious bystander to active participant in the Doctor's world – is underpinned by Piper's gesture. Although this action is included in the shooting script (Davies *et al.* 2005: 24) – indicating that it was not a simple matter of actor choice – there are other scripted directions that do not appear, such as the Doctor and Rose pausing to smile at each other during intended moments of contact between their characters. The fact that the actors instead remain mobile throughout implies a degree of either actor or director choice in the interpretation of their written instructions, dependent on their effectiveness; some are abandoned (the physical pauses) and others retained (the taking of the arm).

Despite the fact that Eccleston and Piper are working to Russell T Davies's script, there is a sense of spontaneous reaction in their delivery of his lines – such as the facetious accusation made by each that the other believes the world revolves around them, and the repeated motif 'Sort of' – which is unfettered by considerations of post-production editing. This delivery illustrates what William Gillette termed 'the illusion of the first time': 'For an actor who knows exactly what he is going to say to behave as tho [sic] he didn't; to let his thoughts (apparently) occur to him as he goes along, even tho they are in his mind already; and (apparently) to search for and find the words by which to express those thoughts, even tho these words are at his tongue's very end' (1915: 40).

The impression in 'Rose' is not of characters delivering lines for an audience's benefit, as was more noticeable in 'An Unearthly Child', but of two people genuinely talking, listening and responding to each other in the moment. While both episodes employ realist modes of performance (for the human characters, at least) which were acceptable to their respective audiences, the more rehearsed, studio-bound style employed in 'An Unearthly Child' has become de-naturalised by the passage of time. In a detailed reading of Eccleston's performance, Matt Hills describes his combination of 'intense naturalism and disruptive moments of stylisation' (2010: 154). Hills makes the case that these tonal shifts are employed to 'convey the Doctor's human-alien duality', citing as an example the contrast between Eccleston's playful use of the Auton arm to wave goodbye to Rose and the subsequent cut to his pensive expression as he walks away (*ibid.*: 157).

The performance mode employed in this scene, which comprises a reaction to the performing environs in which the actors find themselves, with little prior preparation and minimal use of projection and gesticulation, is as near an example of location realism as can be found in the episode. It is notable, however, that it was recorded months *after* the majority of work on the episode had concluded (Davies 2005c), fitted into a subsequent production block. The shots that immediately follow it in the narrative seamlessly combine material filmed months apart in two separate locations; now common practice in television production. Most actors are, however, able to adapt to such potentially performance-dislocating schedules, as Lucy Fleming relates: 'I don't think it's a hindrance ... You can't rely so much on natural instincts, I think, because you have to have thought the story through very carefully in your head, and know where you are for each particular scene ... You kind of have to have gone through the journey in your head, or even not in your head, having done it yourself; probably without the other actors' (2010).

This is a preparation of the type that goes beyond learning lines and outlining general ideas regarding characterisation for a particular scene. Instead, the actor must maintain constant awareness of the point their character has reached in both overall and episodic through-lines and how their given circumstances have altered, adjusting the playing of objectives and super objectives accordingly. Robert Barton describes how some actors cope with the problem of out-of-sequence recording:

> Wise film actors often prepare cards for every scene ... so the actors can see the way the story should unfold. The card includes ... conditioning forces, where you've just been, what you've been doing, where you're going, what you will be doing at the end of the scene, your objective, who will be in the scene with you. Actors can grab the card and take it to the set with them so they have a sense of context.
>
> **(2009: 208)**

Jamie Payne cites *Doctor Who* guest actor David Morrissey as exemplifying the lengths actors will go to in order to prepare for out of sequence filming:

> Knowing that we're shooting out of continuity, knowing that he may get contradictory notes from a director – hopefully not – he does a thing where, per scene, he's got a notebook, and on one side he's got the scene, on the other side he's got all his thoughts related to that scene, and that's in response to what's just happened, where he's been. So if you say to David: 'We're shooting scene seventy-six from episode two,' he goes to his own, 'This is what I think's going on.'
>
> **(2011)**

It is for this reason that Denis Lawson prefers to carry his full-length script with him on the set, rather than 'sides' (one-sheet versions of the scene to be shot) provided by the production crew:

> I want to have my full script with me at all times, because ten to one during rehearsals, or just as we're running up to a take, I'll want to check where exactly this scene comes in the narrative. When did the audience last see me? How long is it since they've seen me? ... If we're doing a series, it could have been a week since they've had certain information. What was my emotional state like in the previous scenes? Where is my character going after this scene? A dozen different questions that can't be answered by sides.
>
> **(2014: 62–63)**

A sequence from the *Doctor Who* episode 'Dalek' presents an example of how accustomed actors have become to out-of-sequence filming. Work began on 25 October 2004 at the National Museum of Wales, before moving to Cardiff's Millennium Stadium between 26 October and 3 November. Production moved to the series' base of Unit Q2 studio in Newport on 4, 5 and 8 November, and filming concluded on 23 and 26 November (Sullivan 2009). Although this schedule allowed Christopher Eccleston and Billie Piper a loose continuity to their characters' through-lines for the episode, they were obliged to film their opening and closing scenes on the same day, while on 23 November they were also filming studio scenes for the later episode 'Father's Day'. Such a schedule meant that the actors had to switch between scenes from two different episodes that were separated in transmission terms by a third, 'The Long Game', which had yet to be filmed. In addition, several of Eccleston's key dialogues were recorded in separate halves, the actor having in effect to perform his lines to thin air, rather than reacting to another performer in real time and creating the organic sense of developing conversation found in the earlier tracking shot with Billie Piper.

Mid-way through the episode, there is a sequence in which the Doctor and his Dalek adversary converse via a television monitor. Having just watched the latter wipe out an entire security force, the Doctor has little sympathy for his foe as it reflects that it is now the last of its species. In response to the Dalek's plaintive cry: 'Where shall I get my orders now?', Eccleston's face twists with rage in what seems a spontaneous and immediate reaction to the Dalek's plea, the actor's chin inadvertently flecked with spittle as he exhorts it to self-destruct.

However, Dalek voice artist Nicholas Briggs later recalled that his and Eccleston's halves of the exchange were recorded entirely separately, Eccleston requesting an additional rehearsal of the lines on set with Briggs prior to recording his section (Briggs 2005). The shooting schedule suggests that Briggs's segments in the Millennium Stadium were completed first, in which case Eccleston might have been able to 'react' to already-filmed shots of the Dalek being played into the screen on the office set. However, Eccleston and the monitor are never clearly seen in shot together, suggesting that a finished 'edit' of the Dalek's dialogue from the monitor's perspective was not played in during Eccleston's lines. In this case the actor would instead have had to select a visual focal point for his eye-line, the majority of his shots being in medium close-up or close-up, meaning that his reactions were in no way a genuinely immediate response to a real-time conversation. Even if Briggs was sitting in the same room, reading his lines (as seems possible), the effect would not be equal to that of Eccleston facing the full Dalek prop. This absence, a direct result of the exigencies of staggered shooting schedules and location availability, requires an additional leap of imagination on Eccleston's part in order to attain the emotional pitch that his performance ultimately reaches, literally spitting out the line 'Why don't you just die?'

Scenes such as this illustrate a need for increased focus as actors are called upon to visualise and react to characters and environments which at the time of filming exist only in their mind's eye. Such requirements are increasingly informing the mode of drama training provided in Britain, which has increasingly begun to intersect with technology.

Training and technology

As seen throughout this book, the determinants of television acting develop at different rates, and are constantly changing in their relation to each other. British drama training since the 1980s has changed significantly in two key respects: the increased visibility in the curricula of Stanislavski; and the extent to which technology – and in particular acting for the screen – has come to the fore. However, these advances did not take place at the same time, acting for the camera only having come to prominence in the 2000s.

Having penetrated drama schools in the 1950s and 1960s only very gradually – and often by stealth – the work of Stanislavski became increasingly prominent in the 1980s, finally being trumpeted in RADA's official prospectus in 1988 (RADA 1988: 4). In addition, the abstracted form of his work that comprised the Method was also now being taught, as Andrew Tiernan recalls of his arrival at the Drama Centre in 1984:

> For 21 years Doreen Cannon had [adhered] to the traditional Stanislavskian codes, and for the first year of our three-year course we enjoyed learning about them in her classes; simple exercises like 'life or death' through simple improvisation to 'playing an action'. I don't know what went on at board level, maybe the school's directors could see that younger generations of actors and actresses were as much influenced by film and TV as they were by any ambitions to work in weekly rep in the theatre. Suddenly we were working with Doreen's replacement, Rueven Adiv, who had studied the Method under Stella Adler and Lee Strasberg at [the] Actors Studio. From that point on, our training was based on this more modern approach. More Strasberg and Adler I would say than pure Stanislavski. The emphasis was on transformation and becoming the character through object exercises and emotional and affective memories, which are used as devices to trigger reactions relating to the scene. Research and character histories were also important as well, and this valuable discipline was designed to give us all we needed before we could start even preparing for the role!
>
> (2011)

Tiernan is emphatic that this training prepared him equally well for stage and screen: 'It taught me to understand the character and the text and to do my homework. The training prepared me to work all hours and not complain and to expect the unexpected' (*ibid.*). Julia Dalkin, who trained in Glasgow the following decade, agrees that Stanislavski's techniques are equally applicable to theatre and television: 'Sense memory and stuff like that, that I think are invaluable even to TV, because TV is very realistic, and you might draw on things that happen to you to create tears, or to create a mood, or to fall in love with somebody that you find very ugly [laughter], that I would also use in theatre' (2010).

This generation of actors, who emerged in the late 1980s and 1990s, clearly feel that television work is a matter of adapting their stage training, Dalkin stating: 'A lot of actors say it's a bit like driving a car; you learn doing it' (*ibid.*). This 'learning by doing' approach was, however, the only option available to such actors given the continuing paucity of screen training at drama schools. After the false start of limited multi-camera input in the 1960s, the majority of academies continued to focus solely on theatre skills. Suzan Sylvester describes the minimal television input provided at the Central School of Speech and Drama between 1981 and 1984:

> I think the only time we did some screen work was either the end of the second year or the beginning of the third year ... It wasn't even called TV Work; Camera Work or something. [It was] about twenty minutes in total on screen, and apart from one producer person who was in the TV studio editing as he went along, the people on camera were stage managers from school, who equally hadn't come to drama school to become cameramen. I mean, we certainly could have done with a lot more of it ... there wasn't enough. I think it made you feel that there was a gulf of difference between the two, and I still feel that way; I still don't feel qualified to be a TV performer.
>
> **(2010)**

Even a decade later, at Webber Douglas, Kemal Sylvester received minimal preparation for the screen:

> In two years we did two weekend workshops in TV acting, and that was in the last few terms, I seem to recall. And it always seemed ludicrous ... Even if you actually knew it or not, the fact is that most people coming out of drama school will be doing a lot of TV stuff, and even if they're doing plays as well, the only way to earn any money is to do the TV stuff. So I did think it was mired a bit in the past.
>
> **(2010)**

One of the few institutions equipped to teach acting for the camera was the Royal Scottish Academy of Music and Drama in Glasgow. While former student Denis Lawson, who attended in the 1960s, regarded himself as fortunate to have gained experience in several multi-camera productions (2014: 7), by the 1990s the effectiveness of such training had lessened, according to Julia Dalkin:

> We had about two, two-week courses of TV in the whole three years. Because, apparently, they were just making more money renting it out. But then, having said that, people who I knew who were training at other schools weren't getting any, so I was getting four weeks more than other schools at the time. But to be honest with you, the people that taught us were a guy that had worked in STV comedy and was retired ... and his wife, who had been a dancer and kept going into first position and swinging her legs about ... So as far as TV acting was concerned, I was learning really over the top sitcom, and I can't even think if I know what I would relate it to. It was bad. Bad; I mean, the only things that I did learn were things like ... hitting your mark, and technical things, not being late to set, but the actual style of acting, TV acting, I don't think I learnt much about.
>
> **(2010)**

Such a set-up, focusing on the multi-camera technique still favoured for sitcom, had little practical application to the single camera that by now predominated in television drama. According to Charlie Higson, who was casting for *Randall and Hopkirk (Deceased)* in the late 1990s, many emerging drama graduates of this time were ill-suited to television work: 'You have to know how to act for the screen, which means: more real, less projection, more nuance ... And a lot of those people, when they come out of drama school, are unemployable on TV; they're too big, too "stagey"' (2010). The National Council for Drama Training subsequently found that 'drama school graduates seem unanimous in their view that their first television jobs were terrifying because they knew so little of how the process works, of who was in the crew, of what was expected of them' (NCDT 2002: 9). Actors' Institute graduate Sasha Oakley was 'paranoid about being too big for the camera' when cast in *The Bill* (ITV, 1984–2010): 'I learned it was all about scale, but you suddenly discover that you use your hands a lot and your facial muscles go crazy!' (cited in Martland 2002). Oakley's comments regarding her sudden increased awareness of hand movements demonstrate the extent to which television acting had scaled down, but reinforce Charlie Higson's assertion that drama school graduates in the late 1990s and early 2000s were simply 'too big'.

In recent years more appropriate camera training has begun to be provided. As a result, directors such as Jamie Payne have noted a greater facility for screen work in British drama graduates; increasingly important now that auditions themselves are videotaped and circulated as part of the casting process:

> Younger actors are more multi-media aware; they're aware of this whole thing like pushing themselves on tape, they're aware of the camera's presence ... In casting now we have video cameras running on every cast interview ... It's been the case since I've been directing, which is ten years, but apparently before that it was very rare. So there's a generation of actors which were at their height before that [who] would not be used to a camera being in the casting situation.
>
> **(2011)**

For *Doctor Who* director Colin Teague, this increased ease in front of the camera is a direct result of training:

> I think there's a different sort of training that's taken place over the last ten or fifteen years, actually, and I see a lot of that with students at RADA, as well. I mean, their confidence and their ability now – what they get trained on – is very different ... Back then there was no such thing as doing any work to camera, or even preparing for auditions, you know. Now that's pretty much there from day one; you're working with the camera, you're looking back on yourselves, you're preparing yourselves for these meetings and how you are in the room. I mean, it's amazing.
>
> **(2011)**

According to actor Denis Lawson, however, British drama schools are only tackling television acting 'with varying degrees of success ... I'm sorry to say that I spent a day not too long ago in a very well-established drama school and was shocked by some of the "advice" the students had been given by a director' (2014: 5).

Although opinions differ as to when exactly camera training came to the fore,[17] former LAMDA Principal Peter James claims that 'all drama courses worth talking about now have a strand of screen acting' (2011). This more comprehensive grounding means students are now able to make their own films, while secondments to working studios and sets help familiarise them with the technological environment (*ibid.*).

However, familiarity with the camera is only one technological aspect that television actors must consider. Of arguably equal importance is the voice, the required projection of which has diminished as audio technology becomes more advanced. The importance of recording equipment has been highlighted by Jacob Smith, who claims the development of radio and microphone technology in the twentieth century as being of equal importance in performance terms to the film camera (2008: 95). According to Denis Lill, this trend has now reached its apotheosis:

> There's a whole new generation of actors coming up who presumably have been taught by their drama schools that they don't actually have to project; that they don't have to push their voice or anything like that. Whereas myself and other actors of my generation will actually probably give it a little more vocal pressure than one might normally do when one is speaking in an ordinary conversational context. I've had to go to some of these kids and say: 'Look, you're just going to have to bring it up a bit, because at my age I can't actually hear when my cue's coming up.' [Laughter] And they say: 'Well, what's the point in speaking up when you've got a microphone right in front of us?' Highly sensitive; it will pick up every little whisper, you know.
>
> (2010)

According to Denis Lawson, the sophistication of recording equipment means that actors only need increase the volume of their speaking voice by degrees: 'If I'm asked to lift the volume up a bit before a take by the sound recordist ... it will be an infinitesimal rise. I will not suddenly start projecting ... all we need to do is squeeze it up a fraction' (2014: 45).

Modern television actors are evidently less reliant on the vocal projection traditionally taught and required for stage work, as Louise Jameson states: 'These kids that go straight into soap [are] very ill-equipped, when they come out, to deal with any classical text, or simply to be able to fill a room with their voice' (2011). While similarly emphasising the need for audibility, Phillip Rhys makes a distinction between the level of projection employed for stage and screen:

> If an actor cannot be heard – whether on stage, screen, on television – he's not doing his job. You need to be able to convey these

emotions; you have to bring the life of all these words onto the page, regardless of training. But [there is] the whole thing of this voice acting that on stage you can get away with ... In places they do the correct intonation in their voice to convey emotion, they assume a position, and they think that's it; which you can't get away with on screen.

(2011)

Despite the increased sophistication of microphones, it is often necessary for actors to re-record their lines in post-production. David Tennant, who in 2005 took the lead role in *Doctor Who*, described this ADR[18] process while commenting on a scene from the 2006 episode 'School Reunion', in which his dialogue with guest actor Anthony Head required re-dubbing due to sound interference from the swimming pool area in which they performed:

[You're] basically lip-synching to yourself. It's something that most actors hate having to do, because you just feel like the scene kind of slips away from you a little bit, as you're not actually in the moment; trying to mimic yourself as you were in that moment ... It's one of those skills that you kind of have to learn, because often the most intimate of emotional scenes are ... the ones you have to re-do.

(2006)

Denis Lawson, however, sees ADR as an opportunity to improve his performance: 'You may find there's a phrase or a line that you want to try in a different way from the original take. The director may suggest something, or it may occur to you on the spur of the moment' (2014: 118).

The fact that the use of ADR for the above scene in 'School Reunion' is undetectable on first viewing illustrates the skill of the actors involved, who need to think themselves back into and replicate an earlier moment of performance; another example of modern production techniques requiring the performer to (re)position themselves in their character's through-line.

ADR is now common practice, but an area more particular to *Doctor Who* is its extensive use of visual effects. This requires a particularly imaginative approach on the part of its cast, who are often called upon to act with artificial characters or environments. For Christopher Eccleston, such work is all part of an actor's repertoire: 'Acting to green screen's imagining; it's just like being a kid again. And I enjoy the challenge. If I'm supposed to be speaking to a six foot two alien and in fact I'm speaking to a yard brush, if I can pull that off then that's what I did all those years training for, and it's all acting, and it's all good' (Eccleston 2005b). Guest actor Simon Callow also saw visual effects work as an extension of his Drama Centre training: 'They're [a] real drama school exercise, actually ... you've got to imagine, you've got to see it, somehow' (Callow 2005).

A sequence from the series one episode 'Father's Day' provides an example of actors utilising their imaginations to react to something that, until post-production, simply isn't there. In this episode, Rose has convinced the Doctor to take her back to the year 1986, when her father Pete (Shaun Dingwall) was killed in a car accident. Unable to stand by and watch, Rose pushes her father out of the path of the car which should have killed him, creating a time paradox. As a result, winged flying creatures known as Reapers are unleashed, attacking attendees at the wedding to which Pete was en route.

The on-screen visualisation of the Reapers via CGI is impressively realistic (Figure 4.18), but at the time of filming all the cast had to focus on in representation of their attackers was an unsophisticated stand-in prop, as Shaun Dingwall relates: 'We're all imagining different things, but basically what you're seeing is some bloke with a long pole with a bit of gaffer tape stuck on it. And that's what you look at, and you have to react to, and that's hard. You know; a grown man and you start reacting to monsters that aren't even there. It's quite strange' (Dingwall 2005). In such circumstances, it is a testament to the flexibility of the actors involved that their reactions are so convincing (Figure 4.19).

Once again, this fantastical element of telefantasy acting complicates the notion of studio and location realism as a pure binary. Rather than reacting to their performing environs, these actors are responding to purely imagined circumstances; not so much suspending disbelief as extending their belief in situations and characters which exist only in their mind's eye. This is not the *un*realism of the type displayed by William Hartnell and Carole Ann Ford in 'An Unearthly Child', when they were performing alien characters; rather, actors such as Billie Piper and Shaun Dingwall are striving to

Figures 4.18 and 4.19 Billie Piper in *Doctor Who*: 'Father's Day'

provide realistic responses to an unreal (in fact, non-existent) situation. For *Doctor Who*, this continues a long-standing use of Colour Separation Overlay (or CSO), an early version of the green screen process, which the series pioneered from the 1970s. The challenge of working with the imagined/imaginary is therefore nothing new.

The fact that experienced actors such as Simon Callow and Christopher Eccleston cite these working conditions as a practical application of their acting training contradicts the stance adopted by David Lavery in his article 'What's My Motivation? The Method Goes Fantastic in Television Acting'. Citing the extraordinary narrative situations in which actors are forced to perform for such programmes as *Buffy the Vampire Slayer* (The WB/UPN, 1997–2003) and *Terminator: The Sarah Connor Chronicles* (Fox, 2008–9), Lavery questions the practical application of Stanislavski-derived acting techniques: 'How do you prepare, as an actor, for something like that? What instructions could a director give? What method would suffice?' (2011). However, Lavery overlooks the important point that, via the use of such principles as emotion memory (for example recalling a horrific or horrifying sight or experience) and adaptation (applying it to the imagined circumstance), actors can make their characters' emotional reactions to the 'fantastic' as 'truthful' as they would be to more acceptably terrestrial (i.e. non-fantasy) threats. This recalls Matt Hills' appropriation of Ien Ang's concept of 'emotional realism' when examining the new series' efforts to add soap-style psychological depth to its characters. In Hills' example this is represented by Rose's desire to stay in touch with mother Jackie while travelling the universe with the Doctor; a realistic, human response in a fantastic, unreal scenario (2010: 100). Ang originally outlined this concept in *Watching Dallas: Soap Opera and the Melodramatic Imagination* (1985): 'the same things, people, relations and situations which are regarded at the denotative level as unrealistic, and unreal, are at a connotative level apparently not seen as unreal, but in fact as "recognizable"' (42). This applies equally to actors striving to provide realistic, 'recognizable' responses to the unreal scenarios in which their characters find themselves. As Phillip Rhys points out:

> The actor's process may be different, but the objective is the same: to live truthfully under imaginary circumstances ... The use of the actor's imagination is also vital when creating a character. One can't always experience the life you're portraying – heroin addict and serial killer come to mind – but the actor can use the imaginary 'as if', to live truthfully under the imaginary circumstances. My teacher would say: 'If you can kill a fly, you can play Othello.'
>
> **(2011)**

Such use of the imagination, as represented by the increased amount of effects work employed in film and television, requires actors to react to given circumstances based entirely in the arena of the fantastic. While *Doctor Who* was an early adopter of CSO, the increasing prominence of such technology illustrates yet again the constantly developing working conditions of television performers.

Actor experience and generational differences

Actor experience with regard to television performance is less a question of type as of quantity and duration. While theatre provided a common starting ground for television actors well into the 1970s, Robert Barton has observed that 'more and more frequently, actors are onscreen before they are onstage' (2009: 207). Whereas *Doctor Who*'s Christopher Eccleston worked extensively in the theatre before finding film success in *Let Him Have It* (1991), colleague Billie Piper did not make her professional stage debut, in Christopher Hampton's *Treats*, until 2007; a year after she left *Doctor Who*. Trevor Rawlins has pointed out that 'in many cases professional [British] actors today rarely, if ever, work in the theatre' (2010: 3), and in a 2010 feature on up-and-coming British actors, Gerard Gilbert stated that 'theatre – the West End, at least – is something to be done once you've arrived' (2010: 13).

With television now the arena in which actors are likely to work, the most relevant focus with regard to performance style is the era in which they began their careers, and the production practices and performing conventions to which they became accustomed. Andrew Gunn's earlier comments regarding the minimal facial projection employed by some younger actors, combined with Denis Lill's observations on use of the voice, make it clear that generational differences exist. The decline of the rehearsal period means that some actors who began their careers in the era of studio realism find the swift execution of modern productions somewhat disorientating, as noted by Mark Gatiss: 'They can get a bit flustered by the fact that ... they haven't met anyone properly, or they haven't established any kind of rapport. I mean, you must mix into that of course every actor's favourite hobby, which is moaning; that's a different part of the equation. But yes, I've noticed a big [generational] difference' (2011). Whereas studio realism was flexible enough to accommodate actors who did not necessarily conform to its conventions, as exemplified by Talfryn Thomas in *Survivors*, modern location realism is more likely to marginalise those who do not – or cannot – adapt. Questioned over the need for actors to prepare characterisations in advance, rather than in extended discussions with the director or showrunner on set, where the clock is always ticking on very tight schedules, *Survivors* showrunner Adrian Hodges stated:

> I think one would expect actors to do that as a matter of course, and the vast majority do. But sometimes the on-set rehearsals throw up unanticipated problems that have to be resolved before the actors can move forward with the scene. That can be time consuming and frustrating and is never ideal, but if the actor can't work something out it has to be dealt with, no matter how long it takes. But of course every director would prefer to work with actors who are well prepared and come to the set with the arc of their character in the scene pretty well thought through in advance.
>
> **(2011)**

In the time-pressurised environment of modern television production, directors are more likely to cast actors whom they know are able to cope, as Jamie Payne points out: 'Budgets are dropping; the machine still needs to deliver the drama, so the actors are relying on their default position. And if you've got brilliant casts ... then you know that their default position is going to be pretty bloody good' (2011).

However, Payne has also observed a discipline in older actors that is occasionally lacking in their younger colleagues:

> How you relate to the company – the cast and the crew around you – is different between generations. The older generation you'll find are very rarely if ever late. Their attitude to company, and all the responsibilities of being a leading artist, are thorough and complete and brilliant. This is a generalisation – not for every actor – but I've noticed a lot in the younger generation, they have to learn that respect, and they kind of kick and scream their way through it.
>
> **(Ibid.)**

Actress Lucy Fleming believes this has more to do with modern distractions of the kind to which older actors were simply not exposed in their youth: 'When I started filming or doing television people didn't have mobile phones. Nowadays, if you're rehearsing or something and the person is maybe fiddling with a mobile phone or texting, it's a different sort of feel' (2010). However, for Payne the difference runs deeper:

> I did a drama recently with a combination of a very young cast, and a very established, respected older cast. And between takes, and between set-ups, with the older cast you'd have considered discussion about where the character is, and the quiet and calm you need to prepare for the rush of going straight to the next scene. One of

the younger cast, who had a predominantly lead part, would just pick up the latest biography they were reading. And basically their motivation for getting into the business – [he] wasn't aware of who any of the other actors were – is different; there's this immediate fame thing, which comes from being a TV star. Their motives are different, whereas when I went to drama school you'd know who all those actors were. The craft of it [is] less studied now, and it's actually less encouraged. You know, the contemporaries you need to know about, or the actors, are the ones doing the stuff you're interested in. And I think that's a shame, and that's affected it; it has a permutated effect on acting styles.

(2011)

Andrew Tiernan concurs that 'generally, people aren't as educated anymore and they don't research' (2011), but not all actors agree, Patrick Malahide stating:

I'm hugely impressed by the younger generation of actors, and my contemporaries will strike me down but I think they take it actually a lot more seriously than we did. I mean, I've just finished *Hamlet* at the National and it's full of youngsters, a lot of them playing tiny parts or just playing mercenaries, just contributing to the feel of this tyrannical court, and they just took it really seriously and had an intellectual framework because of their training, which I've never had. So no, I don't think there is a generational difference, except to say that they're probably better trained and better equipped for the real world.

(2011)

Malahide is speaking here of actors working in a prestigious stage production rather than a one-off episode of a television series, and it is possible that questions of status in terms of the work being done are also at play. However, despite her views regarding technical distractions, Lucy Fleming agrees that many younger television actors are extremely hard-working: 'You have to be disciplined in order to get through something like *Casualty*, where you're doing different episodes in the same day, and connect back to back, inside out; you have to do your homework' (2010).

Discipline aside, a notable difference between modern television performers and their studio era predecessors is the decline in Received Pronunciation. Once a requirement of any television actor, real or adopted RP has now become, if anything, a disadvantage, as original *Doctor Who* director Waris Hussein affirms: 'Friends of mine, because they went to university and have posh accents, they won't get employed' (2011). With an increase in the prevalence of regional accents on television, the mimicking and putting on of accents has become less common, according to Kemal Sylvester: 'There's no real point in casting someone who is trying to do a Birmingham accent when there's two thousand actors from Birmingham out there' (2010). According to Jamie Payne, such decisions are a direct result of increased pressures of time:

> You usually cast them within the first five minutes of when they walk in the room, and you're almost never going to go: 'Oh, I can see they could be northern' ... Asking an actor to do an accent on these schedules, they're often having to think through the dialect before they're starting to act. And on these schedules I just don't think you've got time to go again for dialect.
>
> (2011)

This shift in the acceptable use of voice is reflected in *Doctor Who* by Christopher Eccleston's decision to utilise his real Salford voice, providing a marked contrast with the RP of previous incumbents – including William Hartnell and Liverpudlian Tom Baker. The actor explained his choice thus: 'The defining characteristics of *Doctor Who* to a certain extent are heroism and intelligence, and they seem to be being equationed wrong [sic] with RP, Received Pronunciation; that that was the sole area, really. I felt that it was time, along with the sexism, for that to be kicked out' (Eccleston 2005a). The actor was clearly keen to mark out his working-class origins as distinct from those of former Doctors: 'These authority figures, lecturing me in their upper-middle-class accents. It seemed like everyone in outer space came from Surrey, rather than Salford, where I grew up' (*ibid.*). Like Eccleston, semi-regulars Noel Clarke and Camille Coduri employed their real voices as Rose's working class boyfriend, Mickey Smith, and mother Jackie, while as Rose the Swindon-born Billie Piper was alone in adapting her voice, utilising dropped aitches to mimic the East London accent.

Interestingly, when Eccleston was replaced by David Tennant, the Scottish actor did not use his real voice, instead adopting an 'estuary' English that made his incarnation less geographically specific, without coding him as 'posh' and risking the alienation of a broader cultural demographic. This decision, however, was made not by the actor but by executive producer Russell T Davies, Tennant later admitting: 'I never thought to question it ... I spend half my life not using my own voice, so it doesn't bother me at all' (cited in Russell 2006: 58). Such a move indicates a continuing place in British television drama for the (skilful) mimicking of accent, though the increased use of real regional voice indicates that the more contrived putting on of *The Quatermass Experiment*'s Iris Ballard fifty years earlier is no longer acceptable. In addition, while both Tennant and Eccleston have demonstrated their ability to produce Received Pronunciation in other roles, many younger actors now lack this capacity, as Kevin McNally laments:

> I'm starting to sound like a terrible old fart, but a lot of young people come out of drama school who, for me, I can not only not understand, they have speech impediments, or they actually can't speak ... I was asked by a friend of mine to meet a young, fourteen-year-old boy who wanted to know how to get on in the business, and was plainly just looking for short-cuts, and I said, 'I think you'd be good at drama school; I think your voice needs it.' Well, he was so offended that I thought his voice might need a bit of work; he felt he was absolutely ready to go ... Some young actors say: 'I don't wanna be like that,' and I always say to them: 'Yeah, but wouldn't you like to be considered for more roles?'
>
> **(2010)**

The obverse of this particular coin is that older actors who still focus on voice rather than internal characterisation are seen as somewhat archaic by younger generations – though they can still attract a certain admiration, according to Julia Dalkin: '[There are] a lot of people who act with their voice, and that's pretty much all; there's a few of those. And the thing is, I like listening to them because they've usually got a really beautiful voice [laughter]' (2010). Such generational differences, however, can also extend to use of the body: 'They can often be quite commanding physically; there's something about their posture, the way they hold themselves, but then they start acting, and the acting isn't necessarily dreadful, but it's certainly of a style' (*ibid.*).

Despite the weight of observation presented here that indicates distinct approaches and acting styles resulting from generational differences, director Andrew Gunn believes the majority of actors working in television today have simply adapted to circumstances:

> Most actors of any generation these days are aware of how quickly you have to work, and that they won't get an awful lot of opportunity for take after take after take ... So everybody comes in prepared for that, and I always make sure that I say: 'It's going to be a really busy day, and we're going to be flat out, and you're going to have to be patient, because we're going to be working quickly.' ... And they go: 'Oh yeah, it's just like that now, isn't it?' And that's why it gets done, because everybody's in the same team, on the same side; most of the time.
>
> (2011)

For director Richard Clark, the question of generational difference does not even arise: 'They can all be of an older generation and all trained, and you'll find that they all have completely different working practices and approaches ... Some actors deliver on the first take; some actors, they get going for the third take, and would ideally have [more] time. Every actor has a different approach, and that's just the way it is' (2011).

As noted by Adrian Hodges, 'the general trend in television has been towards younger casts' (2011), and it is possible that modern directors simply have less experience of working with older actors. Although series such as *Midsomer Murders* (ITV, 1997–) and *New Tricks* (BBC, 2003–15) have provided greater employment opportunities for mature performers, such programmes are in the minority. The trend in modern television drama is for more youthful casts, as Mark Gatiss observes: '*Doctor Who* uses less [sic] people of that age ... They tend to be a younger guest cast, so they won't have come from that tradition; they'll be actually more informed by television themselves. So it's just a different energy' (2011). In the first series of *Doctor Who* and *Survivors*, only Christopher Eccleston, Camille Coduri, Paterson Joseph and Julie Graham were aged above forty, and none were over forty-three. As a result, scenes demonstrating the interaction of different generations are somewhat limited, though *Doctor Who* featured guest roles for a handful of more senior actors, including Simon Callow and Richard Wilson. In 'The Empty Child', the latter has a brief but key expositional role as Doctor Constantine, who in the Blitz of 1941 maintains a hospital ward populated by eerie patients with gas masks seemingly welded to their faces. Although Constantine is on screen for mere minutes, his conversation with Eccleston's Doctor provides essential clues to the developing narrative, and Wilson, at this time best known to television viewers as curmudgeonly Victor Meldrew in sitcom *One Foot in the Grave* (BBC, 1990–2001), offers a useful representative of an acting generation who emerged when studio realism was predominant, as compared with Christopher Eccleston, whose television career began in the early 1990s.

In a moment somewhat reminiscent of William Hartnell in 'An Unearthly Child', Constantine makes a notable 'entrance' from stage left, tottering into the ward on his walking stick in medium long shot. Director James Hawes then cuts between medium long shots in which either Constantine (Figure 4.20) or the Doctor face the camera, allowing the opening segment of the script to be played through twice in its entirety; once for each camera. Each actor maintains the continuity of delivery and reaction necessary to edit seamlessly between the two takes, but the use of a medium shot of the Doctor, in which Constantine is clearly not present when spatially he should be (Figure 4.21), makes clear the exigencies for Eccleston of a location shoot on which actor Richard Wilson was available for one day only (Moffat 2005b).

From the moment Constantine seats himself, the focus is more firmly on the Doctor, examining the mask-wearing patients in

Figure 4.20 Christopher Eccleston and Richard Wilson in *Doctor Who*: 'The Doctor Dances'

Figure 4.21 Christopher Eccleston in *Doctor Who*: 'The Doctor Dances'

cutaways while Constantine remains largely motionless, responding to his queries with only the slightest inclination of his head. It is interesting at this point to recall Julia Dalkin's comments regarding 'voice' actors, as Wilson, from his seated position, manages to maintain his character's prominence in the scene – which could easily have been dominated at this point by the Doctor's energetic movements, gabbled observations and surmises – even when limited by the script to at times monosyllabic responses. Wilson's voice, his native Scots accent filtering through the Received Pronunciation of his RADA training, commands attention as he maintains his frozen posture, providing a clarity and resonance born of the theatre – or of voice training – without amplifying or enunciating his lines to the extent that he seems to be projecting. His sole physical movement comes in reaction to the Doctor's observation that all the patients have a gash on their hands, as he moves his head downwards to glance at his own maimed paw.

A body double was used for the subsequent sequence in which Constantine undergoes his own transformation into a gas-masked victim (*ibid.*), but Wilson's brief appearance demonstrates Andrew Gunn's assertion regarding the extent to which seasoned actors are able to adapt to the demands of modern filming processes, while still providing thoroughly rounded characterisations. However, it is notable that the few such appearances in *Doctor Who* by more senior actors typically feature them as either historical period or futuristic characters, as if signifying that their – arguably more traditional – performance approach is better suited to roles in some way outside accepted contemporary norms. Even when older actors are featured as modern-day characters, as with Bernard Cribbins and June Whitfield's appearances in the 2009 episode 'The End of Time – Part 1', they are presented as endearing eccentrics. This follows the trend, long-established in Hollywood, of casting older female stars as 'grotesques'; according to Anne Morey, a form of back-handed compliment: 'Presentation as grotesque was often an acknowledgement of … artistic effort and ability to perform at the margins' (2011: 104). The extent to which Cribbins' character, Wilf Mott, can be considered 'grotesque' or 'marginal' is debatable; initially introduced as a minor character in Christmas special 'The Voyage of the Damned', he was later featured more prominently as companion Donna Noble's (Catherine Tate) grandfather, and ultimately plays a significant – and heroic – role in David Tennant's final adventure. This is balanced by Whitfield's casting as Wilf's friend Minnie 'the Menace' Hooper, whose continuing sexual appetite is played for comic relief, thus drawing upon the actress's sitcom pedigree.[19] Extending Morey's reading to older British actors, *Doctor Who*'s senior castings could perhaps be taken as an acknowledgement of the demands such 'eccentric' roles make upon the creative capacities of the performer, to which more seasoned actors are better able to respond – male and female alike.

Reception

Launched in a blaze of publicity, *Doctor Who* was the focus of much media attention. Showrunner Russell T Davies and lead actor Christopher Eccleston in particular were placed under the spotlight, and in interviews each stressed the new programme's realist approach, despite the fantastical nature of its narrative. Both focused on the programme's more visually cinematic approach, Eccleston claiming that it was the original's 'low production values' that had prevented him from 'believing it was real' (cited in Middleton 2005: 3). However, the awareness that *Doctor Who* was traditionally regarded as a children's programme was also highlighted, Eccleston stating: 'If you make good television for children, the adults will come' (Eccleston 2005a). Davies, meanwhile, echoed predecessor Verity Lambert in his comments on children's expectations of the small screen: 'The youngest audience is more sophisticated in the television it watches. It wants more drama, it wants more emotion; it wants more honesty, and it wants more truth. Simple pictorial thrills are not enough anymore' (Davies 2005a).

Doctor Who was an immediate success, winning audiences of between 6.81 and 10.81 million over its first year (Russell 2006: 139). Eccleston and Piper's performances were singled out for praise by viewers in the *Radio Times*, Hyder Ali Pirwany writing: 'Brilliant *Doctor Who*. Brilliant Christopher Eccleston. Brilliant Billie Piper. Thank you, BBC TV – you've made me young again' (2005: 9). Dave Symes similarly proclaimed Eccleston 'superb', while praising Piper, 'who I didn't expect to be up to the job' (2005: 9); indicative of the widespread perception of the former pop star as a singer rather than an actress, despite her training at the Sylvia Young drama school and an acclaimed appearance in *Canterbury Tales* (BBC, 2003). Critical response was also favourable, though some reservations were expressed regarding the tonal variations of Eccleston's performance, the *Sunday Times*' A.A. Gill stating 'He's an intense, naturalistic actor with a dangerous edge; being a pre-watershed alien with quirky bits isn't really playing to his strengths' (cited in Mellor 2015). Though Patrick Mulkern in the *Radio Times* agreed Eccleston did not always convince in the Doctor's frivolous moments, 'I love the blend of muscularity and sensitivity he brings to the role' (*ibid.*). It is possible that critics were not prepared to see an actor such as Eccleston – whose casting has been read by both Matt Hills (2010) and James Chapman (2013) as an attempt to reposition *Doctor Who* as 'quality' television drama – performing such comparatively manic comedy moments. Recalling his time on the series a decade later, Eccleston himself admitted that he had 'over-pitched' the comedy; 'If I had my time again, I would do the comedy very, very differently – but I think where I did possibly succeed was in the tortured stuff – surprise surprise!' (cited in Jeffery 2015). Billie Piper was, however, unanimously praised, hailed as a 'revelation' by *Digital Spy*'s Dek Hogan, and she and Eccleston subsequently won Most Popular Actress and Actor at the National Television Awards, in addition to being nominated for several others, including the BAFTA Cymru and the Broadcasting Press Guild. This would suggest that both actors' realisation of their characters was more than acceptable to contemporary audiences and critics.

Interestingly, the reception of *Survivors*, with its arguably less fantasy-based *mise-en-scène*, was comparatively muted. Television critic Alison Graham's lambasting of the programme's 'predictable TV archetypes' (cited in Cross 2010: 155) seemed aimed as much at the writing as the acting, though *Digital Spy*'s Ben Rawson-Jones praised the consistency of the performances, singling out Max Beesley 'for creating such a compelling anti-hero in Tom Price' (Rawson-Jones 2008a), and stating that Phillip Rhys and Chahak Patel 'deserve huge plaudits for their emotive acting' (2008b). With ratings of between 4.2 and 6.5 million (Cross 2010: 154) *Survivors* was successful enough to be renewed for a second series, though following its transmission the programme was cancelled in April 2010. Certainly the lack of specific criticism of the cast would seem to indicate that their performances were not a major factor in its comparatively poor reception, and are as representative of television acting in the late 2000s as any production can be.

Conclusion

The conditions that originally contributed to the emergence of studio realism have all but disappeared from modern television drama, and modern location realism is distinct from that which evolved in the 1970s in several ways. The reduction in rehearsal time means that performances are now evolved almost entirely on location,[20] allowing actors to an extent to react to the environment in which they find themselves. However, though comparatively limited contact time with directors would seem to place responsibility for performance more firmly in the hands of the actor, directors and editors are able to mediate this in post-production via the use of editing, sound and visual effects, and non-diegetic music. In addition to being compromised by the need for continuity of performance in repeated takes, actors working in modern single camera productions also face a number of other pressures. Increased limitations of time and money mean that endless re-takes, and the attendant luxury of choice, are not always available, while as a result of the late delivery and frequent re-writing of scripts, a fixed text is sometimes not available even on the day of shooting. Where the possibility of re-takes does exist, it will most probably be more readily available to 'star' performers; the extent of an actor's creative input is therefore limited by their status. This will also affect the range and type of roles available, though this is likely to be more limited still for older performers.

Such a working environment requires a delicate balancing act, in which both thorough preparation and flexibility are paramount. British actor training has begun to meet this demand, combining the self-preparation techniques of Stanislavski with increased screen input. The result is a generation of actors for whom stage work is no longer a career priority, and consequently the perceived need to project, both vocally and in terms of facial expression and gesture, has notably diminished.

Location realism has developed as a result of major changes in the primary conditioning factors of television acting over the last two decades. Between the 1950s and the 1970s the weft and wane of performance determinants was sporadic; some remained relatively static for years, while others underwent more significant changes. Since the mid-1990s, however, these factors have significantly altered both of themselves and in relation to each other. New technology and production processes have combined with training to produce an environment in which actor approaches can be markedly diverse depending on their age and the length of their time in the profession. Those accustomed to the more stage-derived practices of the 1970s and 1980s have been forced to adapt or face unemployment in a market-driven television culture that offers a more limited variety of opportunities than ever before. As seen, modern location realism is a reflection of all these factors, and its future development will, as ever, be contingent upon the various directions and intersections they follow in their continuing realignment.

Notes

1 A 2002 report by the National Council for Drama Training concluded that 'it is in television that today's graduates are most likely to get their first professional acting jobs' (NCDT 2002: 7), while a 2005 Performing Arts Industry Report showed that in February of that year 18 per cent were working in television and 7 per cent in film, as opposed to 10 per cent in various types of theatre (Equity/Skillset 2005).

2 Manuel Alvarado and John Stewart have also cited labour relations as a motivating force in the decision to work on film, the British Film and Television Producers' Association allowing greater flexibility of working hours than the Independent Television Companies Association (1985: 21–29).
3 The BBC anticipated Granada's planned adaptation of *Brideshead Revisited* (ITV, 1981) with a six-part adaptation of John le Carré's *Tinker, Tailor, Soldier, Spy* (BBC, 1979), while crime series *Target* (BBC, 1977–78), *Shoestring* (BBC, 1979–80) and *Bergerac* (BBC, 1981–91) were also all-film.
4 US drama on British screens was nothing new; *Dragnet* (NBC, 1951–59) had become a fixture of UK schedules as early as 1955. The difference was that *Dynasty* and *Dallas* (CBS, 1978–91) belonged firmly in the continuing episodic drama category; in Britain traditionally the province of multi-camera studio.
5 John Ellis has presented inflation-adjusted figures to show that, between 1975 and 1980, 'drama production costs grew at a faster rate ... than at any time before or since' (2005: 51).
6 Speaking at the *On the Boundary* conference in 1998, actor Timothy West repeated a cameraman friend's description of this trend as 'fucks, fights and flashing blue lights' (cited in Caughie 2000b: 171). More recently Tony Garnett's objection that 'not all drama can sensibly be set in a place called Holby' (2009) reflected the fact that the long-running *Casualty* (BBC, 1986–) had spawned both a sister hospital drama, *Holby City* (BBC, 1999–), and a crime drama in *HolbyBlue* (BBC, 2007–8) – aside of the period hospital dramas *Casualty 1906* (BBC, 2006), *Casualty 1907* (BBC, 2008) and *Casualty 1909* (BBC, 2009).
7 Several *Doctor Who* serials in the late 1980s were in fact recorded entirely on location, using OB video. However, in its twenty-six years of production only one serial, 'Spearhead from Space', was made entirely using single camera film.
8 Work began in July 2004 (Gardner 2005) and May 2008 (Cross 2010: 58) respectively.
9 Read-throughs typically occur 'ten days or a week before shooting begins' (Gunn 2011).
10 Due to increasingly limited preparation time the director will not necessarily have met actors cast in minor roles prior to filming, as Jamie Payne explains: 'I used to get eight weeks' prep; you now get four. It often means that the casting director's going to be doing a lot of the little parts, and you end up watching them on tape with everybody else. So sometimes you've not met them until they hit the floor' (2011).
11 A series or 'season' (in US terminology) of *Doctor Who* usually consists of twelve to thirteen fifty-minute episodes, while each series

of *Survivors* was made up of six hour-long episodes (with a ninety-minute series opener).

12 The first director to work on a new series, the lead director will usually be involved in the casting of the regulars, in consultation with the casting director and executive producers.

13 Clark's reference to soap is significant in that programmes such as *EastEnders* (BBC, 1985–) and recurring series *Casualty* and *Holby City* typically allow no time for read-throughs or rehearsal.

14 In guide book *The Actor and the Camera*, Denis Lawson concurs that all key decisions are made by the executive producer and the commissioner: 'From an actor's perspective, the director has less control than we might imagine (particularly in a long-running series)' (2014: 122). Despite his long television career, Lawson admits to still finding this situation 'odd' (*ibid*.: 64).

15 Denis Lawson has pointed out, however, that continuity 'isn't always God', as for example when a close up may be used for a particular part of the edit, meaning that a perfect match with the preceding wider shot is not necessary (2014: 103).

16 The boom microphone is still employed, though this equipment is arguably easier to use in terms of being kept out of shot, e.g. for individual close-ups, than would have been the case in the multi-camera environment. According to Denis Lawson, sound mixers still prefer the sound quality provided by a boom to a throat microphone, though as an actor he is more comfortable with the latter (2014: 60).

17 Trevor Rawlins places it in the early to mid-2000s, citing the film training provided by Edward Hicks at East 15 and latterly RADA as an example (2011).

18 Known variously as Automatic Dialogue Replacement (Lawson 2014: 117) and Additional Dialogue Recording (Russell 2006: 124).

19 Whitfield's comedy roles include June Fletcher in *Happy Ever After* (BBC, 1974–79), June Medford in *Terry and June* (BBC, 1979–87) and Eddie Monsoon's mother in *Absolutely Fabulous* (BBC, 1992–2012).

20 The sets which are used today tend to be of the semi-permanent 'standing' variety, which according to Mark Gatiss can take on the nature of locations in their own right: 'Location has become so cheap, and cameras are so adaptable, the idea of building a set is a curious indulgence unless it's ... a standing set, like the TARDIS. In [a] way, going into the studio is like going to a location' (2011).

5
The return of studio realism?

It is Saturday night, and on the television screen three men can be seen, crouching round a small box, listening intently in the latest scene from live drama *The Quatermass Experiment*. By this point in the story it has become clear that something untoward happened in the depths of space to the crew of Britain's first manned rocket, and the on-screen trio are now playing back a recording of the astronauts' final moments. To the left, the trench-coated Quatermass holds a silencing finger aloft, gesturing at moments of significance as the recorder emits distorted, unearthly sounds. The central figure, Investigator Lomax, holds a finger to his chin as he listens, while on the right Paterson, a scientist from Quatermass's team, alternately rubs his brow, pulls at his beard and bites on his fingers, indicating his growing unease. The blocking is static, the scene's atmosphere of tension deriving entirely from a combination of the performers' concentrated stillness and their use of gesticulation. When the actors speak, their voices are quiet yet urgent; their words can be clearly understood, despite the fact that, though Quatermass is speaking in a London accent, Lomax has an Irish lilt to his voice, and Paterson is clearly from the north-east.

This scene would initially seem to be indicative of studio realism, featuring a deployment of physical gesture on a scale smaller than that required for stage work, yet still relatively projected when compared with everyday behaviour. However, the use of voice and real regional accent – as opposed to mimicked or put on – complicates such a reading, and the almost total lack of vocal projection is more typical of modern location realism. This apparent conflict derives from the fact that the sequence described above was not in fact taken from the 1953 original of *The Quatermass Experiment*, but the live re-mount first broadcast on 2 April 2005 as part of BBC Four's 'Television on Trial' season (Figure 5.1).

The Corporation's first live drama in two decades, this production was a deliberate attempt to evoke the conditions of the earlier serial (Fell 2005), and is useful here both for summarising the key determinants that have been seen to influence television acting, and to illustrate the alterations in performance style that can result when one or more of these factors is adjusted or removed. The 2005 version of *The Quatermass Experiment* is notable for returning to the rehearsal template that was a principal feature of studio realism, while employing sophisticated modern technology and a lead cast[1] who had come to prominence predominantly in the era of location realism. Its live transmission from a Ministry of Defence testing base (Willett 2005), whose buildings and grounds stood in for a variety of exteriors and interiors (including the Turbine Hall of the Tate Modern gallery), represents neither the traditional, constructed sets of the studio nor the typical location shoot, in which repeated takes are the norm. The resulting performance demonstrates the importance of combined conditioning factors with regard to screen acting, the 2005 version of *The Quatermass*

Figure 5.1 Jason Flemyng, Adrian Dunbar and Mark Gatiss in *The Quatermass Experiment*

Experiment representing neither pure studio nor location realism, yet exhibiting traits of each as a result of its peculiar production context.

The clearest link in this production to the determinants of studio realism is the rehearsal process, which began at the American Church on Tottenham Court Road one month before transmission (Varma 2005). The first week was spent reading and editing the script, removing any unnecessary exposition and dialogue that might seem dated to modern audiences (Tennant 2005); a rare luxury when compared to the single read-through allowed for modern television drama. Only in the second week did work progress to blocking, taping out the floor to represent the sets that would be used on the night of transmission (*ibid*.). For many of those involved, this atypical rehearsal process felt reminiscent of theatre processes, as lead actor Jason Flemyng outlines: 'It was nice to have the rehearsals on *Quatermass*, and it felt very much like a play because we kind of taped out the floor … we had to, because you couldn't ask any questions on the day; you had to know exactly where you were going and what you were doing' (2011).

Such sentiments are shared by Flemyng's co-star Mark Gatiss, who states:

> [Rehearsal] was essential … because it was not like the mechanics existed to do it; it's not like it's being done all the time. So, it had to be worked out, how it was simply achievable, which meant that without an existing studio we had to find a location which could do all those things, and then work our way around it. It was like doing a play; it was like rehearsing a play.
>
> **(2011)**

Rehearsals then transferred to the hangar-like Ministry facility, where a 'dress rehearsal' was recorded on the evening of 1 April, the day before transmission (Willett 2005). By this point, timings of scene changes and actor movements between sets were extremely precise:

> By the time we actually came to shoot it, it was choreographed to within an inch of its life in terms of where the cameras were. And each of us were [*sic*] actually assigned a runner who would literally push us into different parts of the place, because there was no room for error. My favourite bit – because it was so exciting – was

getting from the control room when the rocket had landed, down to the crash site in real time, while they cut away to one pre-recorded shot. And having to get into the whatsit suit; it was so exciting. So it was four weeks of rehearsal, but it wasn't any kind of indulgence, it was just the way it had to be because they had to work out camera moves, they had to work out literally how far away each room could be from the other one if the character was going from one to the other; what the film breaks would be, timings, absolutely everything.

(Gatiss 2011)

As Mark Gatiss implies, such extensive rehearsal makes *The Quatermass Experiment* entirely atypical of television drama in the 2000s. Comparison with the 1953 original highlights several of the other changes that have taken place in acting style over the preceding five decades. Each actor, for example, was equipped with a radio microphone (Willett 2005), diminishing the need for vocal projection, while the Received Pronunciation that characterised the original British Experimental Rocket Group was now lost in a sea of real regional voices. Gatiss later explained the use of his recovered Durham accent: 'I took a decision early on to make Paterson a northerner like me, because we were talking initially about getting away from the slightly stilted '50s [thing] of them all being very posh, and I thought it was quite an interesting way to go. It seemed to me early on to make some of those more stiff upper lip lines slightly more say-able' (2005).

As seen in Chapter 4, such developments are now typical. Less representative was the choice by producers to use primarily actors that possessed 'a reasonable amount of stage experience' (Willett 2005). This decision was a direct result of the live nature of the production; as demonstrated in the last chapter, theatre experience has become increasingly irrelevant with regard to casting for television in recent years. In rehearsals, director Sam Miller encouraged his cast to treat the script as 'a theatre piece, because there was nothing else that was comparable to it' (*ibid.*), and this added factor of liveness illustrates how a change in just one production condition can significantly influence performance. *The Quatermass Experiment*'s transmission in real time counteracts and amplifies the restrained scale of location realism and results in acting that is, in the words of producer Jane Willett, 'slightly heightened, which we're not used to … because of the adrenalin that's coursing through everyone's

Figure 5.2 Jason Flemyng and Adrian Dunbar in *The Quatermass Experiment*

Figure 5.3 Jason Flemyng in *The Quatermass Experiment*

veins' (*ibid.*). The performances of Jason Flemyng, Adrian Dunbar and Mark Gatiss in the section described earlier are particularly notable for the use each makes of his hands. Re-watching his performance for the DVD commentary, Gatiss was amused to note his (real life) habit when nervous of pulling at his nose (2005). Dunbar gestures for emphasis as Lomax lists the astronauts in the capsule (Figure 5.2), while Flemyng provides a (literally) pointed reminder of studio realism as he indicates the recorder on Quatermass's line: 'To think, the answer is in there somewhere ...' (Figure 5.3).

While this more notably gestural performance could be seen simply as a means of compensating for static blocking and heavy exposition, it marks an interesting return to the performance style seen in earlier chapters from Reginald Tate, William Russell and Peter Bowles, in which physical gestures underpin the drama, albeit in a more moderated form than the stage-derived performances of W. Thorp Devereux and Van Boolen. Originally allocated a two-hour slot in the schedule, *The Quatermass Experiment* concluded after just ninety-seven minutes due to the accelerated performances of its cast, Jason Flemyng later admitting: 'It's really exciting; you can't help but get invigorated by it, it's really amazing' (2011). However, despite the use of actors with stage experience, television is the medium in which many actors now work most regularly. In *The Quatermass Experiment* this meant that the pressures of live performance produced negative effects in those more accustomed to screen work, as supporting actress Suzan Sylvester observed:

> This sounds awful [laughter] but I loved it partly also because there were an awful lot of TV actors in it ... who freaked out; who really panicked when they realised there was no going back. You know; it was out there, it couldn't be re-done. So there were people like Isla Blair, who's done loads of theatre and stuff, and she just brilliantly sailed through ... I do remember some of the younger actors – who I only know from television – just quaking; probably in the same way that I'd quake if I had a close-up on me in a recorded thing.
>
> (2010)

An example of actor nerves impeding performance came when Adrian Bower suffered a notable 'dry' as journalist Fullalove midway through the broadcast. While the actor quickly recovered, these brief seconds of hesitation stand out in stark relief in an era where such mistakes would normally be re-recorded.[2] According to Mark Gatiss, this was one of two nerve-jangling moments:

> The other brilliant one – it was like a bloody *It'll Be Alright on the Night* (ITV, 1997–2008) story, it was fantastic, and you can detect it – is at the end of the chemist scene. There was an entire wall of flasks, retorts, test tubes, and Adrian Dunbar finally has had enough, and he says: 'Come on, Quatermass!' and he slams the door, and the entire wall went. And the camera cut just before

Jason Flemyng and David Tennant go, because it just smashed to bits; fantastic.

(2011)

Such near-disasters were noted by the *Guardian*'s Nancy Banks-Smith, who described the production as 'adrenaline-fired, if sometimes a bit bumpy' (2005). Clearly, *The Quatermass Experiment* represented a new interaction of the determinants examined throughout this study – production process, technology, direction, actor training and experience – resulting in a style of performance distinct from both modern location realism and classic studio realism. For Mark Gatiss, *The Quatermass Experiment* was a unique television acting experience:

> Well, I can tell you what it is, I've never had it before or since; it felt like something new. It was an awareness that it was like doing a play without an audience, except they were there, and there were five hundred thousand of them.[3] So it was strange. I wasn't scared at all; I was thrilled, and it was a proper kind of hairs on the back of your neck kind of thrill, not a sort of dry-mouthed scared. It was a real buzz ... I do remember very well, Isla Blair, with the green room beforehand we were all just kind of wishing each other good luck, and she kept saying 'Goodbye'; completely unconsciously, as if we were all going into the trenches: 'Goodbye.'

(2011)

The production's uniqueness in modern terms illustrates the value of a multi-perspectival approach when considering the changing causes and conventions of acting style; were the scene described earlier considered *without* supporting contextualisation, it would provide an extremely misleading impression of actors' television work in the mid-2000s.

Since the transmission of *The Quatermass Experiment*, there have been several further excursions into live television drama. However, rather than representing a desire to return to the processes of studio realism, the central attraction of such productions seems to derive from what Mark Gatiss terms 'the car crash element' (*ibid.*); for viewer Christopher Fallis, it was 'the possibility of actors fluffing their lines' which added to *The Quatermass Experiment*'s already suspenseful drama (2005: 9).

One live production to depart entirely from the studio realist model was *Frankenstein's Wedding* (BBC, 2011), a re-telling of Mary Shelley's gothic novel that combined drama, musical and audience participation, and was broadcast in real time from Kirkstall Abbey in Leeds. Rather than being a traditional studio production, director Colin Teague's cast and OB crew were required to perform a feat that was arguably closer in nature to a live concert. The production was subsequently nominated in the Sport and Live Event category at the British Academy Television Awards, rather than drama, and for Teague this approach represented a blend of old and the new: 'I think there was a real clash of cultures. On the one hand we had the youthful side of us, the new people, the new team, wanting to kind of break the mould and do a live show, and incorporate the modern technology of what we could use and possibly try using projectors and modern cameras, and the look and feel of it being a bit more raw' (2011). However, as Teague admits, until this point he was unfamiliar with the processes employed by the established Outside Broadcast crew, and the tendency for the vision mixer to cut between shots on actors' delivery of their lines – something that went again Teague's directorial instincts:

> For me, it's about: feel that emotion – go when you want to know what the person's saying – and this goes against everything that these people have been trained [in] ... So I'm trying to do this in ... forty-eight hours, trying to convince these people: 'It's going to work, it's going to work.' And I tell you it was an uphill struggle. It really was, purely because they were, like: 'But this is the way we do it.' And I'm, like: 'I know it's the way you've done it, and you've done it for twenty-five, thirty years, but I'm trying to actually move it on here, so that the angles are a bit different, right? It's about the drama; you go on the emotion.' And that's the way you cut, and that's the way I feel, and that's the way I see, I suppose; my work is very much driven by that ... I think even with a heightened reality I think there's got to be a certain core realism at its heart, if there's a truth about the product. If there isn't, then I'm just watching something fake. I want to be lost in it.
>
> **(Ibid.)**

Teague's comments represent the instincts of a single camera film director attempting to work within an (extremely ambitious) multi-camera context, and in this respect *Frankenstein's Wedding* was an intriguing experiment; one that has not been repeated. It is clear that, given the unusual nature of its production, *Frankenstein's Wedding* cannot be read as a return to the performance style of studio realism, though in rehearsal terms at least it shared certain of its processes, with the director and cast allocated a week to prepare in the Abbey before the technical crew moved in (*ibid.*).

Given its continuing reliance on multi-camera production, soap is arguably the modern television genre that most closely replicates the conditions of studio realism (though without the prior rehearsal period) and has, perhaps unsurprisingly, featured a number of live 'event' episodes in the 2000s and 2010s. ITV transmitted live episodes of *The Bill* in 2003 (to celebrate the programme's twentieth anniversary) and 2005 (to mark the channel's fiftieth birthday), and *Emmerdale* (ITV, 1972–) in 2012 (celebrating the programme's fortieth anniversary), while live instalments of *Coronation Street* were broadcast in 2000 and 2010 for the programme's fortieth and fiftieth anniversaries; in 2015 a third live episode was mounted to celebrate the sixtieth anniversary of independent television. In addition, the BBC transmitted special editions of *EastEnders* in 2010 and 2015, marking the programme's twenty-fifth and thirtieth anniversaries. The latter saw live scenes inserted into 'regular' episodes throughout the anniversary week, with a fully live instalment performed on the evening of Friday 20 February. Whereas, in the case of *Coronation Street*, it could be argued that the live episodes represented a return to its original production format[4] as an homage to its roots, the decision to mount live episodes of *The Bill* and *EastEnders* might better be read as a publicity generating attempt to increase viewership in the era of multiple channels and technological convergence, which has seen the traditional broadcast audience become increasingly fragmented. Once again, the 'car crash element' plays a prominent role in this process, combined with major plot events: in *Coronation Street*, the deaths of several characters in the aftermath of a gas explosion and tram crash, and in 2015 the apparent death of villain Callum Logan (Sean Ward); and in *EastEnders* the revelation of who killed Archie Mitchell (in 2010) and Lucy Beale (2015).

There is a marked contrast between the 2010 and 2015 live episodes of *EastEnders*. The first, perhaps over ambitiously, features a greater number of exterior shots – culminating in the fall to his death of Bradley Branning (Charlie Clements) – requiring rapid cutting between cameras which occasionally leaves operators unprepared, one particular zoom arriving a second too late. Other technical problems include Max Branning's dialogue not being loud enough in his opening exterior scene, possibly due to a malfunctioning microphone. Perhaps in an attempt to anticipate any possible disasters, scenes in the opening half of the episode are kept very short indeed, but this seems instead to have increased the pressures on actors, Scott Maslen noticeably 'fluffing' his lines in the second scene, less than two minutes after the episode has begun. As Peggy Mitchell, Barbara Windsor later confuses her dialogue in a key scene, making it unclear why – or even whether – her character opted to retrieve her divorce papers upon discovering husband Archie dead. There are also several examples of actors confusing character names,[5] while other continuity errors include Jake Wood, as Max Branning, being caught on camera forcing his fingers down his throat in order to make himself retch, and the hand of Bradley Branning's corpse visibly twitching after his death.

The fact that the episode garnered audiences of sixteen million (Littlejohn 2010) meant such mistakes did not go unnoticed, some viewers even producing their own video compilations on YouTube.[6] It is probable that the production team bore this in mind when planning the thirtieth anniversary episode, which focused on showing the effects on the Beale family of the revelation that ten-year-old Bobby (Eliot Carrington) was unwittingly responsible for half-sister Lucy's death. Rather than mounting an ambitious exterior set-piece, as with Bradley's attempt to elude the police in 2010, the episode features a series of lengthy scenes in the Beale living room, as Ian (Adam Woodyatt), son Peter (Ben Hardy) and daughter Cindy (Mimi Keene) try to extract the truth from Ian's wife Jane (Laurie Brett), who is attempting to take the blame on Bobby's behalf. These emotionally loaded scenes are intercut with shorter sequences at the Queen Vic pub, where landlord Mick Carter (Danny Dyer) and his daughter Nancy (Maddy Hill) are attempting their own cover-up of what they believe is the murder of rapist Dean Wicks (Matt Di Angelo).

In contrast with the 2010 episode, there are no noticeable 'fluffs',[7] despite the extreme pressure that the cast would have been under. Adam Woodyatt in particular is called upon to perform some extremely emotive material, first venting Ian's confusion and rage by destroying the Beales' crockery collection, followed by his gradual realisation that Jane's confession is a lie, to his ultimate decision to participate in the cover-up, not telling Bobby that it was his attack on Lucy that caused her death. The fact that Woodyatt, who was also one of the stronger performers in the 2010 episode,[8] responds so well to the pressures of live, continuous performance could be due to his extensive experience of multi-camera, having appeared in the series since the opening episode in 1985. Over the show's run, Woodyatt had to adapt to the increased production turnaround, doubling from just two episodes a week in 1985 to four in 2015. As seen in Chapter 4, rehearsal does not play a significant part in modern soap production, as Woodyatt confirmed in an interview conducted to promote the live episode: 'We don't usually rehearse; we sort of do a line run, block it for the cameras and then shoot it. For this, we've done that and then rehearsed some more, and some more, and some more' (2015). However, Woodyatt claimed to be eagerly anticipating the live performance: 'There's no point in getting nervous about it. It's no different to being on stage, by the time we get the transmission – we'll have done so many rehearsals' (*ibid.*). Interestingly, Woodyatt's comments contradict those of Mark Gatiss with regard to *The Quatermass Experiment*. While agreeing that the rehearsal process makes the production similar to stage work, the absence of a live audience does not seem to be as relevant a factor to Woodyatt as to Gatiss – perhaps because the *EastEnders* actor is more accustomed to (audience-less) multi-camera studio production.

As seen earlier, multi-camera requires actors to maintain continuity of performance while remaining conscious of various technical issues such as blocking. In his live scenes the experienced Woodyatt demonstrates a keen awareness of the importance of physical positioning, both within the set and in the frame of the camera, which the younger actors in the cast do not always match. An example of this is the moment where Ian, now realising that his wife's confession is false, moves towards Jane to confront her, leaving Peter and Cindy watching from the the rear of the set. The fact that Woodyatt has moved into close up, while Hardy and Keene remain in the background, means that either one or the other of the younger actors is now obscured by Woodyatt's head as Ian questions Jane (Figure 5.4). More experienced actors would

Figure 5.4 Ben Hardy, Adam Woodyatt, Mimi Keene (obscured) and Laurie Brett in *EastEnders*

perhaps have repositioned themselves in the back of the frame so that their faces remained in shot, though given the pressures of the live set-up this is a minor fault, Hardy and Keene otherwise acquitting themselves as well as their more experienced colleagues during some intense sequences.

The live 2015 episode of *EastEnders* attracted twelve million viewers (Hogan 2015), down by four million on 2010,[9] but in general received far more positive reviews, the *Telegraph* lauding the cast's achievement as 'triumphant, heartbreaking and faultless' (*ibid.*). While this would seem to demonstrate that an appetite still exists for live studio realist performance, the fact that such excursions are purposed primarily as 'event' television indicates that a more general return to the methods of studio realism proper is unlikely. Were they once again to become the norm in terms of production practice, the novelty would doubtless diminish – as indicated by the fall in viewing figures between *EastEnders*' 2010 and 2015 episodes, regardless of the latter's superiority. As Mark Gatiss states: 'You can't put the genie back in the bottle, but you could do it as a decision. You could say: "Right, we're going to do a *Play of the Week* in the old style; everybody rehearses it for a month like a proper play, and puts it on, and we record it from 9 to 10.30 and we put the lights out." And see what happens' (2011). However, according to Howard Burch, the same monetary pressures that eradicated the rehearsal process vital to studio realism are now creating a culture in which certain of its skills are once again required:

> You're not getting as much time as you used to do to re-take stuff. So if you're rattling through a schedule, by the end of the day the actors and the director and the rest of the crew know that you're pretty much down to one take. And that's a similar sort of feel to those old studio things, you know; that you've got to nail this in one go ... There's a real pressure on the schedules now that doesn't accommodate six or seven takes, and that's where I think that sort of theatrical experience comes into it; with dividends, because I think everybody again raises their game a little.
>
> (2011)

Burch describes a situation in which certain aspects of studio realism could perhaps again come to prominence: 'I could easily see a scenario in the next few years where we'd go back to a studio drama, just for a run, or just for a one-off, or whatever. Because I think visually it would be interesting in the landscape of drama that's out there' (*ibid.*). As seen in earlier chapters, however, the ability to sustain a one-take performance is only half the equation. Such productions would, as Mark Gatiss points out, also require increased preparation time: 'It would be interesting to see what that would result in, because you'd have the expenditure of keeping people together to rehearse, but then they'd be very, very much more across it than when you turn up on location' (2011).

From the actor's perspective, rehearsal seems to be the key factor missing from modern television production, and if few yearn for the days of multi-camera recording, all prize the benefits of prior preparation. Louise Jameson believes that 'the absolute ideal is film, one camera; hours to light it, hours to rehearse it' (2011). This combination of modern and past production techniques also appeals to Kevin McNally: 'We can learn a lot from the past and, you know, upgrade slightly to the quality that we have nowadays ... Television doesn't get rehearsed now, and I think it would benefit from it' (2010).

Certain directors in modern television already employ a more extended preparatory period, Ben Bolt being cited by several interviewed here for his insistence on a period of discussion and rehearsal prior to filming. After working with Bolt on *Doc Martin* (ITV, 2004–), Louise Jameson recalled: 'We did the full read-through for four episodes, they called me in the next day, we discussed line changes and objectives and the history of the character ... [It] was just a thrilling reminder of how it used to be ... If you'd interviewed me two weeks ago [before working with Bolt], I'd have given you a very different answer' (2011).

Elsewhere, independent producers such as Mark Gatiss also favour an approach more reminiscent of that which helped form studio realism, as regular collaborator Julia Dalkin describes: 'We have a reading, and we rehearse; "This is how we're going to do the scene." You're not spending ages on it, but you're doing it enough so you're meeting the person you're going to be working with' (2010). For Louise Jameson, who worked with Gatiss on *Cleaning Up* (Guerrier, 2011) and *The Tractate Middoth* (BBC, 2013), he represents a new breed of 'dominant, strong, multi-tasking characters within the business, who so love the craft. And also writers, so they understand the respect that that needs; there are lots more of those guys, and some girls, arriving' (2011).

Given the ongoing mutability of television production culture demonstrated herein, such a development is not beyond the bounds of possibility. The period covered within this book, from the live era of the 1950s to the 2010s, demonstrates that while change is, as once famously observed by Benjamin Disraeli, both inevitable and constant (Kebbel 1882: 487), in the television industry it is also gradual – as are its visible effects. While, for the moment, writer/director production companies with the capital and inclination to indulge in the luxury (as many would regard it) of extended rehearsal processes remain in the minority, it is not inconceivable that, in an age of ever-increasing deregulation, they might one day come to represent a new norm. Were such a development eventually to occur, it is not inconceivable that a new form of television acting might gradually emerge; one that could combine the scaled down performance style of location realism with the more lengthy preparation process formerly allocated to studio productions. As illustrated in this chapter, such a move would be welcomed by many actors working in television, but as to whether – or how quickly – it could take place, only time will tell.

Notes

1 The lead roles were played by Jason Flemyng, David Tennant, Mark Gatiss, Indira Varma, Adrian Dunbar, Andrew Tiernan and Adrian Bower.

2 For the subsequent DVD release, the version from the 'dress rehearsal' was included, rather than the live broadcast which featured Bower's 'dry'.
3 The programme garnered a peak audience of 542,000 (Plunkett 2005).
4 However, few of the regular cast would have been with the programme long enough to remember this. In fact, only one of the two episodes broadcast each week was live, and after February 1961 the programme was entirely pre-recorded.
5 As Peggy Mitchell, Barbara Windsor addresses Janine Butcher as 'June', while Lacey Turner calls Bradley Branning 'Charlie' and Dot Cotton (June Brown) forgets her granddaughter's name.
6 Two notable examples include Neon Media's 'EastEnders Live – The Mistakes', which focuses on performance-related errors, while Luke's Stuff's 'Eastenders Live – The Mistakes' features only technical problems. Although the latter poster stresses his admiration for the technical achievement which the episode represented, the careful detailing of errors by each illustrates the scrutiny to which live episodes are subjected – and the appeal of the 'car crash element'.
7 In the earlier 18 February live episode, however, Jo Joyner's delivery of the line 'How's Ian?' as 'How's Adam?', confusing actor and character Christian names, represented a blunder that did not go unremarked by the press.
8 The actor's only noticeable mistake in the earlier episode comes when Ian tells Phil Mitchell (Steve McFadden) to 'Slop it!' instead of 'Stop it!' This is also during an extremely emotive scene, as Mitchell threatens Ian and tears his home apart in search of incriminating evidence which he believes the latter possesses.
9 There was a similar dip in the viewing figures for *Coronation Street*'s 2015 live episode, which was watched by 8.369 million (McGeorge 2015) as opposed to 14.027 million in 2010 (Plunkett 2010). This could, however, be taken as evidence that it is becoming more difficult to attract large audiences in the era of iPlayer catch-up, as much as a decline in any interest in live drama.

Conclusion

The methodological approaches employed herein offer as complete a picture as possible of the determinants of British television acting, and cover distinct historical periods. In the live era, from the mid-1930s up to the early 1960s, the type of experience gained by actors was arguably of greater importance than duration. Many were unaccustomed to the mediating effects of television technology, and had yet to 'scale down' approaches to performance that had typically been acquired and developed through stage experience. The varying backgrounds of *The Quatermass Experiment*'s 1953 cast informs a notably diverse range of acting styles, from the emerging studio realism of Reginald Tate to the more gesturally inflected emoting of Van Boolen. The fact that some – though by no means all – of these performances were deemed worthy of censure by contemporary audiences and critics indicates that a studio 'norm' in acting terms had not, as yet, established itself, though audiences at least were beginning to develop some sense of what was acceptably 'realistic' from the 'new' medium of television.

By the 1960s the introduction of videotape pre-recording had done little to affect either the production process or the pressures upon actors of 'as live' performance. While the majority of the regular cast in *Doctor Who* had begun their careers on the stage, they had also acquired an approximately equivalent amount of television experience. This, combined with the effects being felt in film and television drama of social realism, led to performances that were notably scaled down from those of just ten years before. As studio realism – and the medium of television itself – became more established, small screen acting notably distinguished itself from stage-derived practice via a reduction in vocal projection (though this was still greater than that which would be employed in everyday life), and a gradual eschewal of broad gestural signifiers, aided by the fact that pre-recording meant actors now had the opportunity to assess their own performances after the event.

By the mid-1970s the studio realist style had been refined into a form that was accepted and understood by the majority of actors; in the words of Shaun Sutton: 'Today's actor is television-wise; he has learned the grammar' (1982: 105). This grammar was also understood by audiences, yet there was still room for those who did not entirely conform to its rules; the more stylised, gestural acting of Talfryn Thomas in *Survivors* proved just as acceptable to viewers in 1975 as that of Van Boolen two decades earlier. However, the uniform scaling down among actors working on the programme makes it clear that studio realism was now arguably at its zenith.

If the majority of television actors understood the 'grammar' of small screen performance, the foundations for a linguistic shift were already in place. The increased use of Outside Broadcasting techniques in the 1970s and 1980s began to break down the conditions that had contributed to the development of studio realism, resulting in a further scaling down of vocal projection, and a reduction in physical movement for its own sake. However, this emerging style took time to become established; casts and crews in the 1970s were constrained both technically and by lack of experience, and the development of this nascent form of location realism was stymied by the fact that the shift to all-OB production ultimately proved a blind alley in production terms.

By the mid-1990s single camera film had instead become the norm for most television drama, aside of soaps and situation comedy. This brought its own production processes, which in turn had an impact upon performance. Whereas the multi-camera set-up used for studio work had meant that physical movement and blocking were often conducted on the basis of providing visual interest, in the era of modern location realism this can instead be provided through editing and *mise-en-scène*. In addition, the increasing use of CGI and post-production effects seen in our telefantasy case studies of the 2000s and 2010s allows for a far greater degree of mediation of performance, with actors now literally performing to nothing other than a green screen – a scenario that would have been impossible to imagine for those working in the almost entirely studio-based world of 1950s television drama.

In recent years the increased intersection of technology with UK drama training, which at last provides a practical focus on screen work, has led to a notable reduction of overall scale on the part of many younger actors when compared with previous generations – a development that, as seen in Chapter 4, has led to censure in some quarters, director Andrew Gunn lamenting the lack of projection on the part of some younger actors. More senior performers have, meanwhile, had to adapt to the harsh fact of minimal rehearsals, lack of time to bond with their fellow cast members, last-minute re-writes and, overall, increasingly pressurised working conditions, all of which have taken television drama further than ever before from the production model of the live era. However, in the 2010s renewed interest in the spectacle of live television drama – albeit primarily for 'event' episodes or productions – has simultaneously indicated a continuing fascination with the performance processes of the past, from which modern television would otherwise seem to have distanced itself. Whether this can be taken as an indication that studio realist performance is poised for some form of renewal – or is simply regarded as a welcome novelty when combined with the thrill of live transmission – is open to debate.

Any future directions that British television acting might take fall outside the scope of this book, yet the evidence presented herein suggests that these will not be dependent on any one factor alone. Studio and location realism emerged only gradually from a maelstrom of influences that were constantly waxing and waning in relation to each other, and at the time of writing these factors are no more stable than they have been at any other point in the medium's history. The recent debate over the BBC's Charter renewal calls into question the future of the very institution which produced this book's case studies, and the simultaneous growth of non-broadcast service providers such as Netflix and Amazon Prime means that the very nature of small screen drama production is in a state of flux. At the same time, as viewers increasingly access content on devices such as mobile phones and tablets, the question emerges of what impact this will have upon performance. Could the increased viewing of television dramas via smaller screens in fact result in a move back towards the 'close-up' acting and projection of the 1950s? This is, perhaps, questionable; the large flatscreen television currently shows little sign of becoming extinct – though the number and proportion of adults without a working television set is gradually increasing (Ofcom 2015: 40). However, as these factors take new paths, combined with the other determinants examined herein, so too will the resulting television acting styles of the future.

It is to be hoped that *The Changing Spaces of Television Acting* illustrates the importance of considering contextualising factors with regard to television acting, and that future researchers will now build upon the methodologies and models utilised. Throughout, the book's aim has been to look beyond screen performances as historic curiosities, and examine instead the extent to which they represent the times and environments in which they were produced; any analysis that does not take these determinants into consideration risks failing to fully understand and appreciate the performances that result from them. The suggested models of studio and location realism, while far from all-encompassing, represent an important step towards counter-acting a purely immanent reading of archive texts, which run the risk of being distorted by the passage of time.

While, as noted in the Introduction, academic interest in television acting is building, the field remains largely open for investigation, and possible areas of future research are numerous. Inter-genre comparison might well prove a fruitful path, for example contrasting acting in telefantasy with historical or crime drama. Brett Mills's work (2004) aside, the field of television comedy performance has been largely neglected, and given its commonalities with studio realism (rehearsal process, multi-camera studio production – but with the added ingredient of a live audience) and the more recent move towards a single camera model, this might provide some interesting contrasts and similarities. The particular styles employed for other dramatic formats such as the soap, the episodic drama and the single play also warrant investigation, and given the increased reliance in British drama schools upon Stanislavski – so often confused with the 'Method' style of the Actors Studio – it would be intriguing to compare the development of British television acting with that in the United States.

Whatever direction future research takes, it will be forced always to adapt to changing circumstances, just as television acting – and the various factors that combine to shape it – continue to evolve, throughout the twenty-first century and beyond.

References

'Actor for a Bet', *Radio Times* (9–15 August 1953), p. 13.
ADA. (1906) *Prospectus 1906*, London: RADA.
ADA. (1908) *Prospectus 1908*, London: RADA.
Affron, Charles. (1977) *Star Acting: Gish, Garbo, Davies*, New York: Dutton.
Alvarado, Manuel and Buscombe, Edward. (1978) *Hazell: The Making of a TV Series*, London: BFI.
Alvarado, Manuel and Stewart, John. (1985) *Made for Television: Euston Films Limited*, London: Methuen/BFI.
Ang, Ien. (1985) *Watching Dallas: Soap Opera and the Melodramatic Imagination*, translated by Della Couling, London and New York: Routledge.
Auslander, Philip. (2008) *Liveness: Performance in a Mediatized Culture*, 2nd edition, London and New York: Routledge.
Banks-Smith, Nancy. (2005) 'One-Take Wonder' [online], *Guardian*, 7 April. Available at: www.guardian.co.uk/media/2005/apr/07/television.apprentice (accessed 4 August 2016).
BARB. (2016) 'Television Ownership in Private Domestic Households 1956–2014' [online]. Available at: www.barb.co.uk/resources/tv-ownership/ (accessed 4 August 2016).
'Bards and Beauties', *Manchester Guardian* (12 August 1953), p. 3.
Baron, Cynthia and Carnicke, Sharon Marie. (2008) *Reframing Screen Performance*, Michigan: University of Michigan Press.
Barr, Tony. (1997) *Acting for the Camera*, 2nd edition, New York: HarperCollins.

Barrowman, John. (2005) Commentary on 'The Doctor Dances', *Doctor Who: The Complete First Series*, BBCDVD1770.

Barry, Michael. (1992) *From the Palace to the Grove*, London: Royal Television Society.

Barton, Robert. (2009) *Acting Onstage and Off*, 5th edition, Belmont: Wadsworth/Thomas.

Battin, Tom C. (1959) 'The Television Actor', *The Southern Speech Journal*, 24:4, pp. 210–215.

'BBC to Extend Television at Once', *Radio Times* (12–18 July 1953), p. 3.

BBC WAC R8/261/1 British Actors Equity Association – BBC Transcription Service.

BBC WAC R9/7/8 Viewer Research Reports – May to August 1953.

BBC WAC R9/7/66 Audience Research Reports – November to December 1963.

BBC WAC R9/7/135 Audience Research Reports – May to June 1975.

BBC WAC R9/7/136 Audience Research Reports – July to August 1975.

BBC WAC R37/121/1 British Actors Equity Association – General.

BBC WAC T5/418 *The Quatermass Experiment*.

BBC WAC T5/638/1 *Doctor Who* – Series A Ep. 1 tx. 23/11/63.

BBC WAC T5/647/1 *Doctor Who* – General.

BBC WAC T62/122/1 Studios.

BBC WAC The Quatermass Experiment/Contact has been Established/BBC/18/07/1953 – camera script.

BBC WAC Survivors/The Fourth Horseman/BBC1/16/04/1975 – camera script.

BBC WAC Survivors/Law and Order/BBC1/18/06/1975 – camera script.

Bennett-Levy, Michael. (2001–13) 'Television History – The First 75 Years' [online]. Available at: www.tvhistory.tv/index.html (accessed 4 August 2016).

Bernard, Ian. (1998) *Film and Television Acting: From Stage to Screen*, 2nd edition, Boston and Oxford: Focal Press.

Bignell, Jonathan. (2005a) 'And the Rest is History: Lew Grade, Creation Narratives and Television Historiography', in Catherine Johnson and Rob Turnock (eds), *ITV Cultures: Independent Television Over Fifty Years*, Maidenhead: Open University Press, pp. 57–70.

Bignell, Jonathan. (2005b) 'Space for "Quality": Negotiating with the Daleks', in Jonathan Bignell and Stephen Lacey (eds), *Popular Television Drama: Critical Perspectives*, Manchester and New York: Manchester University Press, pp. 76–92.

Bignell, Jonathan. (2006) 'Exemplarity, Pedagogy and Television History', *New Review of Film and Television Studies*, 3:1, pp. 15–32.

Bignell, Jonathan. (2007a) 'The Child as Addressee, Viewer and Consumer in Mid-1960s *Doctor Who*', in David Butler (ed.), *Time and Relative Dissertations in Space: Critical Perspectives on Doctor Who*, Manchester and New York: Manchester University Press, pp. 43–55.

Bignell, Jonathan. (2007b) 'Citing the Classics: Constructing British Television Drama History in Publishing and Pedagogy', in Helen Wheatley (ed.), *Re-Viewing Television History: Critical Issues in Television Historiography*, London and New York: I.B. Tauris, pp. 27–39.

Bignell, Jonathan. (2008) *An Introduction to Television Studies*, 2nd edition, London and New York: Routledge.

Bignell, Jonathan and O'Day, Andrew. (2004) *Terry Nation*, Manchester and New York: Manchester University Press.

Bignell, Jonathan, Lacey, Stephen and MacMurragh-Kavanagh, Madeleine (eds). (2000) *British Television Drama: Past, Present and Future*, Basingstoke and New York: Palgrave Macmillan.

Billington, Michael. (1973) *The Modern Actor*, London: Hamish Hamilton.

Blum, Richard A. (1984) *American Film Acting: The Stanislavski Heritage*, Ann Arbor: UMI.

Born, Georgina. (2005) *Uncertain Vision: Birt, Dyke and the Reinvention of the BBC*, London: Vintage.

Briggs, Asa. (1979) *The History of Broadcasting in the United Kingdom: Volume IV – Sound and Vision*, Oxford: Oxford University Press.

Briggs, Nicholas. (2005) Commentary on 'Dalek', *Doctor Who: The Complete First Series*, BBCDVD1770.

Burch, Howard. (2011) Interviewed by the author, 17 February.

Burrows, Henry. (1953) 'Letters', *Radio Times*, 26 July–1 August, p. 35.

Butler, David (ed.). (2007) *Time and Relative Dissertations in Space: Critical Perspectives on Doctor Who*, Manchester and New York: Manchester University Press.

Butler, Jeremy. (1991) '"I'm Not a Doctor, But I Play One on TV": Characters, Actors and Acting in Television Soap Opera', *Cinema Journal*, 30:4, pp. 75–91.

Butler, Jeremy. (2010) *Television Style*, New York and London: Routledge.

Callow, Simon. (1984) *Being an Actor*, London: Methuen.

Callow, Simon. (2005) Commentary on 'The Unquiet Dead', *Doctor Who: The Complete First Series*, BBCDVD1770.

Cardullo, Bert, Geduld, Harry, Gottesman, Ronald and Woods, Leigh (eds). (1998) *Playing to the Camera: Film Actors Discuss Their Craft*, New Haven: Yale University Press.

Carney, Jessica. (1996) *Who's There? The Life and Career of William Hartnell*, London: Virgin Books.

Carnicke, Sharon Marie. (1999) 'Lee Strasberg's Paradox of the Actor', in Alan Lovell and Peter Kramer (eds), *Screen Acting*, London and New York: Routledge, pp. 75–87.

Carnicke, Sharon Marie. (2004) 'Screen Performance and Directors' Visions', in Cynthia Baron, Diane Carson and Frank P. Tomasulo (eds), *More Than a Method: Trends and Traditions in Contemporary Film Performance*, Detroit: Wayne State University Press, pp. 42–70.

Carnicke, Sharon Marie. (2006) 'The Material Poetry of Acting: "Objects of Attention", Performance Style, and Gender in *The Shining* and *Eyes Wide Shut*', *Journal of Film and Video*, 58:1, pp. 21–30.

Caughie, John. (2000a) *Television Drama: Realism, Modernism, and British Culture*, Oxford: Oxford University Press.

Caughie, John. (2000b) 'What Do Actors Do When They Act?', in Jonathan Bignell, Stephen Lacey and Madeleine Macmurraugh-Kavanagh (eds), *British Television Drama: Past, Present and Future*, Basingstoke and New York: Palgrave Macmillan, pp. 162–174.

Chapman, James. (2013) *Inside the TARDIS: The Worlds of Doctor Who*, 2nd edition, London and New York: I.B. Tauris.

Clark, Richard. (2011) Interviewed by the author, 9 April.

Coburn, Anthony and McElroy, John (eds). (1988) *Doctor Who – The Scripts: The Tribe of Gum*, London: Titan Books.

Cole, Toby and Krich Chinoy, Helen (eds). (1970) *Actors on Acting: The Theories, Techniques and Practices of the World's Great Actors, Told in Their Own Words*, New York: Crown Publishers Inc.

Cooke, Lez. (2003) *British Television Drama: A History*, London: BFI.

Cooke, Lez. (2013) *Style in British Television Drama*, Basingstoke and New York: Palgrave Macmillan.

Cope, Kenneth. (2011) Interviewed by the author, 7 October.

Cornea, Christine (ed.). (2010) *Genre and Performance: Film and Television*, Manchester and New York: Manchester University Press.

Cornell, Paul, Day, Martin and Topping, Keith. (1996) *The Guinness Book of Classic British TV*, 2nd edition, London: Guinness Publishing Ltd.

Crisell, Andrew. (1997) *An Introductory History of British Broadcasting*, London and New York: Routledge.

Cross, Rich. (2010) *Worlds Apart: The Unofficial and Unauthorised Guide to the BBC's Remake of Survivors*, London: Classic TV Press.

Cross, Rich and Priestner, Andy. (2005) *The End of the World? The Unofficial and Unauthorised Guide to Survivors*, Tolworth: Telos.

Cullen, Ian. (2002) 'Remembering "The Aztecs"' [DVD extra], *Doctor Who: The Aztecs*, BBCDVD1099.

Cushing, Peter. (1955) 'Peter Cushing Talks Shop: This Favourite TV Actor Speaks Here as a Specially Interested Play-viewer', *TV Annual for 1955*, London: Odhams Press, pp. 60–68.

Cushing, Peter. (1986) *An Autobiography*, London: Weidenfeld & Nicolson.

Cushing, Peter. (1988) *Past Forgetting: Memoirs of the Hammer Years*, London: Weidenfeld & Nicolson.

Dalkin, Julia. (2010) Interviewed by the author, 7 November.

Davies, Russell T. (2005a) *The Culture Show*, BBC Two, 17 March.

Davies, Russell T. (2005b) *Doctor Who Confidential: Bringing Back the Doctor*, BBC Three, 26 March.

Davies, Russell T. (2005c) Commentary on 'Rose', *Doctor Who: The Complete First Series*, BBCDVD1770.

Davies, Russell T., Gatiss, Mark, Shearman, Rob, Cornell, Paul and Moffat, Steven. (2005) *Doctor Who: The Shooting Scripts*, London: BBC Books.

Davis, Desmond. (1960) *The Grammar of Television Production*, London: Barrie & Jenkins Ltd.

Davis, Desmond. (1966) *The Grammar of Television Production*, 2nd edition, revised by John Eliot, London: Barrie & Jenkins Ltd.

Davis, Desmond. (1974) *The Grammar of Television Production*, 3rd edition, revised by John Eliot and Mike Wooller, reprinted with corrections, London: Barrie & Jenkins Ltd.

Delaumosne, L'Abbe, Arnaud, Angelique, Delsarte, Francois, Geraldy, Marie, Giraudet, Alfred, Durivage, Francis A. and Berlioz, Hector. (1893) *Delsarte System of Oratory*, New York: Edgar S. Werner.

De Vere Cole, Tristan. (1985) *A Guide to Actors New to Television*, Longmead: Element Books.

Dingwall, Shaun. (2005) *Doctor Who Confidential: Time Trouble*, BBC Three, 14 May.

Durham, Kim. (2002) 'Methodology and Praxis of the Actor within the Television Production Process: Facing the Camera in EastEnders and Morse', *Studies in Theatre and Performance*, 22:2, pp. 82–94.

Dyer, Richard. (1979) *Stars*, London: BFI.

Dyer, Richard. (1998) *Stars*, new edition with supplementary chapter by Paul McDonald, London: BFI.

Eccleston, Christopher. (2005a) *BBC Breakfast*, BBC One, March.

Eccleston, Christopher. (2005b) *Doctor Who Confidential: Special Effects*, BBC Three, 21 May.

Ellis, John. (2005) 'Importance, Significance, Cost and Value: Is an ITV Canon Possible?', in Catherine Johnson and Rob Turnock (eds), *ITV Cultures: Independent Television Over Fifty Years*, Maidenhead: Open University Press, pp. 36–56.

Ellis, John. (2007) 'Is It Possible to Construct a Canon of Television Programmes? Immanent Reading versus Textual-Historicism', in Helen Wheatley (ed.), *Re-Viewing Television History: Critical Issues in Television Historiography*, London and New York: I.B. Tauris, pp. 15–26.

Ellis, Robin. (1978) *Making Poldark*, Cornwall: Bossiney Books.

Equity/Skillset. (2005) 'Working Patterns and Career Development', *Performing Arts Industry Report 2005* [online]. Available at: https://creativeskillset.org/assets/0000/6241/Equity_Performing_Arts_Industry_Survey_2005.pdf (accessed 4 August 2016).

Fallis, Christopher. (2005) 'Living Dangerously', *Radio Times*, 30 April–6 May, p. 9.

Fell, Richard. (2005) 'Bring Something Back – The Making of *The Quatermass Experiment*' [DVD extra], *The Quatermass Experiment*, Simply Home Entertainment 122098.

Fleming, Lucy. (2003) 'Cast Interviews' [DVD extra], *Survivors: The Complete First Series*, DD06482.

Fleming, Lucy. (2010) Interviewed by the author, 25 October.

Flemyng, Jason. (2011) Interviewed by the author, 4 February.

Furness, G. (1953) 'Letters', *Radio Times*, 9–15 August, p. 32.

Gardner, Carl and Wyver, John. (1983) 'The Single Play: From Reithian Reverence to Cost-Counting and Censorship', *Screen*, 24:4–5, pp. 114–124.

Gardner, Julie. (2005) Commentary on 'The Aliens of London', *Doctor Who: The Complete First Series*, BBCDVD1770.

Garnett, Tony. (2009) 'BBC Drama Needs to Change Its Culture' [online], *Guardian*, 15 July. Available at: www.guardian.co.uk/media/organgrinder/2009/jul/15/tony-garnett-bbc-drama (accessed 4 August 2016).

Garnett, Tony. (2010) Interviewed by the author, 5 October.

Gaskill, William. (1988) *A Sense of Direction*, London: Faber & Faber.

Gatiss, Mark. (2005) 'Bring Something Back – The Making of *The Quatermass Experiment*' [DVD extra], *The Quatermass Experiment*, Simply Home Entertainment 122098.

Gatiss, Mark. (2011) Interviewed by the author, 7 November.

Gilbert, Gerard. (2010) 'Right on Cue', *Independent on Sunday*, 7 November, pp. 10–18.

Gillette, William. (1915) *The Illusion of the First Time in Acting*, New York: Dramatic Museum.

Goode, Ian. (2006) 'The Quality of Intimacy: Revelation and Disguise in the Dramatic Monologue', *Journal of British Cinema and Television*, 3:1, pp. 107–114.

Gorrie, John. (2009) Commentary on 'The Velvet Web', *Doctor Who: The Keys of Marinus*, BBCDVD2616.

Gunn, Andrew. (2011) Interviewed by the author, 14 April.

Hagen, Uta. (1991) *A Challenge for the Actor*, New York: Scribner.

Harper, Graeme. (2007) *Calling the Shots: Directing the New Series of Doctor Who*, London: Reynolds & Hearn.

Harper, Graeme. (2011) Interviewed by the author, 22 January.

Hartnell, William. (1965) *Desert Island Discs*, 23 August [online]. Available at: www.bbc.co.uk/programmes/p009y3yj (accessed 4 August 2016).

Hartnell, William. (2005) Interviewed for *Points West*, 1967 [DVD extra], *Doctor Who: The Tenth Planet*, BBCDVD3382.

Hewett, Richard. (2013) 'Acting in the New World: Studio and Location Realism in Survivors', *The Journal of British Cinema and Television*, Volume 10.2, April, pp. 321–339.

Higson, Charlie. (2010) Interviewed by the author, 22 November.

Hills, Matt. (2010) *Triumph of a Time Lord: Regenerating Doctor Who in the Twenty-First Century*, London and New York: I.B. Tauris.

Hills, Matt, Mellor, David and Earl, Benjamin (eds). (2013) *New Dimensions of Doctor Who: Adventures in Space, Time and Television*, London and New York: I.B. Tauris.

Hobson, Dorothy. (1982) *Crossroads: The Drama of a Soap Opera*, London: Methuen.

Hodges, Adrian. (2011) Interviewed by the author, 15 February.

Hogan, Michael. (2015) '*EastEnders* Live Episode Review: "Triumphant, Heartbreaking and Faultless Family Drama"' [online], *Telegraph*, 21 February. Available at: www.telegraph.co.uk/culture/tvandradio/eastenders/11425733/EastEnders-Live-review.html (accessed 4 August 2016).

Hogg, Christopher and Cantrell, Tom. (forthcoming) *Acting in British Television*, Basingstoke and New York: Palgrave Macmillan.

Hogg, Christopher and Cantrell, Tom (eds.) (forthcoming) *Exploring Television Acting*, London: Bloomsbury.

Holdsworth, Amy. (2011) *Television, Memory and Nostalgia*, Basingstoke and New York: Palgrave Macmillan.

Holdsworth, Nadine. (2006) *Joan Littlewood*, London and New York: Routledge.

Hornby, Richard. (1992) *The End of Acting: A Radical View*, New York: Applause.

Hussein, Waris. (2006) Commentary on 'An Unearthly Child, pilot', *Doctor Who: The Beginning*, BBCDVD1882.

Hussein, Waris. (2011) Interviewed by the author, 3 May.

Jacobs, Jason. (2000) *The Intimate Screen: Early British Television Drama*, Oxford: Clarendon Press.

James, Clive. (1975) 'Fleeing and Surviving', *Observer*, 4 May, p. 26.

James, Peter. (2011) Email responses to questions, 15 and 18 January.

Jameson, Louise. (2011) Interviewed by the author, 2 April.

Jarvis, Martin. (2005) Commentary on 'Invasion', *Doctor Who: The Web Planet*, BBCDVD1355.

Jeffery, Morgan. (2015) 'Christopher Eccleston on *Doctor Who* Exit: "I'm Always There in Spirit"' [online], *Digital Spy*, 19 April.

Available at: www.digitalspy.com/tv/doctor-who/news/a642707/christopher-eccleston-on-doctor-who-exit-im-always-there-in-spirit/ (accessed 4 August 2016).

Jenkins, Henry. (1992) *Textual Poachers: Television Fans and Participatory Culture*, New York and London: Routledge.

Johnson, Catherine. (2005) *Telefantasy*, London: BFI.

Johnson, Catherine. (2007) 'Negotiating Value and Quality in Television Historiography', in Helen Wheatley (ed.), *Re-Viewing Television History: Critical Issues in Television Historiography*, London and New York: I.B. Tauris, pp. 55–66.

Johnson, Catherine and Turnock, Rob (eds). (2005) *ITV Cultures: Independent Television Over Fifty Years*, Maidenhead: Open University Press.

Jordan, Marion. (1981) 'Realism and Convention', in Richard Dyer, Christine Geraghty, Marion Jordan, Terry Lovell, Richard Paterson and John Stewart, *Coronation Street*, London: BFI, pp. 27–39.

Kalter, Joanmarie. (1979) *Actors on Acting: Performing in Theatre and Film Today*, New York: Sterling.

Kebbel, Thomas Edward (ed.). (1882) *Selected Speeches of the Late Right Honourable the Earl of Beaconsfield*, 4:2, London: Longmans, Green & Co.

Kennedy Martin, Troy. (1964) 'Nats Go Home: First Statement for a New Drama for Television', *Encore*, 11:2, pp. 20–33.

King, Nicola. (2000) *Memory, Narrative, Identity: Remembering the Self*, Edinburgh: Edinburgh University Press.

Klein, Kerwin Lee. (2000) 'On the Emergence of *Memory* in Historical Discourse', *Representations*, 69, pp. 127–150.

Klevan, Andrew. (2005) *Film Performance: From Achievement to Appreciation*, London: Wallflower Press.

Kneale, Nigel. (1959) 'Not Quite So Intimate', *Sight and Sound*, 28:2, pp. 86–88.

Kneale, Nigel. (2005) 'Cartier and Kneale in Conversation', interviewed by Lynda Miles and John Bush for *The Late Show*, 1990, and *The Lime Grove Story*, 1991 [DVD extra], *The Quatermass Collection*, BBCDVD 1478.

Kuleshov, Lev. (1974) *Kuleshov on Film: Writings by Lev Kuleshov*, translated from the German and edited by Ron Levaco, Berkeley and Los Angeles: University of California Press.

Laban, Rudolf. (1960) *The Mastery of Movement*, 2nd edition, revised by Lisa Ullman, London: Macdonald and Evans.

Lacey, Stephen. (2005) 'Becoming Popular: Some Reflections on the Relationship between Television and Theatre', in Jonathan Bignell and Stephen Lacey (eds), *Popular Television Drama: Critical Perspectives*, Manchester and New York: Manchester University Press, pp. 198–214.

Lambert, Verity. (2002) Commentary on 'The Temple of Evil', *Doctor Who: The Aztecs*, BBCDVD1099.

Lambert, Verity. (2003) Commentary on 'World's End', *Doctor Who: The Dalek Invasion of Earth*, BBCDVD1156.

Lambert, Verity. (2006) Commentary on 'An Unearthly Child', *Doctor Who: The Beginning*, BBCDVD1882.

Lambert, Verity. (2008) Commentary on 'Checkmate', *Doctor Who: The Time Meddler*, BBCDVD2331.

Lavery, David. (2011) 'What's My Motivation? The Method Goes Fantastic in Television Acting', *CST Online*, 13 March. Available at: http://cstonline.tv/telegenic-method (accessed 4 August 2016).

Lawson, Denis. (2014) *The Actor and the Camera*, London: Nick Hern Books.

Lay, Samantha. (2002) *British Social Realism: From Documentary to Brit Grit*, London and New York: Wallflower Press.

Lill, Denis. (2010) Interviewed by the author, 7 December.

Littlejohn, Georgina. (2010) '*EastEnders* Live Episode Gaffes Revealed after Nerves Got the Better of Its Stars' [online], *Mail*Online, 22 February. Available at: www.dailymail.co.uk/tvshowbiz/article-1252911/Eastenders-live-episode-gaffes-revealed-nerves-got-better-stars.html (accessed 4 August 2016).

Littlewood, Joan. (1994) *Joan's Book: Joan Littlewood's Peculiar History as She Tells It*, London: Methuen.

Lloyd Pack, Roger. (2011) Interviewed by the author, 20 January.

Logan, Elliott. (2015) 'How Do We Write about Performance in Serial Television?', *Series: International Journal of TV Serial Narratives*, 1:1, pp. 27–38.

Luke's Stuff. (2010) 'Eastenders Live – The Mistakes' [online], YouTube, 19 February. Available at: www.youtube.com/watch?v=gClD3Y-CDoA (accessed 4 August 2016).

McGeorge, Alistair. (2015) '*Coronation Street* Loses Live Ratings Battle to *EastEnders* after Pulling In Over 8 Million Viewers for Error-Free Show' [online], *Mirror*, 24 September. Available at: www.mirror.co.uk/tv/tv-news/coronation-street-loses-live-ratings-6507540 (accessed 4 August 2016).

McNally, Kevin. (2010) Interviewed by the author, 9 November.

McNaughton, Douglas. (2014) '"Constipated, Studio-bound, Wall-confined, Rigid": The Influence Of British Actors' Equity On BBC Television Drama, 1948–72', *The British Journal of Cinema and Television*, 11:1, pp. 1–22.

'*Maigret*', *The Classic TV Archive* [online]. Available at: http://ctva.biz/UK/BBC/Drama/Maigret1960–63_BBC_RupertDavies.htm (accessed 4 August 2016).

Malahide, Patrick. (2011) Interviewed by the author, 13 June.

'The Man Who Put *1984* Over on Television', *The Times* (1 December 1958), p. 14.

Marshall, Kevin P. (1995?) 'Interview with Carolyn Seymour' [online]. Available at: www.survivorstvseries.com/Carolyn_Interview.htm (accessed 4 August 2016).

Martin, Richard. (2005) Commentary on 'Invasion', *Doctor Who: The Web Planet*, BBCDVD1355.

Martin, Richard. (2006) 'Doctor Who Origins' [DVD extra], *Doctor Who: The Beginning*, BBCDVD1882.

Martland, Lisa. (2002) 'Training Programs for Stage and Screen' [online], *Back Stage*, 22 February. Available at: www.backstage.com/bso/esearch/article_display.jsp?vnu_content_id=1349485 (accessed 4 August 2016).

Mellor, Louise. (2015) '10 Years of New *Doctor Who*: What 2005 Reviews Made of Rose' [online], *Den of Geek*, 24 March. Available at: www.denofgeek.com/tv/doctor-who/34407/10-years-of-new-doctor-who-what-2005-reviews-made-of-rose (accessed 4 August 2016).

Mendlesohn, Farah. (2008) *Rhetorics of Fantasy*, Middletown: Wesleyan University Press.

Middleton, Christopher. (2005) 'Lord's Test', *Radio Times Doctor Who* pull-out special, 26 March–1 April, pp. 3–4.

Miller, Ken. (2013) *More Than Fifteen Minutes of Fame: The Changing Face of Screen Performance*, London and New York: Routledge.

Mills, Brett. (2004) 'Comedy Vérité: Contemporary Sitcom Form', *Screen*, 45:1, pp. 63–78.

Mills, Brett. (2009) *The Sitcom*, Edinburgh: Edinburgh University Press.

Moffat, Steven. (2005a) Commentary on 'The Doctor Dances', *Doctor Who: The Complete First Series*, BBCDVD1770.

Moffat, Steven. (2005b) Commentary on 'The Empty Child', *Doctor Who: The Complete First Series*, BBCDVD1770.

Morahan, Christopher. (2010) Interviewed by the author, 26 October.

Morey, Anne. (2011) 'Grotesquerie as Marker of Success in Ageing Female Stars', in Su Holmes and Diana Negra (eds), *In the Limelight and Under the Microscope: Forms and Functions of Female Celebrity*, New York: Continuum, pp. 103–124.

Mulkern, Patrick. (2010) 'Interview: *Doctor Who*'s William Russell', *Radio Times* [online], 1 November. Available at: www.radiotimes.com/news/2010-11-01/interview-doctor-whos-william-russell (accessed 4 August 2016).

Naremore, James. (1988) *Acting in the Cinema*, Berkeley and Los Angeles: University of California Press.

National Council for Drama Training (NCDT). (2002) *Report of the Recorded Media Working Party*.

Neale, Steve. (1990) 'You've Got to Be Fucking Kidding! Knowledge, Belief and Judgement in Science Fiction', in Annette Kuhn (ed.), *Alien Zone*, London: Verso, pp. 160–168.

Neale, Steve. (2000) *Genre and Hollywood*, London and New York: Routledge.

Nelson, Robin. (1997) *TV Drama in Transition: Forms, Values and Cultural Change*, Basingstoke and New York: Palgrave Macmillan.

Neon Media. (2010) 'EastEnders Live – The Mistakes' [online], YouTube, 16 March. Available at: www.youtube.com/watch?v=TaNQFxbeBQ8 (accessed 4 August 2016).

Newman, Sydney. (2006) 'Doctor Who Origins', interviewed for *BBC Oral History Project*, 1984 [DVD extra], *Doctor Who: The Beginning*, BBCDVD1882.

Norman, Bruce. (1984) *Here's Looking at You: The Story of British Television: 1908–1939*, London: Royal Television Society/BBC.

Ofcom. (2015) 'Changes in TV Viewing Habits' [online], *The Communications Market Report 2015*, August. Available at:

http://stakeholders.ofcom.org.uk/binaries/research/cmr/cmr15/CMR_2015_Annex_Changes_in_TV_viewing_habits.pdf (accessed 4 August 2016).

Paget, Derek. (2011) Interviewed by the author, 12 May.

Parker, John (ed.). (1947) *Who's Who in the Theatre*, 10th edition, London: Pitman.

Parker, John (ed.). (1952) *Who's Who in the Theatre*, 11th edition, London: Pitman.

Payne, Jamie. (2011) Interviewed by the author, 12 April.

Peacock, Alan T. (Chairman). (1986) *Report of the Committee on Financing the BBC*, London: HMSO.

Pearson, Roberta. (1990) '"O'er Step Not the Modesty of Nature": A Semiotic Approach to Acting in the Griffiths Biographs', in Carole Zucker (ed.), *Making Visible the Invisible: An Anthology of Original Essays on Film Acting*, Metuchen: Scarecrow Press, pp. 1–27.

Pearson, Roberta. (1992) *Eloquent Gestures: The Transformation of Performance Style in the Griffith Biograph Films*, Berkeley and Los Angeles: University of California Press.

Pearson, Roberta. (2010) 'The Multiple Determinants of Television Acting', in Christine Cornea (ed.), *Genre and Performance: Film and Television*, Manchester and New York: Manchester University Press, pp. 166–183.

Pearson, Roberta, and Messenger Davies, Maire. (2014) *Star Trek and American Television*, Berkeley and Los Angeles: University of California Press.

Pirwany, Hyder Ali. (2005) 'Saviour of Earthlings...', *Radio Times*, 9–15 April, p. 9.

Plunkett, John. (2005) 'Norton Dance Show Trips Up' [online], *Guardian*, 4 April. Available at: www.guardian.co.uk/media/2005/apr/04/overnights2 (accessed 4 August 2016).

Plunkett, John. (2010) '*Coronation Street* Live Show Draws Show's Biggest Audience for Seven Years' [online], *Guardian*, 10 December. Available at: www.theguardian.com/media/2010/dec/10/ratings-coronation-street-live (accessed 4 August 2016).

Powell, Jonathan. (2010) Interviewed by the author, 2 February.

Pudovkin, Vsevolod. (1953) 'Stanislavski's System in the Cinema', *Sight and Sound*, 22:3, pp. 115–118, 147–148.

Purves, Peter. (2008) Commentary on 'A Battle of Wits', *Doctor Who: The Time Meddler*, BBCDVD2331.

Purves, Peter. (2010) Commentary on 'The Death of Doctor Who', *Doctor Who: The Space Museum/The Chase*, BBCDVD2809.

RADA. (1926) *Prospectus 1926*, London: RADA.

RADA. (1928) *Prospectus 1928/29*, London: RADA.

RADA. (1959) *Prospectus 1959*, London: RADA.

RADA. (1960) *Prospectus 1960*, London: RADA.

RADA. (1988) *Prospectus 1988/89*, London: RADA.

Rakoff, Alvin. (2011) Interviewed by the author, 27 April.

Rawlins, Trevor. (2010) 'Screen Acting and Performance Choices', *Networking Knowledge: Journal of the MECCSA Postgraduate Network*, 3:2, pp. 1–27.

Rawlins, Trevor. (2011) Interviewed by the author, 21 May.

Rawson-Jones, Ben. (2008a) '*Survivors* S01E01: Part One' [online], *Digital Spy*, 23 November. Available at: www.digitalspy.com/tv/survivors/review/a136434/survivors-s01e01-part-one/ (accessed 4 August 2016).

Rawson-Jones, Ben. (2008b) '*Survivors* S01E02: Part Two' [online], *Digital Spy*, 25 November. Available at: www.digitalspy.com/tv/survivors/review/a136452/survivors-s01e02-part-two/ (accessed 4 August 2016).

Rebellato, Dan. (1999) *1956 and All That: The Making of Modern British Drama*, London and New York: Routledge.

Redgrave, Michael. (1946) 'The Stanislavski Myth', originally published in *New Theatre*, 3:1, and reprinted in Cole, Toby and Krich Chinoy, Helen (eds). (1970) *Actors on Acting: The Theories, Techniques and Practices of the World's Great Actors, Told in Their Own Words*, New York: Crown Publishers Inc., pp. 403–408.

Rhys, Phillip. (2011) Interviewed by the author, 19 February.

Ridgman, Jeremy (ed.). (1998) *Boxed Sets: Television Representations of Theatre*, Luton: John Libbey Media.

Ringham, John. (2002) 'Remembering "The Aztecs"' [DVD extra], *Doctor Who: The Aztecs*, BBCDVD1099.

Rixon, Paul. (2011) *TV Critics and Popular Culture: A History of British Television Criticism*, London and New York: I.B. Tauris.

Roberts, Pennant. (2003a) Commentary on 'The Fourth Horseman', *Survivors: The Complete First Series*, DD06482.

Roberts, Pennant. (2003b) 'Cast Interviews' [DVD extra], *Survivors: The Complete First Series*, DD06482.

Ross, Lillian and Ross, Helen (eds). (1962) *The Player: The Profile of an Art*, New York: Simon & Schuster.

Russell, Gary (ed.). (1995) *Doctor Who Yearbook*, London: Marvel.

Russell, Gary. (2006) *Doctor Who: The Inside Story*, London: BBC Books.

Russell, William. (2003a) Commentary on 'The Daleks', *Doctor Who: The Dalek Invasion of Earth*, BBCDVD1156.

Russell, William. (2003b) Commentary on 'The Waking Ally', *Doctor Who: The Dalek Invasion of Earth*, BBCDVD1156.

Russell, William. (2005a) Commentary on 'Escape to Danger', *Doctor Who: The Web Planet*, BBCDVD1355.

Russell, William. (2005b) Commentary on 'Invasion', *Doctor Who: The Web Planet*, BBCDVD1355.

Russell, William. (2006a) Commentary on 'The Firemaker', *Doctor Who: The Beginning*, BBCDVD1882.

Russell, William. (2006b) Commentary on 'An Unearthly Child', *Doctor Who: The Beginning*, BBCDVD1882.

Russell, William. (2009a) Commentary on 'Desperate Measures', *Doctor Who: The Rescue*, BBCDVD2970.

Russell, William. (2009b) Commentary on 'The Powerful Enemy', *Doctor Who: The Rescue*, BBCDVD2970.

Ryan, Marie-Laure. (1991) 'Possible Worlds and Accessibility Relations: A Semantic Typology of Fiction', *Poetics Today*, 12:3, pp. 553–576.

Sanderson, Michael. (1984) *From Irving to Olivier: A Social History of the Acting Profession in England 1880–1983*, London: The Athlone Press.

'Saturday Serial', *Manchester Guardian* (5 August 1953), p. 3.

Sendall, Bernard. (1982) *Independent Television in Britain: Volume 1 – Origin and Foundation, 1946–1962*, London and Basingstoke: Macmillan.

Sexton, Max. (2015) 'Philip Jackson: The Craft of Acting', *Journal of British Cinema and Television*, 12:1, pp. 121–126.

Shatner, William and Kreski, Chris. (1999) *Get a Life!*, London and New York: Pocket Books.

Smart, William. (2010) *Adaptations of Classical Theatre Plays on BBC Television 1957–1985*, unpublished PhD thesis, Royal Holloway.
Smith, Andrew. (1975) 'Letters', *Radio Times*, 2–8 August, p. 53.
Smith, Jacob. (2008) *Vocal Tracks: Performance and Sound Media*, Berkeley and Los Angeles: University of California Press.
South West England Vintage Television Museum (2011) [online]. Available at: www.tvmuseum.co.uk/ (accessed 4 August 2016).
Stanislavski, Constantin. (1924) *My Life in Art*, translated from the Russian by J.J. Robbins, London: Geoffrey Bles Ltd.
Stanislavski, Constantin. (1934) *An Actor Prepares*, translated from the Russian by Elizabeth Reynolds Hapgood, London: Geoffrey Bles Ltd.
Stanislavski, Constantin. (1949) *Building a Character*, translated from the Russian by Elizabeth Reynolds Hapgood, New York: Theatre Arts.
Stanislavski, Constantin. (1961) *Creating a Role*, translated from the Russian by Elizabeth Reynolds Hapgood, New York: Theatre Arts.
Sullivan, Shannon. (2009) 'Dalek', *A Brief History of Time (Travel)* [online], updated 17 October. Available at: www.shannonsullivan.com/drwho/serials/2005f.html (accessed 4 August 2016).
Susi, Lolly. (2006) *The Central Book*, London: Oberon Books.
Sutton, Shaun. (1982) *The Largest Theatre in the World*, London: BBC.
Sylvester, David. (1954) 'The Kitchen Sink', *Encounter*, December, pp. 61–63.
Sylvester, Kemal. (2010) Interviewed by the author, 7 November.
Sylvester, Suzan. (2010) Interviewed by the author, 7 November.
Symes, Dave (2005) 'Saviour of Earthlings...', *Radio Times*, 9–15 April, p. 9.
Taylor, Don. (1990) *Days of Vision: Working with David Mercer: Television Drama Then and Now*, London: Methuen.
Teague, Colin. (2011) Interviewed by the author, 29 March.
Tennant, David. (2005) 'Bring Something Back – The Making of *The Quatermass Experiment*' [DVD extra], *The Quatermass Experiment*, Simply Home Entertainment 122098.
Tennant, David. (2006) Commentary on 'School Reunion', *Doctor Who: The Complete Second Series*, BBCDVD2122.
'Television', *Sunday Times* (22 June 1975), p. 32.

'This Week', *Radio Times* (12–18 April 1975), p. 3.

Tiernan, Andrew. (2011) Email response to questions, 12 January.

Tucker, Patrick. (2014) *Secrets of Screen Acting*, 3rd edition, New York and London: Routledge.

Tulloch, John and Alvarado, Manuel. (1983) *Doctor Who: The Unfolding Text*, London and Basingstoke: Macmillan.

Turner, Victor. (1986) *The Anthropology of Performance*, New York: PAJ Publications.

Turnock, Rob. (2007) *Television and Consumer Culture: Britain and the Transformation of Modernity*, London and New York: I.B. Tauris.

Varma, Indira. (2005) 'Bring Something Back – The Making of *The Quatermass Experiment*' [DVD extra], *The Quatermass Experiment*, Simply Home Entertainment 122098.

Watson, Moray. (2010) Interviewed by the author, 5 November.

Watson, Moray. (2011) Interviewed by the author, 7 June.

Weston, Judith. (1996) *Directing Actors: Creating Memorable Performances for Film and Television*, Studio City: Michael Wiese.

Wheatley, Helen. (2005) 'Rooms within Rooms: *Upstairs Downstairs* and the Studio Costume Drama of the 1970s', in Catherine Johnson and Rob Turnock (eds), *ITV Cultures: Independent Television Over Fifty Years*, Maidenhead: Open University Press, pp. 143–158.

Willett, Alison. (2005) Commentary on *The Quatermass Experiment*, Simply Home Entertainment 122098.

Williams, Raymond. (1983) *Keywords: A Vocabulary of Culture and Society*, London: Fontana Press.

Willis, Susan. (1991) *The BBC Shakespeare Plays: Making the Televised Canon*, Chapel Hill: University of North Carolina Press.

Woodyatt, Adam. (2015) '"I Want Tuesday to Arrive!" – Interview Chat' [online], *EastEnders Ultra*, 16 February. Available at: www.eastendersultra.co.uk/news/interviews/13597/adam-woodyatt-i-want-tuesday-to-arrive-interview-chat (accessed 4 August 2016).

Zucker, Carole. (1995) *Figures of Light: Actors and Directors Illuminate the Art of Film Acting*, New York: Plenum.

Zucker, Carole. (1999a) *In the Company of Actors: Reflections on the Craft of Acting*, New York: Theatre Arts/Routledge.

Zucker, Carole. (1999b) 'An Interview with Ian Richardson: Making Friends with the Camera', in Alan Lovell and Peter Kramer (eds), *Screen Acting*, London and New York: Routledge, pp. 152–164.

Index

A for Andromeda 18
Absolutely Fabulous 222n.19
Academy of Dramatic Art 56–57, 69n.16
Acton Hilton 117, 122–125, 131–132, 164n.10, 170–171, 175
Actors Studio 69n.19, 71, 85, 200, 242
actor training 8, 56–62, 67, 71, 109–113, 118, 145–153, 162–163, 164n.13, 165, 199–208, 211, 220, 222n.17, 240
ADA *see* Academy of Dramatic Art
Adair, Hazel 99
Adam, Kenneth 72
Adiv, Rueven 200
Adler, Stella 115n.16, 200
ADR 205
Adventures of Sir Lancelot, The 75, 89–91, 111
Affron, Charles 7, 19
Alexander, John 180, 182–183
Alexandra Palace 14, 42, 45, 47
Alvarado, Manuel 15, 18–19, 83, 126, 221n.2
Amyes, Julian 49

Anderson, Lindsay 71, 75
Ang, Ien 208
Armchair Theatre 67n.1, 72, 84, 87
Army Game, The 75
Arrow to the Heart 27
'as live' recording 12, 70, 74, 98–99, 103, 179, 238
Atkins, Ian 49
Audience Research Report 112, 161–162
see also Viewer Research Report
Auslander, Philip 9–10
Avengers, The 153

Baker, Tom 212
Bakewell, Michael 114
Ballard, Iris 52, 53–54, 55, 60–61, 67, 69n.23, 78, 129, 213
Banks–Smith, Nancy 229
BARB *see* Broadcasters Audience Research Board
Barkworth, Peter 110
Baron, Cynthia 7, 9, 187
Barr, Patrick 50
Barr, Tony 164n.6
Barrowman, John 178

Barry, Michael 1, 22n.1, 27, 42–44, 46–47, 49, 52, 68n.6, 125
Barton, Robert 69n.19, 115n.16, 177, 179, 197, 209
Bates, Alan 85–86
Battin, Tom C. 109–110
BBC2 72, 118
Beautiful One, The 42
Beerbohm-Tree, Herbert 56
Beesley, Max 219
Bennett-Levy, Michael 68n.9, 115n.14
Benson, Frank 74
Bergerac 221n.3
Bernard, Ian 164n.6
Bignell, Jonathan 3, 11, 14–15, 73, 115n.11, 119, 168
Bill, The 202, 231
Billington, Michael 147–148
Blair, Isla 229
Blake, Gerald 119
Blaker, Hugh 111
Blum, Richard A. 8, 69n.19
Boak, Keith 175, 177
Bolt, Ben 235–236
Boolen, Van 52–53, 55–56, 60, 67, 78, 129, 228, 238–239
Borderers, The 119
Born, Georgina 167–168
Bower, Adrian 228, 236n.1, 237n.2
Bower, Dallas 42
Bowles, Peter 127–128, 130, 153, 228
Brando, Marlon 85, 115n.16
Bratby, John 84
Brecht, Bertolt 149
Brett, Laurie 232, 234
Brideshead Revisited 221n.3
Briggs, Asa 26n.3, 68n.3
Briggs, Nicholas 199
Brighton Rock 75
Bristol Old Vic School 58, 146, 149

Broadcasters Audience Research Board 71, 118
Broadcasting Act (1990) 166, 168
Brown, June 237n.5
Buffy the Vampire Slayer 207
Burch, Howard 171–172, 234–235
Bury, Margaret 114n.1, 147
Butler, David 15, 83
Butler, Jeremy 22n.2

Callow, Simon 147, 206–207, 214
Cannon, Doreen 200
Canterbury Tales 218
Cantrell, Tom 5
Cardullo, Bert 24n.20, 176
Caretaker, The 145
Carleton Greene, Hugh 71, 73
Carney, Jessica 75, 111
Carnicke, Sharon Marie 7–9, 152, 160, 187, 195
Carrington, Eliot 232
Cartier, Rudolph 24n.18, 26–28, 30, 32, 34, 36, 40, 44, 47–49, 51–52, 55, 68n.11
Carry On Sergeant 111
Cassidy, Gary 5
Casualty 211, 221n.6, 222n.13
Casualty 1906 221n.6
Casualty 1907 221n.6
Casualty 1909 221n.6
'Cathy Come Home' 120, 167
Caughie, John 5–6, 9, 20, 71, 93, 115n.15, 221n.6
Central School of Speech and Drama 56–58, 69n.17, 109–110, 147, 149, 201
CGI 4, 166, 206, 239
see also special effects; visual effects
Chapman, James 15, 218
cinema performance
analysis of 6–7, 36

influence of 71, 85
Clark, Richard 171–172, 214, 222n.13
Clarke, Noel 212
Cleaning Up 236
Clements, Charlie 231
Coburn, Anthony 116n.29
Coduri, Camille 212, 214
Cole, Toby 24n.20, 58
Colin, Ian 59
Compact 72–73, 95, 99
Conti, Italia 111
Cooke, Lez 5–6, 22n.4, 87, 93
Cope, Kenneth 58, 187
Cornea, Christine 15
Coronation Street 84, 86–87, 89, 231, 237n.9
Courtenay, Tom 85, 110–111
Crawford, Ann 50
Cribbins, Bernard 217
Crisell, Andrew 26
Cross, Rich 119–120, 122, 130–132, 134, 160, 163n.4, 164n.10, 189, 219, 221n.8
Cruttwell, Hugh 146–148
Cullen, Ian 99–100, 106
Curtis, Simon 168
Cushing, Peter 5–6, 22n.4, 22n.5, 44–46, 68n.13
cut-key 45

Dad's Army 153–154
Dalkin, Julia 177, 185–186, 200–202, 213, 216, 236
Dallas 221n.4
Danes, Clare 22n.2
Daniels, Jeff 176, 179
Davies, Rupert 91
Davies, Russell T 169, 175, 194–196, 213, 217–218
Davis, Desmond 116n.21
Dean, Isabel 30, 32–39, 48, 51, 59–60, 67

Dean, James 85
Delsarte, Francois 57, 69n.18
Desert Island Discs 116n.31
determinants, 2, 5–9, 22, 26, 40, 113–114, 138, 162, 166, 199, 220, 224–225, 229, 238, 241
De Vere Cole, Tristan 120–121, 124, 130–131, 133
Devine, George 71
Di Angelo, Matt 232
Digital Spy 21, 218–219
Dikij, Aleksei 149
Dingwall, Shaun 180, *184*, 206
director training 49, 101, 116, 139
Disraeli, Benjamin 236
Doc Martin 235–236
Doctor Who
  'Dalek' 198
  'Doctor Dances, The' 178–179, 215–216
  'Empty Child, The' 214
  'Father's Day' 198, 206–207
  'Long Game, The' 198
  'Rose' 175–176, 194, 196
  'School Reunion' 205
  'Unearthly Child, An' 13, 21, 70, 74, 78–79, 81, 83–84, 87–88, 91–93, 95–97, 101–103, 105, 107–108, 110, 112–113, 120, 194, 196, 206, 215
Doctor Who Confidential 175–176
Dragnet 221n.4
Drama Centre London 109, 113, 147, 200, 206
Dudley, Stephen 134, 161
Dudley, Terence 119, 163n.4
Du Maurier, Gerald 86
Dunbar, Adrian 224, 227–228, 236n.1
Dunning, Ruth 86
Durham, Kim 165, 185
Dyer, Danny 232

Dyer, Richard 7
Dynasty 168, 221n.4

East 15 School 71, 109, 113–114n.1, 147, 222n.17
EastEnders 177, 179, 184–185, 222n.13, 231–234, 237n.6
Eccleston, Christopher 112, *175–179*, 194–196, 198–199, 205–207, 209, 212–218
Ellis, John, 6, 168, 221n.5
Ellis, Robin 123
Emerald Soup 74
Emitron cameras 14, 47, 131
Emmerdale 231
Emperor Jones, The 55
Equity 114n.6, 116n.25, 117, 126, 220n.1
Escape 75
Euston Films 167
Exton, Clive 119, 158

Fabian of Scotland Yard 167
Fallis, Christopher 229
fantastic, the 15–19, 23n.17, 23n.18, 65, 84, 92, 206–208, 217
Fernald, John 110, 115n.17, 146
Fettes, Christopher 147
Finney, Albert 85–86, 111
Five Children and It 69n.23
Flanagan, Anthony 189, *192–193*
Fleming, Lucy 119–120, 131, 133, 134, *135–136*, 138, 149, 155, 186, 192, 197, 210–211
Fleming, Tom 37
Flemyng, Jason 186, 224–225, 227–229, 236n.1
Fligg, Anny 61
Fogerty, Elsie 56
Ford, Carole Ann 75, 92, *93*, *96*, *97*, *103*, *108*, 206
Frankenstein's Wedding 230–231

Gardner, Carl 168
Gardner, Julie 221n.8
Garnett, Tony 70, 85–86, 98, 110, 167, 221n.6
Gaskill, William 149
Gatiss, Mark 38, 40, 173–174, 209, 214, 222n.20, 224, 224–229, 233–236
Gielgud, Val 22n.1
Gilbert, Gerard 209
Gillette, William 196
Glasgow College of Dramatic Art 145
Gorrie, John 76
Goode, Ian 5
Gover, Michael 151
Graham, Alison 219
Graham, Julie 180, *181–182*, 183, *184*, 185, *192*, 214
Granada Television 86, 221n.3
Grandstand 115n.11
Grove Family, The 86
Gunn, Andrew 174, 177, 188, 191, 193, 209, 213–214, 216, 221n.9, 240
Gynt, Greta 37

Hagen, Uta 57, 65
Haigh, Kenneth 86
Hampton, Christopher 209
Happy Ever After 222n.19
Hardy, Ben 232–234
Harper, Graeme 1–2, 125, 139, 174–175
Hartnell, William 74–78, 79, 80, 81, 104, 106, *107–108*, 111–112, 115n.13, 116n.29, 116n.30, 116n.31, 194, 206, 212, 215
Hawes, James 215
Head, Anthony 205
Heavens Above 111
Helmsby, Eileen 136

INDEX

264

Higson, Charlie 169, 186, 202
Hill, Jacqueline 75, 78, 79, 80, 82, 87, 89, 91, 93, 96, 97, 98, 104, 105, 106, 108, 109, 111, 113
Hill, Maddy 232
Hills, Matt 15, 196, 208, 218
Hobson, Dorothy 5
Hodges, Adrian 169, 172, 209, 214
Hogan, Dek 218
Hogan, Michael 234
Hogg, Christopher 5
HolbyBlue 221n.6
Holby City 179, 221n.6, 222n.13
Holdsworth, Amy 20–21
Holdsworth, Nadine 61
Hollywood 6–7, 20, 115n.16, 176, 186, 217
Homeland 22n.2
Hornby, Richard 69n.19, 149
Howell, Jane 164n.7
Hussein, Waris 73, 88–89, 96, 98, 101–104, 106, 116n.27, 116n.28, 211

I, Claudius 37–38, 39, 60
Inspector Morse 60, 185
It is Midnight, Dr Schweitzer 36–37, 60, 92
It'll Be Alright on the Night 228
ITV 13, 71, 73, 112, 114n.2, 114n.3, 114n.6, 118, 231

Jackson, Philip 24, 177, 186
Jacobs, Jason 6, 10, 22n.4, 22n.5, 23n.8, 25–27, 68n.4, 68n.7
Jamaica Inn 4
James, Clive 161
James, Peter 203
Jameson, Louise 125, 145, 147, 150, 185, 204, 235–236
Jane Eyre 30
Jarvis, Martin 104

Jeffery, Morgan 218
Jenkins, Henry 21
Jewesbury, Edward 38, *39*
Johnson, Catherine 13, 15, 18–20, 48, 93, 114n.2
Johnson, Katie 28, 52, 60
Jones, Elwyn 114n.7
Jones, Gareth 67n.1
Jordan, Marion 87
Joseph, Paterson 191, *192*, 214
Journey's End 30
Joyner, Jo 237n.7
Joyous Errand 82
Juke Box Jury 115n.11

Kazan, Elia 71
Kebbel, Thomas Edward 236
Keene, Mimi 232–234
Kelly, Hugh 30, 69n.21
Kemp, June 110
Kennedy, John F. 74
Kennedy Martin, Troy 9
King, Nicola 20
kitchen sink drama 84, 89, 111
Klein, Kerwin Lee 20
Klevan, Andrew 7
Kneale, Nigel 27–28, 36–38, 44, 51, 60, 66, 69n.22, 115n.14
Knox, Simone 5
Kreski, Chris 16
Krich Chinoy, Helen 24n.20, 58
Kuleshov, Lev 187–188

Laban, Rudolf 57, 61–62, 71, 147, 149
Lacey, Stephen 87–88
Lambert, Verity 73, 75, 94, 96, 99, 115n.10, 218
LAMDA *see* London Academy of Music and Dramatic Art
Lamont, Duncan 66
Lavery, David 207–208

Lawson, Denis 22n.18, 175, 179, 198, 201, 203–205, 222n.14-16
Lay, Samantha 83–84, 87
Life Class 85–86
Life in Her Hands 61
Lill, Denis 121, 126, 132, 138, 148–149, 161, 204, 209
Lime Grove 14, 42, 96, 114n.4
Ling, Peter 99
Littlejohn, Georgina 232
Littlewood, Joan 57, 61, 71, 109, 114n.1, 115n.20, 147
live television 1, 9–10, 12, 14, 22n.4, 25, 27–28, 40, 42–47, 50–52, 72, 95, 98–99, 103, 120, 167, 223–224, 226–234, 237n.2, 237n.4, 237n.6, 237n.9, 238, 240
Lloyd Pack, Roger 110–111, 123–125, 137–138, 145, 147, 149–150, 172
Loach, Ken 70, 167
location realism 2–5, 9–10, 12, 21–22, 117–118, 136, 138, 153, 155, 161, 163, 165–166, 170, 173, 178–179, 194, 196, 206, 209, 219–220, 224, 226, 229, 236, 239–241
Logan, Elliott 22n.2
London Academy of Music and Dramatic Art 57, 203
Look Back in Anger 71, 84–85
Lovett, Annie 192, *193*
Lyons, Heather 88

McCulloch, Ian 119, *135*, 149, *190*, 192
McElroy, John 116n.29
McFadden, Steve 237n.8
McGeorge, Alistair 237n.9
McGrath, Pat 48

McNally, Kevin 122–123, 126, 132–133, 146, 148, 164n.13, 213, 235
McNaughton, Douglas 12, 116n.25, 117, 126
McWhinnie, Donald 121
Maigret 91–92, 111
Malahide, Patrick 121, 123–124, 126, 167, 178, 211
Man with the Gun, The 32
Marshall, Kevin P. 132, 152
Martin, Daphne 40, 42
Martin, Richard 96, 100, 104
Maslen, Scott 232
Mayor of Casterbridge, The 164n.15
Meisner, Sandford 115n.16
Mendlesohn, Farah 23n.17
Messenger Davies, Maire 20
Messina, Cedric 164n.9
'Method', the 69n.19, 71, 85, 115n.16, 146–149, 164n.12, 195, 200, 207–208, 241
microphone 29, 31, 43, 47, 80, 99, 110, 128, 137, 194, 204–205, 222n.16, 226, 232
Middleton, Christopher 217
Midsomer Murders 214
Midsummer Night's Dream, A 23n.15
Miller, Ken 7
Miller, Sam 226
Mills, Brett 20, 241
Minder 167
Moffat, Steven 178, 215
Month in the Country, A 137
Morahan, Christopher 85–86, 168
More O'Ferrall, George 49, 125
Morell, Andre 5, 37
Morey, Anne 217
Morrissey, David 197
Mother Courage and Her Children 55

Mulkern, Patrick 111, 218
multi-camera 2, 5–6, 8, 10, 75, 91, 101, 127–128, 134, 138–139, 143, 146, 165, 168, 184–186, 189, 202, 230–231, 233, 235, 239

Naremore, James 7, 9, 36
Nation, Terry 119, 161, 166
National Council for Drama Training 202, 220n.1
Neale, Steve 18
Nelson, Robin 169
Neubert, Julie 131
Newman, Sydney 72–73, 82, 84, 86, 96, 114n.8, 116n.24
New Tricks 214
Nicholas Nickleby 75, 89
Nichols, Peter 85–86
Nicholson, Jack 176–177
Nineteen Eighty-Four 5–6, 44, 55, 60
Nine O'Clock News, The 119
Norman, Bruce 47

Oakley, Sasha 202
OB *see* Outside Broadcast
O'Day, Andrew 119
Oh! What a Lovely War 115n.20
On the Waterfront 71
One Foot in the Grave 215
Osborne, John 71, 84
Outside Broadcast 12–14, 21, 23n.15, 117–118, 130–134, 136–139, 156, 162–163, 164n.9, 164n.15, 221n.7, 230, 239

Paget, Derek 114n.1
Parker, John 59
Patel, Chahak 189, 191, *192*, 219
Payne, Jamie 174, 177–178, 197, 203, 210, 212, 221n.10

Peacock, Alan T. 118
Pearson, Roberta 3, 6, 9, 16, 20
Peck, Brian 192, *193*
Performance 168
Persuaders!, The 153
Pinfield, Mervyn 73
Piper, Billie 175, 177, 194, 196, 198, 206, 207, 209, 212, 218
Play for Today 70, 120, 167
Play of the Month 164n.9
Plunkett, John 237n.3, 237n.9
Points West 116n.30
Poldark 123
Polonsky, Vitold 187
Powell, Jonathan 167–168
Pravda, Hana Maria 136, 149, 161
Pride and Prejudice 45
Priestner, Andy 119–120, 122, 130–132, 134, 160, 163n.4, 164n.10, 189
Producer Choice 167–168
Pudovkin, Vsevolod 8, 22n.6
Purves, Peter 75, 95, 106

Quatermass and the Pit 55, 56
Quatermass Experiment, The (1953)
'Contact has been Established' 13, 21, 26, 30, *33*, 35, 36–38, 41, 47, 52, 53–54, 61–62, 63, 66, 68n.10, 69n.22, 78, 89, 95, 113, 120
Quatermass Experiment, The (2005) 223–229
Quatermass II 38

RADA *see* Royal Academy of Dramatic Art
Rakoff, Alvin 28–29, 45, 47–51, 54, 95, 113
Randall and Hopkirk (Deceased) 169, 202
Ranson, Mavis 88

Rawlins, Trevor 147, 209, 222n.17
Rawson-Jones, Ben 219
realism 3
Rebellato, Dan 71, 84
Received Pronunciation 10, 59–60, 110–111, 113, 161, 211–213, 216, 226
Redgrave, Michael 58
rehearsal 1, 3, 8, 25, 29, 40–46, 48–52, 68n.11, 72, 95–96, 101–102, 116n.22, 117–118, 120–127, 132, 162, 163n.1, 164n.7, 165, 170–176, 179, 198–199, 209–210, 219, 222n.13, 224–226, 231, 233–236, 240–241
rehearse/record 12, 117, 126–127, 132, 162, 175
Reisz, Karel 71
Reynolds Hapgood, Elizabeth 23n.7
Rhys, Phillip 172–173, 188, 204–205, 208, 219
Richardson, Ian 24n.22
Richardson, Tony 71, 85
Ridgman, Jeremy 168
Ringham, John 98–99
Riverside 96, 114n.4
Roberts, Pennant 118–119, 122, 125, 127–128, 130–132, 134, 139, 142, 144, 151, 155, 157, 163n.4, 164n.9
Robinson, John 38, 40
Ronder, Jack 119
Ronder, Tanya 134, 161
Rosenthal, Jack 87
Ross, Helen 24n.21
Ross, Lillian 24n.21
Royal Academy of Dramatic Art 57–58, 61, 69n.16, 69n.20, 85, 110–111, 115n.17, 118, 145–148, 200, 203, 222n.17
Royal Court 71, 84–85, 149

Royal Scottish Academy of Music and Drama 200–201
RP *see* Received Pronunciation
Russell, Gary 115n.13, 218, 222n.18
Russell, William 75–80, 82, 87, 89–90, 92–97, 100, 104–109, 111, 116n.29, 228
Ryan, Marie-Laure 17, 23n.16

Saint, The 153, 167
Sanderson, Michael 28, 56, 68n.8, 72, 74, 114n.6, 145–146
Saturday Night and Sunday Morning 85
science fiction 2, 4, 15–19, 24n.19, 73–74, 92, 94, 115n.9
see also telefantasy
Scully, Terry 134
Search for the Nile, The 119
Sendall, Bernard 84
Sexton, Max 24n.22, 177, 186
Seymour, Carolyn 119, 127–129, 132, 137, 140–143, 144–145, 149, 151–153, 161–162, 183, 189, 190, 192
Shakespeare, William 94, 125, 164n.7
Shatner, William 16–17
Sherlock 173
Shoestring 221n.3
Silent Witness 173
single camera 2, 5, 8, 10, 14, 29, 49, 101, 109, 120, 122, 127, 136, 139, 163, 164n.6, 166–167, 170, 183, 185–186, 189, 202, 219–221n.7, 230, 239, 241
Smart, William 23n.15, 131, 136–137, 164n.9
Smith, Cyril 90
Smith, Jacob 204

social realism 9, 70, 72, 83–84, 87, 92–94, 111, 113, 161, 238
special effects 4, 18, 186
　see also CGI; visual effects
Stanislavski, Constantin 8, 11, 22n.6, 30, 57–58, 69n.19, 71, 109, 113, 118, 137–138, 146–151, 153, 163, 164n.12, 165, 199–201, 208, 220, 241
Stanton, Barry 193
stardom 6–7
Star Trek 16–17, 20, 23n.17, 24n.18
Stewart, John 221n.2
Storey, David 85–86
Strasberg, Lee 69n.19, 85, 115n.16, 147–149, 195, 200
Streetcar Named Desire, A 71
studio realism 2–4, 9–10, 14, 21–22, 30–31, 38, 46, 48, 50, 55, 62, 67, 70, 74, 83, 86, 91, 93, 109, 113, 117–118, 122–123, 127–129, 153, 161–163, 165, 167, 169, 173–174, 192, 209, 215, 219, 223–224, 227, 229, 231, 234, 236, 238–239, 241
studio unrealism 92
Survivors (1975)
　'Corn Dolly' 121
　'Fourth Horseman, The' 13, 21, 118–120, 127, 130, 134, 139–140, 143, 155–157, 160, 180, 182
　'Gone Away' 188–190, 193
　'Law and Order' 13, 21, 118, 133, 135–136, 150, 152–153, 156–161
　'Lights of London' 130
　'Starvation' 161
Survivors (2008)
　'Episode 1' 179, 181–182, 183–184
　'Episode 2' 189, 191–192, 193
Susi, Lolly 57, 147, 164n.12

Sutton, Shaun 23n.10, 41, 51, 124, 130–131, 136, 239
Sweeney, The 167
Sylvester, David 84
Sylvester, Kemal 173, 177, 201, 212
Sylvester, Suzan 187, 201, 228
Sylvia Young drama school 218

Take Three Girls 119
Target 221n.3
Tate, Catherine 217
Tate, Reginald 30–32, 34, 36–37, 40, 48, 58, 60, 62–64, 66–67, 69n.26, 80, 92, 128, 228, 238
Taylor, Don 50, 72–73, 116n.27
Teague, Colin 174, 203, 230
telefantasy 15–17, 19, 23, 206, 241
　see also science fiction
telerecording 27
Television Centre 14, 72, 101, 113, 117, 127, 134, 160, 163n.1, 163n.4, 167, 175
Tenko 125
Tennant, David 205, 212–213, 225, 229, 236n.1
Terminator: The Sarah Connor Chronicles 208
Terms of Endearment 176
Terry and June 222n.19
Thames Television 146, 167
Theatre Workshop 71, 109, 147
This Sporting Life 75
Thomas, Talfryn 132, 149, 151, 153–162, 209, 239
Thorp Devereux, W. 30, 61–64, 69n.21, 78, 155, 228
Tiernan, Andrew 171, 200, 211, 236n.1
Tinker, Tailor, Soldier, Spy 221n.3
Touch of Frost, A 177
Tractate Middoth, The 236
Tranchell, Chris 134, 135, 149, 161

Treats 209
Tucker, Patrick 164n.6
Tucker, Thea 57
Tulloch, John 15, 18–19, 83
Turner, Lacey 237n.5
Turner, Victor 19
Turnock, Rob 13, 71, 96, 114n.2

Ure, Mary 86

Vance, Dennis 32
Varma, Indira 225, 236n.1
verisimilitude 18, 60–61, 66, 87, 89, 94, 106, 161
Viewer Research Report 13, 21, 61–62, 65–66
  see also Audience Research Report
visual effects 205–208
  see also CGI and special effects

Waiting for Gillian 50
Ward, Sean 231
Watson, Moray 28, 30, 40–41, 45, 51–52, 57–60, 72, 99
Way Ahead, The 75

Webber Douglas Academy 57, 201
Wednesday Play, The 70, 120
Wesker, Arnold 85
Weston, Judith 149, 164n.6, 187
Wheatley, Helen 5
Whitaker, David 73
Whitfield, June 217, 222n.19
Whitsun-Jones, Paul 65–67
Willett, Alison 224–226
Williams, Raymond 3
Williams, Terence 119, 189
Willis, Susan 164n.7
Wilson, Donald 96, 114n.7, 115n.9, 115n.10, 116n.24
Wilson, Neil 52–54
Wilson, Richard 214–216
Windsor, Barbara 232, 237n.5
Wood, Duncan 96
Wood, Jake 232
Woods, Aubrey 91
Woodyatt, Adam 232–234
Worth, Brian 69n.24
Wyndham, Denis 65, 67
Wyver, John 168

Zucker, Carole 24n.21, 24n.22

EU authorised representative for GPSR:
Easy Access System Europe, Mustamäe tee 50,
10621 Tallinn, Estonia
gpsr.requests@easproject.com

www.ingramcontent.com/pod-product-compliance
Ingram Content Group UK Ltd.
Pitfield, Milton Keynes, MK11 3LW, UK
UKHW021839140426
5217IPUK00022B/1525